NO GOD

But God

NO GOD

But God

EGYPT AND THE TRIUMPH OF ISLAM

Geneive Abdo

OXFORD
UNIVERSITY PRESS

OXFORD

UNIVERSITY PRESS

Oxford   New York
Auckland Bangkok Buenos Aires
Cape Town Chennai Dar es Salaam Delhi Hong Kong Istanbul
Karachi Kolkata Kuala Lumpur Madrid Melbourne Mexico City Mumbai
Nairobi São Paulo Shanghai Singapore Taipei Tokyo Toronto

and an associated company in

Berlin

Copyright © 2000 by Geneive Abdo

First published by Oxford University Press, Inc., 2000
198 Madison Avenue, New York, New York 10016
First issued as an Oxford University Press paperback, 2002

Oxford is a registered trademark of Oxford University Press

Library of Congress Cataloging-in-Publication Data
Abdo, Geneive, 1960-
No God but God: Egypt and the triumph of Islam / Geneive Abdo.
p. cm.
Includes bibliographic references and index.
ISBN 0-19-512540-1 (cloth) ISBN 0-19-515793-1 (pbk.)
1. Islam--Egypt--History--20th century
2. Islam and state--Egypt--20th century
3. Islam and politics--Egypt--20th century
4. Egypt--Politics and government--1981--
I. Title.
BP64.E3 A25 2000
297'.0962'09049--dc21
99-058415

1 3 5 7 9 10 8 6 4 2
Printed in the United States of America
on acid-free paper

FOR JONATHAN

CONTENTS

ACKNOWLEDGMENTS

The religious transformation of Egyptian society appeared obvious to me shortly after I stepped out into the Cairo breeze one December evening in 1993. Convincing the publishing industry in the United States of the great importance of this process, however, was difficult. Only when I met Professor John Esposito of Georgetown University did I finally feel an influential ear was listening. Over a cup of coffee in a hotel restaurant in Amman, Jordan, he returned to me the hope I had lost. This book would never have been published without his wisdom and dogged determination to help me present the true face of Islam.

My greatest source of inspiration and enlightenment came from the hundreds of Islamists who sat through the years of interviews I conducted during my research. I have tried to present their views accurately and to give them a voice in a world ordinarily closed to them. Journalists and editors at *al-Shaab* newspaper helped me to gain access to sources who otherwise would have been unwilling to meet me. I owe special thanks to Abu al-Ela Mady, who gave me the benefit of the doubt and endured my many tedious inquiries.

Among the handful of researchers who assisted me, Hasan Mroue was exceptional. He managed to charm potentially reluctant sources; he provided a sharp eye for significant detail; and he tried patiently to grasp my idea and purpose during the early months. His persistence in plowing through the forest of Egyptian bureaucracy was commendable. He gave up only when all avenues had been exhausted. Sherine Azzam spent months translating complex, and often convoluted, Arabic texts into cogent English. Her talent for identifying the substance amid the rhetoric was critical to my understanding of the Egyptian literature written on subjects related to this book. John Iskander also translated many Arabic works.

This project was funded in part by the United States Institute of Peace. The opinions, findings, and conclusions or recommendations in this work are those of the author and do not necessarily reflect the views of the United States Institute of Peace.

Members of the Cairo expatriate community offered knowledge gleaned from many years spent in Egypt. I am most grateful to Ernst Herb for his keen memory of historical detail and his analytical mind. He offered his books, his computer skills, and his unwavering companionship during some frustrating times.

The Program for Near Eastern Studies at Princeton University, where I was a fellow from 1992 to 1993, gave me grounding in contemporary Islamic movements. My studies at Princeton enabled me to develop a deep understanding of the Islamic societies I would later observe in my work. I am particularly grateful to Professor L. Carl Brown, who admitted me to the program.

Finally, my greatest thanks goes to my husband, Jonathan Lyons. His brilliant insights and editing have touched every page. He was a constructive critic and listened tirelessly to my monologues as I tried to articulate the ideas I would later put on paper. His intellectual generosity was matched with personal sacrifice. He was just as supportive the night I boarded a plane for Cairo, only months after our wedding, as he was five years later when we were finally reunited for good. He understood what few people ever do— that fulfilling a dream is the reason for living. I am grateful to him, not only for this book, but for everything.

Tehran
January 2000

NOTE ON TRANSLITERATION

Transliteration has been presented with an eye toward ease of use. As a result, I have avoided most diacritical marks and have tried to standardize the system wherever possible around the approximate pronunciation of Egyptian Arabic. Exceptions include well-known figures, where traditional spellings are preferred, and those cases in which the subject expressed a preferred transliteration. Thus, Egypt's leading film director is rendered as Yussef Chahine, his preferred spelling, while the litigious *sheikh* is written as Abd al-Sabour Shahin.

NO GOD

But God

1

THE NEW FACE OF ISLAM

The scene from my balcony, in one of Cairo's wealthiest districts, offered a view the world had somehow failed to notice. Each Friday, within minutes of the awe-inspiring refrain of *Allahu Akbar*, God is Great, dozens of men flocked to a small plaza below, each clinging to a green prayer mat. They laid them out in unison, turning a small triangle in the street into a sea of green—the color of the Prophet Mohammed. They removed their shoes and prostrated themselves toward the mosque and, far beyond, toward Mecca itself. I was intrigued not by the sound of the muezzin, whose eloquent echo can be heard in various keys across most Muslim cities five times a day, nor by the instant field of green, which I soon learned was commonplace wherever Cairo's faithful gathered to pray. Rather, I was struck by the fact that the worshippers hunched over their mats were not the kind of men commonly seen in the streets and coffeehouses of Cairo. One glance revealed their social class: The smooth feet of this well-groomed set stood in sharp contrast to the rough calluses many Egyptian men develop from dragging their bare heels over the edges of their ill-fitting shoes.

I was stunned that middle and upper middle-class men would leave their luxurious apartments and villas in Zamalek, once home to Egypt's pashas and kings, to pray on a dusty corner of Ahmed Hishmat Street. Nearly everything I had read before coming to Egypt in 1993 described the Islamic revival as a movement reserved for the poor. The common explanation in press accounts and academic circles for Egypt's return to its Islamic identity had become a cliché: After experimenting with socialism, Arab nationalism, and capitalism under successive leaders Gamal Abd al-Nasser, Anwar Sadat, and Hosni Mubarak, a vast majority of Egyptians were left poverty-stricken and embittered toward the West. The failures of Western-oriented ideologies

3

and economic development, went the argument, fueled a rejectionist movement—hence, the nostalgic search for Islamic "roots."

But as I watched the men dressed in imitation Pierre Cardin sweaters and
fine starched cotton shirts sprawled out along the green mats in the street,
that theory rang false. In the months that followed, I met wealthy women
from Dokki, another upper-crust district, who followed the teachings of a
conservative *sheikh*, known for bringing wayward actresses and wives of government ministers back into the Islamic fold. After attending his religious
lessons and listening to his Friday sermons at the local mosque, women who
were once slaves to fashion took the veil and gave their expensive French
wine to the secular friends they left behind. Instead of preparing lunch for
their husbands in the mid-afternoon when the workday ends, they fasted and
prayed, provoking tensions within their families.

There were ample outward signs that religion was penetrating nearly every
sector of society. At Cairo University, a campus that is representative of
middle-class Egyptian society, a majority of female students were veiled. And
no matter where I went at noontime, whether it was a bank, an athletic club,
the central telephone office, the grand bazaar downtown, or even the government press center, all business stopped for prayer.

The overwhelming Islamic sentiment on display begged an obvious question: What effect, beyond the symbols of veils and prayer mats, was the
Islamic revival having on the spirit and values of ordinary people? I found
my first clues in the two or three taxi drivers I met each day as I roamed
the city. The behavior of the drivers, who were always male and most of the
time no older than forty, followed either one of two predictable patterns. If
I heard cassettes on the tape player of popular *sheikh*s or religious music, if
the drivers were dressed in a *gallabiyya,* the long Islamic tunic, I felt at ease.
Unlike those who played Egyptian pop music, attached photographs of bikini-
clad women to their dashboards, contorted their necks to stare at my legs as
I sat in the back seat, or adjusted their mirrors to fix their eyes on my face,
hoping the unmanned steering wheel would find safe passage through the
chaotic traffic, the men of religion were interested only in driving. When I
heard the Koran playing as I hopped in a cab, I knew I would not be pep-
pered with the questions Egyptian men typically toss at foreign women: Was
I married, did I have children, would I go on a date? I also knew a reasonable
fare would suffice. There would be no haggling over money.

Thus began my search for the underlying causes of the Islamic revival in
Egypt. It was clear from the beginning that the "economic determinist" theory, redolent of nineteenth-century European philosophy and so readily accepted in the West, particularly in the United States, did not hold up. Egyptians were clearly more concerned with bringing about social reform than
they were with establishing economic equilibrium between the rich minority

4

and impoverished majority. The Islamic revival was broad-based, touching Egyptians in every social class and all walks of life. All you had to do was look at the feet of the faithful on Ahmed Hishmat Street.

Two potent factors have allowed this revival to proceed largely unnoticed. It has been obscured on the one hand by the West's need to cast Egypt as a "democratic" and "secular" outpost in a bewildering and hostile Arab sea, and on the other by the distraction of Islamic militant groups waging a persistent, but ultimately ineffective, twenty-year challenge to the state. The 1979 Iranian revolution and the bloody struggles under way in Algeria, in Afghanistan and, to a lesser extent, in southern Lebanon, have left a lasting impression in the Western consciousness of what to expect from the "Islamic threat." For a time, Egypt's own militants, led by the *al-Gama'a al-Islamiyya*, did their best to fulfill these expectations and reinforce Western stereotypes. From the late 1970s to the mid-1990s, militants killed dozens of foreign tourists, bombed banks, tour buses, and a cafe in a five-star Cairo hotel, assassinated cabinet ministers, attempted to kill president Mubarak himself, and carried out the bloodiest massacre in modern Egyptian history in the Pharaonic town of Luxor, in November 1997. Fifty-eight foreign tourists and four Egyptians were killed, some hacked to death with knives.

Generally, however, the militant movement inside Egypt has largely succumbed to the tenacity of the state security forces, the enmity of ordinary pious Egyptians, and the poverty of its own proclaimed ideology. Groups such as *al-Gama'a al-Islamiyya*, which emerged from the student protest movement in universities in the late 1970s, now find few supporters today on college campuses. Their leaders, the ideologues who vowed after the 1981 assassination of President Sadat to overthrow the secular state, have been killed by the security forces, thrown in jail, or forced to flee abroad.

In place of the militant threat, a new type of Islamic revival, untested in the casbah of Algiers, the mountains of Afghanistan, and the back alleys of Tehran, has quietly taken shape and poses a far more significant challenge to Western interests in the Middle East. Egypt's "Popular Islam," a grassroots movement emerging from the streets, aims to transform the social structure of Egyptian society from the bottom up, creating an Islamic order.

Leading institutions, once under complete government control, have begun eroding the state's secularist policies. Universities, the courts, the official religious caste, or *ulama*, and in fact much of the middle class, including doctors, lawyers, and engineers, have created their own avenues to apply religious values in society. Students have kept political and religious activities alive on campuses, despite a state ban, by organizing underground Islamic-oriented groups and unions. Middle-class professionals developed a syndicate movement that offered hundreds of thousands of doctors, lawyers, and engineers a system of social services and an Islamic way of life independent from the

state. Likewise, the *ulama* at al-Azhar, a thousand-year-old institution of Islamic learning, have shed their historical role as henchmen for the state and
have challenged government policies on social issues ranging from female
circumcision to birth control. They have asserted themselves as the moral and
political guardians of Egyptian society. In doing so, they have extended their
authority beyond the strictly religious sphere to ban books and films that they
deem offensive to Islam and the Muslim community of believers.

The judicial system has also fallen under Islamic influence. In recent years,
the courts have banned from cinemas films that were considered blasphemous
to Islam. A film directed by Yussef Chahine, Egypt's most famous filmmaker,
was withdrawn after years of legal wrangling, with one court instructing the
parliament to issue a law banning the depiction on screen or stage of the lives
of Islamic holy figures. The ruling argued that while existing Egyptian law
was ambiguous on the matter, religious law, the *sharia*, was not. Perhaps the
most celebrated case involved a university professor who was declared an
apostate for his writings about Islam. A court agreed with the charge against
him and ordered the professor to divorce his wife, citing a law that a non-
Muslim is prohibited from marriage to a Muslim woman. In both cases, the
judges set what secularists regard as dangerous precedents. They exceeded
their civil authority by interpreting religious texts, an exercise generally reserved for Islamic scholars.

The current religious revival has evolved from three waves of Islamic
activism in Egypt, beginning in the nineteenth century. At that time, Jamal
Eddin al-Afghani and his disciple, Mohammed Abdu, argued that Islam was
a rational religion and should be interpreted in ways that could be applied
directly to modern life. They believed tradition-bound Muslim leaders had
led society astray, and that religious thinking should instead be reformed and
used as a vehicle for progress. Their movement emerged in response to foreign intervention in Egypt, first through the Napoleonic invasion and later
through British colonialism. Afghani and Abdu viewed the West as both a
rival and a model, and offered a formula for Muslims that would incorporate
some aspects of foreign culture and achievements while adjusting Islam to
compete with the advances made in the non-Muslim world.

A second phase of Islamic revivalism occurred in Egypt in the early part
of the twentieth century with the emergence of the Muslim Brotherhood.
Founded in 1928 by Hasan al-Banna, it is still the Middle East's most vener-
able such group. Unlike the ideologues and theorists Afghani and Abdu, al-
Banna aimed to apply religion directly to politics and popular life. A special
apparatus was created within the Brotherhood to fight the British in Egypt
and the Jews in Palestine. The Brotherhood's strategy was based on proselytizing and spreading the word through *al-dawa*, the Islamic call. It sought to
gain political power, if necessary, by force. The Brotherhood became increas-

ingly radical during the 1940s and 1950s. It demanded that women wear the veil, and ruled that nightclubs, cinemas, and theaters were sacrilegious and must be closed. Committed to the scriptures of Islam, to an Islamic social and political identity, and to the adaptation of religious principles to the demands of the modern world, the Brotherhood sought to reform Egyptian values, the economy, and the political system in order to create a Muslim society.

For a time it seemed that the Brotherhood would take control in Egypt, but the group was eclipsed by the Free Officers' coup in 1952, which brought Gamal Abd al-Nasser to power. Ideologically, Nasser's regime aimed to satisfy the desires and needs of society through a secular, rather than a religious approach. With the Soviet Union as his financial patron and sometime ideological model, Nasser sought to establish a state based on socialist principles that would address the economic needs of people. Through policies based in pan-Arab nationalism and state domination of the economy, he held out the promise of social mobility through education and economic development.

Nasser banned the Muslim Brotherhood and imprisoned hundreds of its members in the largest crackdown to date on the Islamic movement. To neutralize public criticism, he also coopted members of the *ulama*, the official religious caste, to certify the policies of his government as "Islamic socialism." Nasser drew a clear separation between religious and social matters, which he largely ignored, and political and economic reform, which he promoted, resting his legitimacy on his ability to improve the standard of living for the average Egyptian. With the subsequent failures of his economic policies, society at large began shifting its focus back to religion, and Nasser's credentials as a ruler of a Muslim country were called into question.

In 1967, Egypt's disastrous war with Israel was enough to expose the major social and ideological fault lines in Nasser's Egypt. When the Israeli military humiliated the Egyptian army, the country entered into a period of soul-searching and began to question the principles upon which its national identity was based. There were no foreign powers to inflict defeat, no imperialists depriving the masses of the economic gains they were promised under the veil of Arab socialism. Egyptians had only themselves to blame. It was natural then for the country to seek to reestablish its national collective identity as a way to heal its wounds. That identity was Islam, summed up in the absolute profession of faith: *There is no God but God, and Mohammed is His Prophet.*

The third wave of Islamic activism, beginning in the 1970s and still under way, benefited greatly from the experience of the previous decades. The Islamists leading the revival were more organized and methodical than their predecessors had been. By the end of the decade, the movement had split into those who advocated the creation of an Islamic society by peaceful means, and those who believed force was the only method by which to overthrow the government and establish an Islamic state. The moderates joined the

Muslim Brotherhood, which by that time had renounced violence, and focused their efforts within the universities. They took over student unions that were once controlled by leftists, organized a network of religious activities, ranging from summer camps to meetings in mosques and dormitories, and provided affordable textbooks and religious literature on campuses. The radicals, meanwhile, carried out their first in a series of violent attacks in 1977, when militants kidnapped and then killed Egypt's minister of religious endowments. By 1981, the militants had gained enough organizational strength to assassinate President Anwar Sadat.

With radicals operating along the fringes, the moderate Islamists set about building widespread support within the broader society. Unlike the period of Afghani, and, later, Hasan al-Banna and the early days of his Muslim Brotherhood, contemporary Islam has penetrated deeply into the Egyptian consciousness. Now, there is a widespread feeling that the cause of society's malaise stems primarily from a betrayal from within, rather than a domineering force from without. Here lies the greatest difference between the past and current revivals: Islamic thought in the late 1800s, and again in the 1940s and 1950s, focused on anti-imperialist sentiment and socioeconomic concerns, while the contemporary Islamic fervor emphasizes family values, traditional sexual mores, and cultural authenticity.

This new focus is reflected in a change in the players leading the revival. Where society once looked to those with prophetic zeal, such as al-Banna, to lead them along the Islamic path, today's revival is more evenly diffused throughout Egyptian society. It relies neither on one man, nor one group, nor one institution. At the center of this new religious milieu, a powerful alliance of *sheikh*s, informal street preachers, scholars, doctors, lawyers, and women are groping their way toward a new, Islamic order. Today, the middle class, not what remains of the upper-class cultural elite, is defining social and religious norms. This broad base in turn supports a potent social movement that represents a formidable challenge to the secular state.

Contemporary Islamic movements can be plotted on a scale between revolutionary Iran, in which violent insurrection overthrew a secular regime and replaced it from the top down with an Islamic republic, and quietist Egypt, in which social reform is leading toward the Islamization of society at large from the bottom up. To date, the revolutionary path has left little lasting mark on the Arab world. The Iranian revolution, once regarded as a model for Islamic renewal, lost its credibility in the eyes of Muslim Arabs when the ayatollahs fell into internal power struggles and became bogged down by economic crisis and isolation from much of the Western world. Similarly, the Arab world's moderate Islamists have dismissed insurrections in Algeria and Afghanistan as being un-Islamic for the brutal and savage tactics adopted by the leaders of the Islamic Group in Algiers and the Taliban in Kabul.

Egypt stands alone today for the progress it has made along this second path, characterized by moderate Islamists challenging state policies, rather than the state itself. Followers of radical Islamic movements maintain that living a fully integrated religious life will only be possible if their rulers govern by the word and law of God. Moderate Islamists in Egypt, however, are willing to live with a mixture of man-made laws and Koranic law, the *sharia*, which, according to Egypt's constitution, should be the "primary" source of legislation but in reality is not strictly applied. The flexible nature of Egypt's revival stands to make a profound contribution to the development of Islamic movements in the twenty-first century and will chart a new course for other countries to emulate in much the same way that the Iranian revolution captured the imagination of the Muslim world twenty years ago.

The Egyptian experience reflects centuries-old conflicts and contradictions among Sunni Muslims over the idea and role of the state. According to religious doctrine, the state was a divine institution responsible for carrying out God's intentions. However, the state was also perceived as a source of evil, and the less the citizenry had to do with it the better. The division of labor between the caliphs and the sultans came down to distinguishing between two kinds of authority, one prophetic and the other monarchical, but both religious.[1] In modern terms, the struggle under way in Egypt among moderate Islamists is how to make state policy coincide with religious doctrine laid out by the *ulama* at al-Azhar and the thousands of independent and unlicensed *sheikh*s.

Egypt's nonviolent approach to integrating a modern state with God's laws reflects the historical influences of the country's earliest political culture and, later, its relationship to Islam after the Muslim Arab conquests of the seventh century. Egyptians under the rule of the Pharaoh had few individual rights. They were not allowed to question the form and nature of the state. Unlike the Greeks, they were excluded from participation in the political process; they could not debate, discuss, or oppose government.[2] The Pharaoh's divine status placed him above the law; all functions of government were religious, not civil. The ruler's divine nature meant that obeying him and the laws he imposed was an act of faith. As a result, society was divided between believers and nonbelievers, not between citizens and noncitizens.[3] This political experience wherein the citizenry survived by avoiding or ignoring, rather than confronting, an alien state has existed since time immemorial.

The Arab invasion of the seventh century shaped Egypt's character as an Islamic and Arabic-speaking nation, and for centuries loyalty to Islam was supreme over devotion to the state. For three centuries, between 1250 and 1520, Egypt was the center of religious activity in the Arabic-speaking part of the Islamic world. It remained the focus of spiritual and intellectual life until the Ottoman conquest, when Istanbul replaced Cairo as the center of religious authority.

Egypt's relationship with its new Muslim rulers was consistent with its history. Once Egyptians embraced Islam, Muslim leaders were no more interested in the welfare of the citizenry than their pagan predecessors had been. Until the nineteenth century, Egyptians identified with Islam on a broad scale, independent of their ruler, and tended to their economic needs on a community and personal level. Under Ottoman rule, the hierarchy of the religious establishment, the *ulama*, stepped in to offer religious guidance through their interpretation of religious texts, even when they had no influence on the rule of law in the state. Lower religious functionaries, such as the leaders of prayer and religious teachers in the countryside, led the faithful and helped establish a traditional, religious society independent from the state.[4]

The political culture of Egypt has prompted some historians to conclude that revolution on a massive scale, whether politically or religiously motivated, is alien to the country's experience. Even when Egyptians were ruled for centuries by foreigners, from Alexander the Great in 332 B.C. to the fall of the last monarch, King Faruq, in 1952, they rebelled infrequently against their alien oppressors. Thus, the submissiveness and docility often associated with Egyptian citizens in their relationship to the state is not new; it remains firmly entrenched in the Egyptian psychology. More to the point, out of need during periods of foreign rule and out of inertia during Muslim dominance, Egyptians learned to rely on themselves and institutions outside the state for religious interpretation and moral guidance.

No God But God documents and analyzes the religious transformation of contemporary Egyptian society. Separate chapters detail how central pillars of the state—the universities, the professional unions, or syndicates, the *ulama* at al-Azhar, the courts—have become influential players in the grassroots religious revival. The book will introduce the activists leading this quietist revolution, who are virtually unknown in the West, and allow them to speak in their own voices.

Other chapters will show the great diversity of religious interpretation in Egyptian streets and neighborhoods. In the impoverished district of Imbaba, activities deemed "Islamic duties" are dismissed by members of the *ulama* as based in peasant tradition, rather than religious doctrine. In the upscale Cairo community of Dokki, however, *nouveaux riches* women under the influence of a radical *sheikh* have taken the veil, surrendered their material possessions for Islam, and drastically altered their family lives to accommodate their new religious lifestyles.

The Islamists featured in the following pages defy nearly all the conclusions, theories, and generalizations put forward about Islamic movements

10

over the last few decades: They believe in coexistence with the secular government of President Mubarak, and they are willing to wait years for their vision to materialize. They have eschewed violence to concentrate their energies largely on changing the individual through preaching and worship, in a gradual process of enlightenment known in Arabic as *tarbiyya*.

My first objective is to present Egypt as a new model for the transformation of a secular nation-state to an Islamic social order without the violent overthrow of the ruling power. Western academics, who have written about this process from a theoretical point of view, have given this phenomenon different labels. "Re-Islamization" from below, a process of changing individuals rather than states, is one such description. Other scholars label it "neo-fundamentalism."

My second objective is to provide a human dimension to the Islamists often described in the Western media simply as "fundamentalists." Debate has raged for years within academic circles over the use of the word "fundamentalist" to describe this aspect of modern Islam. Nonetheless, it is generally used indiscriminately in the popular press and in Western political discourse to refer to any Islamist, no matter whether his aim is violent revolution or peaceful transformation. The origins of the term further belie any utility it may retain; it was first applied in the early 1890s to conservative Protestants seeking a return to what they saw as the "fundamentals" of Christianity. Its current usage to describe activist Muslims is almost always pejorative and obscures their thoroughly modern views on society and religion. Egypt's Islamists do not wish to return to the Islamic period under the Prophet; they seek to adapt their religious values to the modern world. For these reasons, the term "fundamentalist" is best avoided.

Instead, I will call the activists featured in the following pages "Islamists," a word that reflects their unique blend of religious and political motivations. My aim is to move beyond their rhetoric and bring understanding to their value system—notions of the role of religion in daily life, social justice, the function of the family, and ideas concerning male and female sexuality. These values, sharply different from those of the West, lie at the core of why Islamists are often demonized and dismissed as repugnant in Western circles. This value system underlies the central thrust of the current revival: to reestablish morality and reclaim social and moral life from what Muslim critics deride as *jahiliyya*, the pre-Islamic period characterized by ignorance, godlessness, and injustice.

The third aim of *No God But God* is to show how this grassroots movement in Egypt poses a far greater challenge to Western interests than the militant movement now on the decline. Since the Iranian revolution, Western governments have taken a practical approach to curtailing what they perceive as a formidable challenge to their political and economic interests. They have pumped energy and resources into combating Islamic militancy, even at the cost of backing repressive secular governments that lack popular support.

The United States has deposited billions into Egyptian government coffers, hoping to douse the Islamic flame. Since the assassination of President Anwar Sadat in 1981, Washington has continued to believe the money is well spent, casting Egypt in the comforting role of the "good Arab" nation. Rewarded with $2.1 billion in annual U.S. aid for mediating between Arabs and Jews, Egypt has emerged as a symbol of secular moderation in a terrifying and unstable region. But how accurate is this picture?

The precepts outlined previously do not hold up under scrutiny. Because the West has been so blinded by a narrow definition of Islam, it has failed to notice that the one nation long considered an outpost of democracy and secularism in the Arab world is quietly being transformed into an Islamic order.

But how can a society, saddled with a secular regime since the Free Officers' coup in 1952, undergo such a profound transformation without violent upheaval?

The answer lies in the flexible and realistic approach of today's Islamists. The figures leading the revival have matured since their forefathers led a crusade to oust the British from Egypt, beginning in the 1930s. Today's Islamists do not reject modernity; instead, they are searching for ways to marry their religious value system with the contemporary needs of their adherents. They intend to achieve this goal through the application of the *sharia*. This demand is not new to Egypt; it has been the core of the Muslim Brotherhood's program since its inception in 1928. As a concession to the Islamic movement, the Egyptian parliament in 1980 passed an amendment to the constitution making the principles of the *sharia* the main source of legislation. But despite the change, the law of the Koran has yet to be enforced.

The founders of the Muslim Brotherhood at one time favored a rigid interpretation of *sharia*. But today's Islamic modernists, some of whom have left the Brotherhood, generally believe Islamic law should be adapted to contemporary society. Egypt's Islamists, for example, say that if they came to power they would not require all women to be veiled, nor would they advocate cutting off the hands of thieves as is done in Saudi Arabia, where a strict interpretation of *sharia* is enforced.

The ideas of Egypt's Islamists during the last half of this century stem from thinkers such as al-Banna and Sayyid Qutb, the Trotsky of the modern Islamic movement. Unlike al-Banna, who believed in creating an Islamic society within the existing Egyptian state, Qutb advocated transforming society through proselytization and militant *jihad*, or holy struggle. This harder line later helped inspire the militant offshoot of today's Islamic movement, which took Qutb at his word. But both thinkers took as the starting point of their philosophies the all-consuming nature of Islam, which unifies religion and politics, the state and society.

"Islam cannot fulfill its role except by taking concrete form in society, rather, in a nation, for many do not listen, especially in this age, to an abstract theory which is not seen materialized in a living society," Qutb wrote in his landmark manifesto, *Milestones*.[5] This volume stands alongside Lenin's *What Is to Be Done?* as a classic of the revolutionary genre and remains widely read in Egypt despite an official ban.

Many of Egypt's Islamists say they now find Qutb's ideas too radical and out of step with the times. Still, his books, as well as those of al-Banna, are eagerly consumed among university students, and serve as symbols of political resistance. At the very least, the ideas of Qutb and al-Banna have had an indirect influence on today's religious revival. Both men argued, for example, that Westernization of Muslim society and Western models for modernization should be rejected because they had failed the Muslim world and were responsible for political corruption, economic decline, social injustice, and spiritual malaise. This theme has clearly struck a chord with Egypt's professional classes, traditional engines of Western modernity, now turning against what they see as a flawed value system that undermines family and social bonds.

The power of such thinking, and its potential to mobilize political and social protest, should not be underestimated. In fact, similar sentiments provided significant impetus, particularly among disaffected intellectuals, for the 1979 Iranian Revolution, the greatest upheaval in this century carried out in the name of Islam. The Iranian intellectual Jalal Al-e Ahmad could just as easily have been referring to Egypt when he warned of "the fundamental contradiction between the traditional social structures of the Iranians and all that is dragging our country toward colonial status, in the name of progress and development but in fact as a result of political and economic subordination to Europe and America."[6] Writing in the 1960s, Al-e Ahmad went on to identify what he called the disease of *gharbzadegi*, often translated as "occidentosis" or "Westoxication." The term, refined and popularized a decade later, became a permanent fixture of the Iranian, and later the global, vocabulary of Islamic dissent.

In Egypt, the deep penetration of Muslim sentiment beyond state control first emerged during Sadat's presidency, in the late 1970s. This religious revival expressed itself in many ways: increased attendance at the mosque; the broad adoption of Islamic dress by men and women; a proliferation of religious literature and taped cassettes; and a burgeoning of Islamic organizations. Sadat encouraged the Islamic movement in universities to counter socialist and leftist holdovers from the Nasserite era opposing his government, until it became evident a decade later that the militant strand of the revival could no longer be contained.

Declared an apostate for making peace with Israel and condemned for aligning Egypt too closely with the United States, Sadat was assassinated by the same Islamic radicals he had helped strengthen a decade earlier. Sadat's assassins denounced his government as illegitimate primarily because it did not enforce religious law, and they determined the only solution was direct, armed confrontation. The assassins heralded the murder as a great Islamic victory over an infidel ruler. "I have killed Pharaoh and I do not fear death," proclaimed the lead gunman as he sprayed the president with automatic rifle fire.

The assassination inspired the militant groups, and the *Gama'a al-Islamiyya* turned its fire on cabinet ministers, foreign tourists, prominent intellectuals, and President Mubarak himself. But by the time the militant movement reached its apogee in the early 1990s, ordinary Egyptians had come to reject the radicals who killed in the name of religion. As the masses embraced Islam and a renewed value system, they became more and more alienated from the militant movement and more determined to tell whomever would listen that their religion had little to do with violence. In a rare opinion poll conducted at the end of 1994 by *al-Ahram* weekly, an English-language newspaper, 86 percent of Egyptians surveyed declared that Islamic groups that resort to violence do not work to the benefit of the country. Conversely, 73 percent of the respondents said nonviolent Muslim groups did benefit society.

The populist Islamic revival indeed charted its own course, free of violence and coercive tactics. According to government estimates, four thousand new mosques were constructed by the early 1980s, at least one thousand of which were erected through private initiatives, outside state supervision. Religious programming on state radio and television exploded, with both moderate and radical *sheikh*s spreading their message more effectively than ever. Koranic and religious schools mushroomed, and Islamic mystical orders increased fourfold.

President Mubarak's government has responded to the populist-led Islamic revival by conveying a conflicted message that is overreactive and tolerant, aggressive and compliant, often at the same time. The Islamic resurgence has made significant gains as a result of this schizophrenic policy toward religion. On the one hand, Mubarak's government has brutally attacked the militant trend, arresting thousands of suspected radicals, some of whom were tortured in prison and held for years without charge, according to human rights lawyers. The state has also imprisoned on minor charges moderate Islamists who never engaged in violence and tried to choke off informal channels feeding popular Islam, such as closing unlicensed mosques and banning unorthodox preachers from the pulpit.

Yet, like his predecessors, Mubarak has also sought to accommodate the Islamic tendency and earn a religious seal of approval. Like them, he is paying an increasingly steep political price, as a changing society pulls the president and the rest of the secularist ruling elite along in its wake. Firebrand preachers, for example, now spread their word on state-run television programs, and the government has turned a blind eye to members of the *ulama* at al-Azhar who have effectively replaced state censors as arbiters of which books and films violate accepted social values. In the spring of 1998, the Minister of Higher Education banned a textbook being used in a course at the American University in Cairo, a bastion of Egypt's secular elite. The book, a biography of the prophet Mohammad written by a renowned Marxist, was outlawed twenty-four hours after Islamists complained in state-run newspapers. There was no review of its political content, and no discussion concerning the book's role in providing intellectual balance in the course. The ban was issued immediately to prevent a scandal that would certainly spark anti-American rhetoric and raise questions over why the state would allow such a Western-style institution to exist on Egyptian soil.

Although state repression has led to victory over militant groups trying to overthrow the government, this same policy also produced a backlash within society and helped feed the nonviolent Islamic revival. The state's fatal flaw lies in its inability to distinguish the militant, who seeks its violent overthrow, from the peaceful Islamist, who seeks accommodation. By 1994, the rhetoric unleashed by authorities had one message: "All Muslim activists are terrorists." The tough talk soon became deed as thousands of students in universities across the country were arrested for participating in peaceful activities in the name of their religion. Dozens of Islamic engineers, lawyers, and doctors were also imprisoned after they swept to victory in professional union elections. As Egyptian students and the professional classes watched their nonviolent peers arrested for peaceful protest, they became increasingly determined to challenge the state's Islamic credentials. The state was winning the battle against the militants, but it was simultaneously losing the support of the common man and forcing society to create autonomous institutions through which to express its religious loyalties.

Mubarak's regime has clung to power by closing down all avenues of political participation. The Islamists have been banned from forming political parties, and impeded from election as independents through widespread fraud and vote rigging, according to Egyptian and international human rights organizations. The professional unions, of which they took control in free and fair elections, have been placed under state guardianship and effectively closed. But while the political process is not within the Islamists' reach at the moment, the social transformation of Egyptian society continues unabated with or without accommodation from the regime.

Despite its underlying power and dynamism, "grassroots Islam" remains very much a phenomenon of the shadows, hidden by the sheer difficulties of penetrating Egyptian society and obscured by the accumulated weight of the country's postcard image. For centuries, the West has been drawn to Egypt as a romantic land of pyramids darting up toward a desert sky at sunset. It is known as the home of the ancient Pharaohs who mobilized entire populations to build lavish tombs filled with gold and jewels.

The first European explorers to venture into Egypt in the sixteenth century endured arduous trips by sea to comb the Valley of Kings in Luxor and Aswan. One of the country's most seductive attractions is the Nile River, which unites Egypt's two cultures, the African-oriented southern rim and the Mediterranean traditions of the north.

Gustave Flaubert, in a letter from Cairo dated January 15, 1850, captured something of the Western fashion for what was then known as the Orient: "So here we are in Egypt, 'land of the Pharaohs, land of the Ptolemies, land of Cleopatra' (as the sublime stylists put it). . . . What can I say about it all? As yet I am scarcely over the initial bedazzlement. It is like being hurled while still asleep in the midst of a Beethoven symphony . . . It is such a bewildering chaos of colors that your poor imagination is dazzled as though by continuous fireworks as you go about staring at minarets thick with white storks, at tired slaves stretched out in the sun on house terraces, at the patterns of sycamore branches against walls, with camel bells ringing in your ears."[7]

Much of that sentiment, stripped perhaps of its lavish romantic style, retains its hold on the Western visitor of today. Travel brochures and package tours to the Land of the Pyramids still peddle the same tired picture, updated for modern tastes but largely unchanged since Flaubert's time. I was determined, however, to chart my own Egyptian experience through a society that remains virtually invisible to the outsider. So began my five-year search for the roots of today's Egypt, the country foreigners rarely penetrate.

As a modern-day traveler through Egypt's back alleys and congested streets, I encountered the unexpected. Many of the hundreds of people I interviewed had never before met a journalist. Depending on their occupation and social status, their reaction ranged from pleasant surprise to suspicion to downright reluctance and fear. In many cases, repeated phone calls over several months were required to convince them to meet me. In poor neighborhoods, Egyptians assumed I was working for the *mukhabarat*, the state intelligence police who often went undercover in their communities to gain information about Islamic militants. If I were not a state agent, they thought, I must be working for the U.S. Central Intelligence Agency, which they believed was determined to quash the rising strength of Islam across the world.

If I were indeed writing a book about Islam, many were reluctant to cooperate; they assumed I would be promoting the Western media image of Muslims as violent, militant, and medieval people who work to overthrow secular governments. When I explained that my mission was to unshackle the stereotypes from the Western consciousness and present the true face of today's Islamists, some found it inconceivable that a non-Muslim would hold such a point of view. "Are you planning on converting to Islam?" they asked. They assumed my Arab-American background had brought me halfway down the Islamic path, and that my research was the final stage toward conversion. When asked about my religion—one of the most common questions put to any outsider in the Middle East—I always answered truthfully. I explained that I was born into a Maronite Christian family and had no plans to adopt a new religion. My reply generally sparked disappointment among those who were willing to cooperate with my research in the hope that I would become a Muslim.

During the years of my research, a radical *sheikh* accused me of costing him his job as the editor of the magazine published by al-Azhar, which at the time was critical of the state. A former actress who took the veil and led weekly Koranic lessons at a neighborhood mosque charged me with working as a "Zionist spy." A doctor who performed female circumcisions as part of what he described as a duty under Islam was convinced I would file a report of our conversation with the CIA.

Despite these and other setbacks, a generation of moderate Islamists, Egypt's only hope for a brighter future, shared their lives and dreams with me during many interviews over the years. They were courageous enough to take the risk of exposing themselves to a Westerner. They were patient at my initial lack of knowledge about their aspirations, and delighted in a foreigner's determination to tell their story to the world. They were sharp enough to correct false conclusions I reached early on, which they identified as "Western prejudice," and helped me step outside my own Judeo-Christian orientation to understand their value system. And, contrary to the popular notion among outsiders that Islamists treat women as second-class citizens, the hundreds of men I interviewed, sometimes alone in their offices or homes, treated me with the utmost respect and, in fact, may have been more cooperative because of my sex. Their only reluctance was in opening up to self-analysis and introspection. I argued that this was necessary for readers to understand their motivations, but such an approach is alien in Middle Eastern cultures. Yet some did their best to help me understand how their family backgrounds and personal histories contributed to the development of their political and religious ideas.

Through them my insights into the application of modern Islam became more sophisticated with each new encounter. For every clue into the Islamic revival, there existed a counterpoint, a caveat that served as a warning to its complex nature. By the time my research ended, I realized, for example, that the national struggle was not only between the Islamists outside government and the state, but also involved Islamists inside the system who were trying to establish a religious society through institutional channels. Seemingly independent nongovernmental organizations created to promote family planning and improved legal rights for women, in fact, perpetuate the state's ideas and political goals. Islamists inside the state on the other hand have designed unofficial organizations to promote what they see as society's broader interests, which may be in conflict with those of the secular government.

I understood that religious symbols dismissed as distasteful by Westerners reflected self-esteem and collective identity. For women these included loose skirts, headscarves, and long-sleeved shirts. For men, the *zabeeb*, a dark callus formed on the forehead from touching the ground in prayer, was a sign of piety. When I witnessed Egyptians glued to their television sets, their faces drenched in tears, the day the country's most popular *sheikh* died, I observed the public loss other societies reserve for royalty or sports heroes. But just as readily as they mourned the demise of a spiritual hero, they changed the channel to worship the commercial idols of the temporal world.

From experiences such as this, it is clear that Islamic revivalism in Egypt does not fit neatly into categories of premodernism or postmodernism. The new Islamists in Egypt seek to pick and choose from that which the outside world, including the often demonized West, has to offer. As an ayatollah in the Iranian holy city of Qom told me, explaining an official state ban on satellite television: "We are not against satellite television. We just want to pick and choose the types of programming that can enter the Islamic Republic. Because this is not possible, we must ban it all together."

The national struggle under way in Egypt cannot be simplistically classified as a clash between "Jihad" and "McWorld," as the scholar Benjamin R. Barber has described the confrontation he sees between Islam and modernity. Instead, the goal is a marriage between the two. When Islamist leaders in Egypt's medical union, which represents hundreds of thousands of middle-class professionals, designed a health insurance program for its members, they used an American model. But they adapted it to fit their moral and religious beliefs. "Our insurance is American and Islamic at the same time," the architect of the program told me. "It's American because we have instituted a payment system for those who suffer from terminal diseases, such as cancer. It is Islamic because we never cut off the payments, no matter what happens. We keep paying until the patients are either cured or dead."

2

STREETS OF GREEN

Mohammed al-Hudaiby put down his Koran one damp December morning and found the Egyptian government had declared war on his neighborhood. Rage and fear gathered inside him. He had always resisted the forces of the state, first as a drug dealer and then as a street preacher. But on this day, Hudaiby could feel the state's wrath at his doorstep. Elite paramilitary forces in Rayban sunglasses and starched white uniforms, their rifles set on full automatic, had come to create order in the ghetto.

Hudaiby thought back over all the years he had wasted peddling cocaine, heroine, hashish—anything a wiry teenager could get his hands on in a Cairo slum. It was an easy job with many benefits. The ten Egyptian pounds he earned each day, the equivalent of about $3.50, was enough to live on. Best of all Hudaiby could pass his time slumped on a chair in his favorite teahouse. He spent a decade, in fact, high on drugs and glasses of sugary mint tea.

Burned out at twenty-six, he traded in the drugs for chickens and opened a poultry shop. The nervous energy he once got from chemicals and caffeine gave way to his natural passive temperament—helpful in tolerating the restless birds. He put on weight, got married, grew a long beard, and taught himself to read the complex Arabic of the Koran. With his bushy, curly locks buried in the Holy Book, he could forget everything else around him and still remain conscious.

Now the outside world was intruding once again. Hudaiby collected his young son and walked out his front door into Cairo's Imbaba district. Fresh from the allied victory in the Persian Gulf War, thousands of Egyptian troops descended on the miles of rutted roads and dusty alleyways that crisscross the area.

Vast stretches of Imbaba were blocked off, and a layer of tear gas hovered

19

overhead. In a matter of minutes, thousands of soldiers were clubbing a path through the throngs of hysterical people running for cover in all directions. Officers used women and children as human shields against the surging mob, leaving behind wailing choruses of black-veiled mothers. Security forces raided homes and shattered shop windows, dragging residents from their houses and turning the streets into a sea of broken glass.

Like most Egyptians, the residents of Imbaba woke to the news the morning of December 8, 1992: the government had declared war on *al-Gama'a al-Islamiyya*, the country's most powerful Islamic militant group. Convinced the *Gama'a* had seized control of the district, the government of President Hosni Mubarak decided to take it back.

It was Egypt's biggest security operation in recent history. For five weeks Imbaba became an island of terror, completely cut off from greater Cairo. Hundreds of people were arrested, most of whom were later released without charge. The idea behind the massive sweep was to gain information about the clandestine group. Nothing was left to chance, no one was innocent. Men with beards, the trademark of the *Gama'a*, were hauled off to jail in a massive search for the big prize: a young man known as Sheikh Gaber, viewed by the government as the ringleader of the *Gama'a*.

"The government unleashed the dogs of hell," Sheikh Hudaiby told me when I sat with him over a cup of tea two years later. "It was like one of those cowboy movies. You see this *gallabiyya* I'm wearing," he said, pointing to a beige floor-length cotton gown. "The police tore it to shreds. I sewed it back together so I can keep it as a souvenir."

Sheikh Gaber Mohammed Ali, the thirty-five-year-old who provoked the wrath of Pharaoh, was an illiterate electrician, barely known outside the confines of the district. He revolutionized Imbaba by offering order to a community in which the only scheduled activities are daily meals and the muezzin's call to prayer. Gaber had the charisma of Ayatollah Khomeini, the street smarts of a Mafia don, and the empathy of Robin Hood. The *sheikh* sought to impose his vision of a proper Islamic lifestyle on a community scratching out a living and searching for its place in modern Egypt. He maintained three wives, who lived together in the same house, and a mistress, Fatin Abd al-Fattah, who became something of a celebrity. Gaber secretly visited Fatin each day between 2 A.M. and dawn. He entered and left her flat along the rutted Ibrahim Khila Street dressed in drag—a long, flowing black veil covering his head and body to escape detection by the state security forces.

Gaber's sexual appetite was the talk of Imbaba. At one point when the gossip spread too far, he claimed to have married Fatin through *orfi*, a verbal agreement recognized by some Muslims. But his fatal flaw was not his womanizing; it was his big mouth. The same hyperbole and flowery language that had lifted Imbaba's spirits brought the garbage-strewn slum down. In interviews with foreign journalists a month before the security sweep, Gaber emerged from the obscurity of the ghetto into the media limelight. He boasted about *al-Gama'a al-Islamiyya*'s grip on Imbaba. The *Gama'a*, Gaber bragged, had turned Imbaba into a "state within a state," guided not by secular officialdom but by the group's unbending interpretation of the Koran and the *hadiths*, the collected sayings of the Prophet Mohammed.

"Islamic Law is applied in many areas of Imbaba. We first use our tongue. If people don't listen, we threaten them and if they still don't adhere we use force," Gaber said at the time. "It annoys the government that we are a state within a state. But thank God we are not only a state within a state, we have become a state in itself...God willing, Holy Law will be applied in all Egypt."

Stories were told of how Gaber's foot soldiers, bearded young men who wore white crocheted skullcaps and white *gallabiyyas*, had formed vigilante squads intent on enforcing Islamic morality. When locals hired belly dancers for their wedding parties, as popular custom dictated, Gaber's so-called *emirs* declared the dancers *haram*—forbidden under Islamic teaching. They gave the bride and groom a stark choice: get rid of the dancers or we will do it for you. Beer and hashish, often the highpoints at local weddings, were ruled immoral. The *emirs* burned video shops and hair salons, also declared sacrilegious, and warned women not to leave their homes without the *hijab*, the Islamic shawl that covers the hair, neck, and shoulders.

Sectarian conflict between Coptic Christians and Muslim extremists contributed to the violence in Imbaba in the three months before the raid. In September, a Christian butcher had shot and seriously wounded a Muslim who wanted him to slaughter a chicken while reciting the Koranic injunction, "God is Great." The incident sparked a wave of sectarian clashes. Muslim militants defaced Christian religious portraits hanging in the streets, wrecked shops owned by Christian Copts, and burned churches.

When the militants were not applying their religious and moral codes directly to Imbaba's residents, they were engaging in Islamic agitprop. Every Tuesday, they organized meetings along al-Buhi Street, a main thoroughfare, between the afternoon and evening prayers to condemn the failings of the Egyptian government. In the evenings, they lined up television sets in rows along the street to replay videos of the 1981 assassination of President Anwar Sadat. They hung banners with the signature of *al-Gama'a al-Islamiyya* to convey their message: "First it was Sadat ... and tomorrow it will be whoever dares to oppose Islam," read one popular poster.

After the militants took control of an entire district within Imbaba called al-Muneera al-Gharbiyya, home to about 300,000 people, Sheikh Gaber's role as judge and jury emerged. He settled disputes among residents, and mediated between them and the militants. One of Gaber's friends and admirers told me a story illustrating the *sheikh's* multifaceted role in the community. "I had a friend whose sister had rented an apartment. She went abroad briefly and the landlord wanted to keep her furniture and all her possessions inside the flat," explained Fauzi Hamid, a corpulent man with thick gray hair and a dark mustache who was a leader in al-Muneera al-Gharbiyya. "Two months passed and there was no resolution to the problem. The police couldn't enter the area to settle the dispute, because the militants controlled the streets. So I went to Sheikh Gaber. He listened to us and then organized a meeting with the landlord. In the end, we were able to take the furniture and all the things out of the apartment."

The actual power and scale of Sheikh Gaber's fiefdom remain in dispute to this day. An Egyptian sociologist who spent years interviewing Gaber's wives and confidants told me the threat his "state within a state" posed to secular rule was highly exaggerated. Gaber and his *emirs* indeed dominated the Muneera al-Gharbiyya neighborhood, an impoverished area orphaned by the central government. Nearly half of the citizens living there had migrated from other parts of Egypt, seeking the promised land. But with an average monthly income of about $40, a housing shortage, and limited sewage and water systems, it was hardly paradise. Sheikh Gaber may have held ambitious notions of a *coup d'etat*, but his adherents were more interested in whether he could deliver on life's more mundane requirements.

Still, Sheikh Gaber and his *emirs* provided good copy for the Western media and appeared to justify foreign and domestic fears that a new, virulent strain of Islam was afoot in the Egyptian capital. The widely published stories could not have come at a worse time for the government. A fierce wave of Islamic militancy was raging some 200 miles to the south in the Assyut region of Upper Egypt. Now it appeared the Egyptian government was losing control in Imbaba, right in the middle of Cairo. At stake was Egypt's prized position as the leading "moderate Arab state." Under Mubarak, Egypt had cashed in on the West's yearning for a loyal Arab friend in the Middle East. The trade-off was simple: Egypt received huge grants of aid and military support in return for an implicit pledge to take whatever steps necessary to undercut the Islamic movement.

With billions of dollars worth of annual Western assistance on the line, it was time for Mubarak to earn his keep. It was left to lowly Imbaba to pay the price. As far as the government was concerned, the facts on the ground did not really matter; the country's reputation was at stake. If Sheikh Gaber and hundreds of his disciples could be put behind bars, then the Islamic tumor eating away at society would wither away and disappear from Egyptian history.

That was the theory, one lifted straight out of the memoirs of Gamal Abd al-Nasser and Anwar Sadat, Mubarak's secularist predecessors. Nasser had launched a series of purges in the early 1950s to suppress the Muslim Brotherhood. An aggressive secularist, Nasser ordered the group disbanded and its leaders sentenced to life in concentration camps after a failed assassination attempt in October 1954. And when prison proved an effective breeding ground for new strategies against the state, death was deemed the final solution. Sayyid Qutb, the godfather of the contemporary Islamic movement, was hanged by Nasser in 1966, but not before he had produced a prison manifesto, *Milestones*, that helped chart the future course for Islamic renewal. Qutb's writings were a direct assault on the secular state: they defined the Islamic concept of *jihad*, or sacred combat, as a struggle against Nasser's socialist policies. The manifesto itself was shaped, in part, by Qutb's experience of several years of self-imposed exile in America, whose society he denounced as decadent and immoral. Qutb's influence and basic philosophy provide much of the foundation for today's Islamic transformation.

When Sadat came to power in 1970, he at first tolerated and even encouraged the revival inspired by Qutb and the Muslim Brotherhood. His motivation was to counter socialist holdovers from the Nasserite era. But the strategy backfired, and a decade later the militant strand of political Islam had gained so much strength that it was no longer under state control. Sadat's counterattack was too little, too late. In 1981, the Islamic radicals Sadat had nurtured took his life in the spectacular assassination that was the militants' finest moment.

In deploying 14,000 soldiers from the elite paramilitary force, *amn al-merkazi*, and at least 100 armored trucks in Imbaba, Mubarak was only picking up where the previous chapter in the state's handbook on extinguishing Islamic extremism had left off. In the cyclical political theater that has become Egypt's modern history, the state justified the Imbaba raid despite widespread condemnation from human rights organizations and many Egyptians. In the state-run press, Sheikh Gaber was blamed for plotting attacks on cinemas, nightclubs, hotels, and other decadent havens. Security officials portrayed Gaber as a petty criminal and a religious impostor. "Gaber started his life as a thug in a bus station in the Bashtil area of Imbaba. He was imposing 'taxes' on the owners of cars, and anyone who objected was beaten up.... Suddenly he became a *sheikh* and a man of religion and an Islamic preacher by exploiting the widespread poverty and ignorance of people," said one security official.[1]

The hunt for Sheikh Gaber lasted four days, and reflected the determination of the security forces to prove they were tougher than the militants. Gaber had been visiting Fatin when the dawn raid began. He was trapped inside her small flat, fearful that word of his veiled disguise had leaked out and that he could no longer deceive the security forces simply by putting on the long black cloak. Every resident living within a one-mile radius of Fatin's flat was virtually under house arrest. Every apartment was searched and turned upside down. "We weren't allowed to go outside for days," recalled one of Fatin's neighbors. "I was grateful that I had a large bag of lentils in the house. We ate lentils for breakfast, lunch, and dinner until Sheikh Gaber was captured." Egyptian press reports said it was hunger that in the end gave Gaber away. Security forces spotted young boys escaping from a flat near Fatin's house and making periodic food runs to the nearest grocery. They assumed the person giving the order was important; no parent in the besieged neighborhood would risk sending children out to face the army's firepower.

The harsh treatment of the innocent, ordinary citizenry did not end with Gaber's arrest. The Egyptian Organization for Human Rights issued a report in March 1993 charging that state violence had replaced militant terror in Imbaba. The police broke into the houses of suspected militants, destroying the possessions inside. Dozens of Imbaba residents were arrested off the streets merely because their beards and Islamic dress looked suspicious. The wives, mothers, and sisters of wanted militants were arrested and detained for up to a month at a time. They complained of being tortured at the Imbaba police station and ordered to strip naked before giving forced confessions for crimes they had never committed. Children between eight and fifteen years old were beaten by security police aiming to coerce information from them about their wanted relatives, according to the Egyptian Organization of Human Rights.

Overkill and brute force were precisely the impressions the authorities wanted to leave behind. President Mubarak claimed that security forces were correct when they boasted that they had arrested 90 percent of the militants in Imbaba. "We prefer to be accused of being tough rather than neglect and fail to do what ought to be done in facing the dangers threatening our country," Interior Minister Abd al-Haleem Mussa told Egypt's Consultative Council, a legislative body.[2]

When I first met Sheikh Hudaiby in February 1995, it was clear that this time around history had failed the Egyptian government; the tired old script of force, firing squads, and the gallows had lost its effectiveness against the Islamic threat. An unexpected turn in the struggle was taking place unnoticed. The country's attention and military might, shaped in part by the deep-set fears among Egypt's Western patrons, were still focused on the militants in the south. Meanwhile, ordinary people who had nothing to do with the violence of *al-Gama'a al-Islamiyya* were in the grips of a grassroots piety that saw the mosque and the *sheikh* displace the state as their guidepost in life.

Nowhere was this dramatic change more clear than in the packed streets of Imbaba. The heavy-handed repression of 1992 had indeed put an end to the fiery sermons against the regime that once blared from the loudspeakers of Imbaba's mosques. The *emirs*, self-proclaimed moral guardians of the "state within a state," were either in jail along with Sheikh Gaber or in hiding.

And nearly everyone had a story to tell of torture, arrest, and abuse at the hands of the security police during the days of rage that December. The mere mention of Gaber's name was enough to make people shudder; the *sheikh* with the big mouth had somehow imposed a vow of silence on his followers from his Cairo jail cell. Two months after the raid, even Gaber's critics remarked sarcastically that "the hell of the *Gama'a* was better than the heaven of the police."

Outsiders were regarded with suspicion and assumed to be working for the *mukhabarat*, the intelligence service. But through Sheikh Hudaiby I learned that Imbaba has emerged from its ordeal with its faith intact. In these streets of green, Islam is the solution. Popular *sheikh*s now exercise authority, despite the repressive powers of the state. The leaders of *al-Gama'a al-Islamiyya* were not simply boasting back in 1992. Imbaba has become an Islamic state, where every act of life is defined by religion. It is not so much a "state within a state" as a state of grace. And this transformation reflects the stirrings of a religious revival that is steadily reshaping Egypt as a whole.

Islam's lack of separation between God and Caesar strikes the Westerner as alarming, if not downright threatening. Since the Iranian revolution in 1979, Islam conjures up stereotypes of backwardness and barbarism in the Western mind. Many experts explain the Islamic revival as a turn to religion for comfort against the pain of impoverished lives. But ask any Egyptian and he will say that the years the country muddled through secularism were the exception, not the rule. The integrated nature of Islam, with its doctrines that encompass all aspects of man's existence, has guided Muslims since the Arab conquests in the seventh century. It is only natural, therefore, for Egyptians to rely on religion as their only compass.

The religious revival that was exposed in Imbaba was often compared to the Islamic movement in Algeria. But its real strength lay in a quiet revolution in the homes and back streets, one that cannot be enforced by Islamic extremists or stamped out by gun-wielding police brigades. Although the *Gama'a* warriors are still making headlines with their shoot-outs with security forces in southern Egypt, the militants have been fatally weakened by mass arrests and an unstated shoot-to-kill policy. In raids that occurred routinely, police confrontations with suspected militants often ended in the militants' deaths. Witnesses and human rights groups over the years said that the goal in such police actions was to shoot the suspects rather than arrest them. Security police in Upper Egypt are notorious for rounding up hundreds of residents in a rural village to catch a half dozen militants. Collaborators, who once sympathized with the extremists but then switched sides, have given the state an added boost. The militants enjoy little popular support. In the minds of most Egyptians, extremism has given Islam a bad name.

The religious transformation of Egyptian society has occurred through the back door. Major institutions, including schools, universities, and professional unions are now in the hands of moderate Islamists, some of whom are former or current members of the Muslim Brotherhood, which renounced violence in the 1980s. In neighborhoods and districts across the country, popular *sheikh*s, free of government control, are making decisions on matters ranging from divorce to land ownership and the role of women in society.

In my hunt for the key to Egypt's religious revival, I soon found that all roads led one way or another to Imbaba, named after a famous *sheikh* of the nineteenth century. As I made my regular passage into Imbaba from the outside world, I retraced the great migrations into the district over the past seventy years. Superstitious peasants from Upper Egypt took refuge in the district's simple dwellings and once vast agricultural lands. Guestworkers back from the Persian Gulf states imported the austere Islam of their temporary homelands. Even the defeat in the 1967 war with Israel shaped Imbaba; many saw it as a warning from Allah that people had strayed too far from Islam. Most newcomers to Imbaba were Muslim peasants from the south, where rivalry with the minority Coptic Christians fed Islamic extremism. Islamic warlords in towns stretching from Minya to Sohag and Assyut were leading the modern militant wave against the state. So many moved, in fact, that areas of Imbaba are named after well-known *sheikh*s from Upper Egypt: Izbit Sheikh Abd al-Naeem is one such neighborhood, virtually an entire village transplanted in the 1920s by residents in search of work and better living conditions. Typically, after one villager made the move, others would follow. According to government statistics, in 1947 only 5,923 people lived in Imbaba. By 1960, the population had more than doubled to 13,584. And now, four decades later, the number of people has reached approximately one million.

This historic pattern of migration has been repeated in recent years, much to the chagrin of the state. Since the late 1980s, when a new period of confrontation erupted, those fleeing the security forces in Upper Egypt have found refuge with their relatives in Imbaba. Two groups within the *Jihad* organization left Assyut for Cairo in 1980, settling in Imbaba and Ain Shams, another district in the heart of the capital. The move created a strategic triangle, giving the militants two bases in Cairo from which to carry out their operations, and refuge in Assyut, where their leaders plotted their attacks and the foot soldiers retreated to escape capture.[3]

Modern Imbaba, separated from central Cairo by the great swath of the Nile, is a microcosm of Egypt and its chronic problems. Despite huge population growth, it remains at heart a village, punctuated by dirt roads and alleyways no more than two yards wide. A thick layer of soot hangs overhead from the choking traffic. On most days, when the black air mixes with smoke from smoldering piles of garbage strewn across the paths, Imbaba suggests a weathered fresco of Dante's Inferno. Emblematic of the district's transformation, one of Imbaba's leading mosques was once the Kit-Kat Klub, the favorite watering hole of King Faruq, Egypt's last monarch.

Along the main roads, men beat their donkeys to keep pace with battered cars. Dusty-faced children run barefoot down the alleyways, dodging the cars as they go. When they are not running, they sit on the muddy roads, caked with patches of dried camel dung, and play with tin cans and plastic bottles taken from garbage heaps. On rare occasions, boys dash over the garbage, pulling white kites made from old newspapers and tape from cassettes in lieu of expensive string.

Home for some is a mud-brick hovel, usually painted a shocking green or orange on the inside. For the less fortunate, it is a filthy canvas tent on the verge of collapse. There are no telephones, electricity, toilets, or running water in many of the houses. At the sound of a bell, women and young girls run out with tin buckets to collect water from roving tanker trucks.

The sights, smells, and sounds of Imbaba are typical of any primitive eastern village: the water bell; the hooves of horses hitting the pavement; the constant human chatter in the streets, where every crevice has been turned into a vegetable or meat bazaar; the old men smoking waterpipes in bedraggled cafes; and the black-garbed women.

As in nearly every corner of Egypt, the state has failed to provide adequate social services, infrastructure, and education to keep pace with the population growth. A startling 85 percent of Imbaba residents are either illiterate or below average in level of education, according to a recent study conducted by Cairo's Center for Criminal and Social Studies. The schools are so crowded that children attend classes in three shifts, the last beginning in late afternoon and ending in early evening. Seventy percent of the children living in Muneera al-Gharbiyya have never been to school, according to a 1995 report by the state-sponsored Al-Ahram Strategic Center.

The only sign of hope at the time of Sheikh Gaber and his *emirs* was the daily rhythm of drills and hoes hitting the pavement. In the late 1980s, there was virtually no running water in parts of Imbaba. Residents constructed homemade pipes to funnel sewage from their homes into cesspools dug along the streets. The struggle between survival and decay was clearly on display: loaves of freshly baked bread were for sale on large wooden boards balanced over the cesspools filled with excrement. But beginning in 1989, the United States Agency for International Development, an American development fund, invested more in Imbaba than in any place in the world. A new system was installed, making running water available in a majority of houses.

Hussein Ghazali, the elderly governor of the Giza province, boasted of the water project that was aimed at transforming Imbaba from a slum into a thriving metropolis. "Go there and see for yourself," Ghazali instructed. "You'll see how happy people are."

The state was so proud of the USAID improvements that celebrities, United Nations envoys, and U.S. congressmen often paraded through Imbaba to take note. England's Prince Charles was the last visitor given the royal tour. "Eddie Murphy came here and ate bread and thought it was good," said Ghazali, unable to suppress a note of surprise.

While Governor Ghazali pats himself on the back, Imbaba residents curse the authorities' ineptitude for the lack of running water, sewers, and other basic services. The solution, they believe, lies not in the secular world of bureaucrats, commissions, and governors but in their religion. In the Criminal and Social Studies survey, 90 percent of young people interviewed said that the spread of Islam would solve problems ranging from sewage running in the streets to the housing shortage.

Hundreds of mosques are tucked along Imbaba's alleyways. Many are *masjid hukoomi*, government-run mosques placed under the Ministry of Religious Endowments—one of many moves by the state to control the *sheikh* and the pulpit. Since the time of Nasser, the state has tried to regulate all mosques. In 1979, Sheikh Abd al-Munim al-Nimr, then the Minister of Religious Endowments, released figures showing the total number of mosques in Egypt had reached 34,000, of which only 5,600 were under state supervision. In 1996, the Minister of Religious Endowments ordered the most aggressive directive to date: Every year, 6,000 mosques should be returned to state control. By 1999, the ministry boasted it had taken over 41,400 of the 67,000 mosques across Egypt, a claim that remains widely disputed. In taking over the private mosques, the state demanded the prayer leaders be accredited from official seminaries or have equivalent qualifications. Those who failed the licensing test were removed from the pulpit and replaced by state-appointed preachers.

The new directive was aimed squarely at communities such as Imbaba, where the private mosque, *masjid ahli*, has captured the Muslim imagination. There, activities similar to those once carried out by Sheikh Gaber are commonplace. At the Hossary mosque, the national network *al-Dawa* recruits worshippers for month-long pilgrimages around the country to spread a conservative interpretation of Islam. Islamic radicals controlled many private mosques in the 1980 and early 1990s, and outsiders to the community were unwelcome. At the Assyuti mosque in Imbaba, named after the hometown of its founder, members of the *Jihad* carefully monitored who attended daily prayers. In an attempt to learn the message being conveyed there, I asked a young Egyptian man to attend the sermon one afternoon and report back.

But as soon as he entered the mosque, he was detected as a stranger. Once he explained his mission, he was ordered to leave.

Just as the mosque has slipped from the state's grasp, so have the street *sheikh*s, who are leading the grassroots Islamic revival. The state defines a *sheikh* as one who has studied at the prestigious center of Islamic learning, Cairo's al-Azhar University. However, the people have a different definition. Most Egyptians use the term "sheikh" loosely. Generally, it is a word reserved for a man who encourages people to become more religious. But it is also used as a reverential title applied to a senior member of a group or office.

In Hudaiby's case, the street is his only pulpit; the state forbids him to give sermons in a mosque. As a self-made cleric, he learned to recite the Koran on his own and only in recent years did he seek instruction from a religious scholar at al-Azhar. "To tell you the truth I take pride in the title, but I don't think I deserve it," he confessed.

His neighbors, however, think he does. Hudaiby's odyssey to being anointed *sheikh* by the community began the day he decided to change his life. "I was an ordinary man. I did not pray. Between the age of sixteen and twenty-six I was lost in drugs. But I started reading the Koran."

He also began charity work. Each day around one o'clock, Hudaiby gathers the young men along Mudaris Street, a large, well-paved avenue, and escorts them to the Nasser mosque for the midday prayer. If a mother has a discipline problem with her son, Hudaiby makes a house call to give advice. Shortly after I began visiting Imbaba, the men in the neighborhood sought Hudaiby's opinion over whether it was forbidden in Islam to shake my hand. To greet a local woman in such a manner would be a violation of religious and social custom. But I was a guest, and some form of formal greeting was in order.

We gathered around the sweets stand where Hudaiby ekes out a living selling grape juice and sweetened couscous topped with cream. Mohammed, a clean-shaven elderly man who walks with a limp, argued that physical contact was permitted, provided the shake was not a shake at all, but a slight touch of a man's fingers onto the palm of a woman's hand.

Hudaiby thought a moment, his small black eyes gazing off into the distance, and proudly recited a verse from the Koran: "O ye who believe! Approach not prayers in a state of intoxication . . . until after washing your whole body. If ye are ill . . . or ye have been in contact with women." It was okay to shake my hand as long as the men washed their hands before praying.

Later that day, I visited a local barbershop, a small, green room off an alley with a ragged curtain serving as a door. Khalid, the barber, is known for his engaging conversation and trademark cuts. For sixty cents, he crops hair so close to the head, men are guaranteed they will not have to return for months.

Khalid was describing in detail what he did on his wedding night a few months before. "When we were about to consummate our marriage, the first thing I did was wash my hands," he explained, before a captive audience of three male customers.

"There is a phrase in the Koran that a man must recite, and your hands must be clean. I then bowed down toward the floor and began reading the verse about how God ordered the people of Israel to slay a cow. It's a special *sura* that is read on wedding nights. It is supposed to keep the devil away for three days."

Khalid was quiet for a moment. "I can't say more because in Islam we are not permitted to reveal what goes on between a man and his wife."

I pressed Khalid to continue the story. I had spent many afternoons in the barber shop over several months and felt at liberty to ask personal questions.

But he shied away from further details, except to say he then performed his other "Islamic duties." In Islam, a woman can legally divorce her husband if he refuses to make love. Bearing children is the primary reason to be married in the first place, he explained.

We sat in silence for a few moments. Then Sheikh Hudaiby walked into the barber shop. "*Al-Salam aleikum,*" he said. "Peace be with you." Hudaiby stood with perfect posture at the entrance of the shop as if he were making his debut in a play or film. He glared at me as I perched on a brown plastic stool facing the barber's chair. He seemed annoyed at my independence. I had come to the barber shop without asking him to escort me there. He gave me an icy stare.

"*Wa aleikumu al-salam,*" Khalid and Mohammed, the man getting his hair whacked, greeted Hudaiby in reverential tones. It was clear Hudaiby wanted to take over the conversation. And it was expected everyone would let him.

He began explaining why more and more women are wearing the veil. "Women wear the veil not because of threats from their husbands, but because it is a Koranic command and people are becoming more religious."

"Does your wife wear the veil?" I asked Khalid.

"Yes," he replied. "And I'm sure she wears it wherever she goes, even when I'm not with her. I know I can trust her."

Hudaiby nodded with approval. "Then, she has proved she is a good Muslim and you made the right decision in choosing her as your wife," he said.

It is the thousands of Hudaibys across Egypt who are enforcing their own vision of Islamic law. Using the street as their pulpit, the homegrown vigilantes operate completely outside the official *ulama*, the state-sponsored religious leadership. With straggly beards and tattered *gallabiyyas*, they stand in stark contrast to the official preachers in their *imma,* or rounded maroon felt caps with a dark silk tassel, and white starched robes.

Popular *sheikh*s are gaining widespread legitimacy for two reasons. First, their lives reflect the tragedies and hardships experienced by their followers. Sheikh Hudaiby holds sway in the community as a former drug dealer who saw the light. Other *sheikh*s now commanding astonishing popularity in Egypt have also risen up from the bowels of poverty and crime in the worst slums in the country. In recent years, some street *sheikh*s have become so influential the state has banned them from preaching in mosques or even placed them under house arrest.

Second, the popular *sheikh* has become an antidote to official preachers co-opted by the state. Over the last century, Egyptians have seen *sheikh*s schooled in traditional Islamic scholarship at al-Azhar engage in collusion with the state. When President Nasser needed support in the 1967 Arab-Israeli war, he turned to al-Azhar, which declared the conflict a holy struggle against the Zionist enemy. And when Anwar Sadat confronted vehement opposition to making peace with Israel in the late 1970s, he too turned to al-Azhar to codify his actions. The state-controlled institution duly issued an opinion, declaring that the time had come to reconcile with the Jews.

Today, keeping step with the religious revival, some *sheikh*s at al-Azhar have dared to part ways with the official orthodoxy. While the current head of al-Azhar, Sheikh Mohammed Sayyed Tantawi, continues to support government policies, the preachers below him are asserting their independence for the first time in nearly a century. Al-Azhar *sheikh*s have clashed with the state on a range of issues from female circumcision to birth control and literary works written by secular authors.

I wanted to meet one of al-Azhar's rebels, so I asked Hudaiby to introduce me to his mentor, Sheikh Ismail Sadiq al-Adawy. After several weeks, Adawy agreed to receive me, provided I appeared fully veiled.

At five o'clock one afternoon in March, I left my flat wearing a long black *hijab* fastened tightly around my face and extending down to the waist. Usually, when traveling to Imbaba, I tied the *hijab* loosely around my head just before I reached the district. But my meeting with Sheikh Adawy required that the veil completely cover my upper body, and I decided I should fasten it in front of a mirror to make sure it was done properly. When the young men who work in the building washing cars and collecting trash saw me, they did a double take. Then, they gave me a thumbs-up sign and a smile, assuming I had converted to Islam at last.

I nervously approached the iron door of the centuries-old al-Azhar mosque. I had never met a high-ranking religious figure in Egypt, and I worried about the etiquette required for such an encounter. Hudaiby was waiting for me in his familiar beige *gallabiyya*. He asked that I remove my shoes and carry them through the mosque, holding the soles together. He explained that dirt from shoes must not fall onto the carpets spread across the mosque floor.

The moment I saw Sheikh Adawy I felt at ease. A husky man in his late sixties with a long gray beard, he sat hunched in a large chair with the tassel of his *imma* dangling near his dark, gentle eyes. When he rose slowly to greet me, he declined to shake my hand, but stared into my eyes, unlike many pious Muslims who believe it is forbidden to look directly at a woman who is not related by blood or marriage.

"This is Mademoiselle Abdo," Hudaiby said, with a reverential tone in his voice I had not observed before.

"Abdo? But why are you not a Muslim?" Sheikh Adawy asked.

"Although Abdo is a common Muslim name, my ancestors are Maronite Christians from Lebanon," I explained. As if to apologize for what seemed a genealogical shortcoming, I mentioned I had studied classical Arabic and struggled through courses in reading the Koran.

Sheikh Adawy invited me to stay in the mosque to listen to his sermon and *dars*, or religious lesson. By the end of the evening, I understood why he was so popular. Like a New York performance artist, Adawy turned the mosque into a stage. He transformed himself from a subdued, contemplative cleric into an animated stand-up comedian or talk-show host. Standing before a mostly male audience of about 200, he fielded questions on subjects ranging from whether using facial cream was against Islam, to whether children were allowed to take revenge against a father who had killed their mother.

"I yelled at my wife," one young man confessed to the crowd and the *sheikh*. "She cried, and I told her, 'If you go on crying I will divorce you.' "

With an exaggerated look of disgust, Adawy snapped: "This is an example of how men can be jerks! You should have consoled her and asked what was wrong. The Koran says God created love and sympathy between a man and a woman. A man like you can never be a husband. You better go and raise rabbits instead."

The key to influencing people and making them better Muslims is to speak in a language they can understand, Sheikh Adawy told me. "I try to reach the average person in a simple way. This is in accordance with the *hadith* of the Prophet. People who feel this sincerity can only respond in a positive way. This is exactly how I influenced Sheikh Hudaiby."

Clearly, Sheikh Adawy's charisma and skilled oratory are partially responsible for his popularity. But in the hearts of many Egyptians, it is his daring declarations that challenge state policy that make him superior to his peers in the offical *ulama*. Adawy has called on the Egyptian government to stop accepting $2.1 billion a year in aid from the United States. He is a leader in a growing crusade to cut Egypt's umbilical cord with the West in order to draw closer into the Islamic orbit. Adawy opposes the Palestinian-Israeli peace process, another cause championed by the Egyptian government. While President Mubarak boasted of frequent meetings with Palestinian leader Yasser Arafat and Israeli Prime Minister Shimon Peres at the presidential palace in the suburb of Heliopolis, Adawy was unleashing bellicose rhetoric against the Jews from his al-Azhar pulpit.

One Friday, in the spring of 1994, thousands of Adawy's followers gathered at the al-Azhar mosque to stage a protest against the United States and Israel. But faced with an army of security police, carrying batons, machine guns, and tear-gas canisters, the Islamists called off the protest. A few days later, Sheikh Hudaiby proudly displayed a front-page photograph in the Islamist opposition newspaper *al-Shaab*, featuring thousands of worshippers gathered inside the mosque. As I sat at his sweets stand, he pointed out his own face, which appeared in the middle of the photograph. I told him I had been standing next to the security forces that afternoon and I wondered if the protesters were afraid the police would kill them.

"We were afraid because we knew what might happen," Hudaiby said. "But everyone in this country is really disgusted, and we don't have any hope. The day has come when we don't care about the police. I have divorced life. It is only because I have children that I have not gone all out for Allah."

The nature and scope of the revolution quietly at work in Egypt's streets of green have so far eluded the sharp eyes of the pervasive security apparatus. Mesmerized by the same alarmist headlines and sound bites that the Western media reserve for deadly Muslim militancy, the secular state has overlooked the far more dangerous threat to its survival that Egypt's grassroots piety has come to represent. Like any order teetering on bankruptcy, the regime has nurtured the seeds of its own destruction.

Take the case of Hasan "Karate" Sultan, Cairo's Exhibit A in the fight against the militant threat. A swaggering former sympathizer of *al-Gama'a al-Islamiyya*, Sultan was paraded before university audiences as the embodiment of a repentant militant and an abject lesson in zealous youth gone bad. A handsome man with a day-old beard and almond-shaped dark eyes, he looks like a model for a fashion magazine. As he walks, he sways his hips slightly, showing off his muscular build. For years he was a black belt in karate, the inspiration for his neighborhood nickname, "Hasan Karate."

Karate came to Imbaba as a boy from Assyut. His father found a cheap apartment for his mother and six siblings in Izbit al-Mufti, a district of clay houses and unpaved roads. When he was eleven, Karate was drafted by groups in the neighborhood to attend prayers at a local mosque. Religious discussions soon turned to politics. When the troubles struck his neighborhood in December 1992, Hasan was caught up in the security sweep and spent four months in jail before returning to Izbit al-Mufti.

The story told about him typifies the simplistic, good-versus-evil melodrama the state disseminates to the world. After years devoted to violent activities aimed at overthrowing the state, it is said, Karate reformed in prison and emerged a peace-loving leader in his community. That is the way Hasan is presented by Saad Eddin Ibrahim, the jet-setting sociologist touted as one of Egypt's leading experts on the radical Islamic movement. Ibrahim often brought Karate along to university gatherings and introduced him as a former *"emir* in Imbaba." He described again and again the young man's journey from militant madness to Imbaba Boy Scout.

But on examination, it became clear Ibrahim's story was just that: another tale concocted by the government, which when repeated often enough somehow stands in for reality in Egypt. The "new" Karate, in fact, was far more dangerous to the regime than the alleged *Gama'a* partisan of old.

I met Karate in a small, freshly painted flat in Izbit al-Mufti. He told me how he had broken with the militant Islamists over their violent tactics and fled to Saudi Arabia, just a few months before the assault on Imbaba in December 1992. He had only returned home briefly to marry his childhood sweetheart when he fell into the hands of the security forces.

The former black belt talked enthusiastically about how he was preaching strict Koranic law in the mosques and community centers in hopes of making people more religious. He was now a leader in *al-Dawa*, a firebrand group tolerated by the state. His good deeds had recently earned him the title "Sheikh Sultan."

I asked him if this was the kind of activity that had provoked the state to crush Imbaba.

"No," he replied. "The police raided Imbaba to get Sheikh Gaber. What we're doing now is teaching people the *sharia* and how to follow the right path of Islam."

Karate led me through the maze of alleyways to a minibus shuttling passengers through the mud to the main roads, where buses and taxis wait. He politely paid the fare, even after I insisted on paying myself. Then, appearing puzzled and hurt, he said: "But you didn't ask about the torture."

"What torture?" I asked.

"The torture in prison. Do you realize what it's like to be in jail in this country? First, the interrogators ripped out my fingernails. And when I kept telling them I didn't know the things they were asking about the *Gama'a*, they beat me. Then, they attached wires to my body and gave me electric shocks."

Later that day, inside my apartment and a world away from the trauma of Imbaba, I listened to a recording of Saad Eddin Ibrahim's portrayal of Hasan "Karate" Sultan, the repentant militant.

"Hasan fought with government troops, and he was proud that with 600 fighters from the neighborhood he was able to keep 12,000 police outside

Imbaba," Ibrahim told an audience at the American University in Cairo. "But he reformed in prison, where he was treated well, and now he is seeking a better life."

I played the tape over and over and thought of Karate in his freshly painted flat, seeking refuge from a state that had tormented his mortal flesh and reciting the *suras*, or verses, of the Koran.

I asked Montassir al-Zayyat, a lawyer and spokesman for the *Gama'a*, what he thought about the idea of "repentant militants." I asked him if the convicted Islamic radicals often pictured on television shouting "Allahu Akbar" from the bars of their prison cells would change if they were sent to a rehabilitation center, rather than the execution chamber.

"Repentant militancy is a contradiction in terms," al-Zayyat answered. "The reason they are militants is that they are ideologues. They are on a mission. In their minds, they have nothing to repent for ... This idea is just state propaganda. If someone claims to be a 'repentant militant' it means he was never a militant in the first place."

The next day, I asked Sheikh Hudaiby what was different about Imbaba today from Imbaba in the time of Sheikh Gaber and his *emirs*. "Did the invasion succeed in extinguishing the Islamic flame? Are fewer women wearing the *hijab*? Are there more belly dancers at weddings?"

"There are more security police here now," he quipped.

"But surely life is different," I insisted.

"If that were true, I wouldn't be sitting here, drinking tea. I'd be in jail."

I left Imbaba that afternoon and did not return for four years. I remained in Cairo, but somehow I could never muster the courage to cross the modest bridge that separated my contemporary home in Zamalek from the premodern world of Imbaba. The months I spent there had left a profound impression. Imbaba was so unlike any other downtrodden district in Cairo. Areas such as Shobra and Bulaq were just as impoverished as Imbaba. The mudcaked paths were just as dirty and smelly. Sheep tied to sticks and poles along the streets were as straggly and malnourished. Donkeys competing for a few inches of space in nonstop traffic jams were beaten just as relentlessly by their masters. But somehow the decay and struggle in Imbaba created an unusual dynamic. When you step into Imbaba, you feel the friction, the energy of a captive society. Egyptians often say Imbaba is a collection of extremes: the drugs, crime, and religious violence reach greater heights there than anywhere else.

Why then was Imbaba so different? That was the question often asked. The most cogent answer I received came from Gamal Qutb, a *sheikh* at al-Azhar who grew up in the district. "Many people in Imbaba came from villages, particularly from Upper Egypt. They brought with them habits and rituals which are cultural, rather than religious. Yet they believe these habits are somehow Islamic. This is where the misinterpretation comes in. The Imbaba resident can't ever forget about his village, so he recreates it . . . I left the mosques in Imbaba because people were always asking me for personal favors, which is what goes on in their villages."

By the time I returned to the district in the spring of 1998 so much had changed throughout Egypt. The government had declared victory against the militants, a claim largely unfazed by the attack on Western tourists at Luxor in the fall of 1997, when renegade militants carried out the most spectacular assault on tourists in their twenty-year campaign against the state.

The militants had also attempted to assassinate President Mubarak during a visit to Ethiopia in 1995. The *Gama'a* had split into rival factions, prompting Montassir al-Zayyat, the lawyer and spokesman who had represented them nearly since their inception, to announce publicly that he had given up the fight. The West congratulated President Mubarak on his physical and political triumph against the militant threat. The world and the Egyptian state attributed his success to a new policy in 1994 that made no distinction between militant and moderate Islamists. The result was the arrest and imprisonment of dozens of nonviolent, moderate Islamists in the syndicates and universities.

Many radical *sheikh*s also fell victim to this strategy of collective punishment. They were banned from the pulpit and retreated underground, where they held secret sessions with their hard-core followers. On the surface, there seemed to be a freeze on the militants and a stalemate with the moderate Islamists. But, in reality, after the heated days of the early 1990s, society had made its choice. The radical Islamic movement that left its imprint on Egyptian history was displaced by a social movement among the masses who chose to apply religion in every aspect of their lives. I returned to Imbaba after four years away to observe this religious transformation. I knew Imbaba, the land of extremes and extremism, would bring the picture sharply into focus.

I soon picked up where I had left off. I spotted a sausage stand off Muneera Square. Aluminum Coke cans and ripe tomatoes were displayed in the front glass of the kiosk near a hotplate where sandwiches were made. Brown sausages hung on each side from strings, framing the kiosk. A large icebox where cold drinks were stored stood to the right of the stand. A banner hanging in front of the stand proclaimed: *God is Great, starring Hasan Karate.* Other signs carried verses from the Koran, culminating in the affirmation of the proprietor's faith: *There is no God but God.*

In four years, Karate Sultan had grown from model repentant militant in Egypt's obscure English-language newspapers to an international media star. He had appeared in nearly every major foreign newspaper, with his sandwich stand as material evidence of his personal rehabilitation. By 1998, Saad Eddin Ibrahim claimed to have reformed forty-one militants like Karate who wanted to "return to society." Through his Ibn Khaldun Center, a fancy brick structure located in the Moqattam Hills overlooking Cairo, Ibrahim's large staff raised foreign funding for his programs and opened a satellite office in Imbaba. But when foreign journalists arrived in the capital and requested interviews with a sample of Ibrahim's repentant militants, the only exhibit on offer was Karate. What about the other forty? Somehow, they remained elusive. Karate would dutifully give the interviews at his sandwich stand, collect $100, the fee he charged as an international celebrity, and the story would go through the spin cycle of the foreign media machine and be hung out to dry, as if it were fresh material.

Karate had become wealthy enough that he himself no longer worked at the sandwich stand. His minions sold the sausages for him, at about ten cents apiece. When I visited that afternoon, a young vendor told me Karate was on his way. I waited and returned periodically for several hours, but he never arrived. I gave up the search.

Hasan Karate's new life as part-time entrepreneur and sometime media hound was typical of Imbaba in the post-militant era. The district appeared to have retreated inward into a more mundane existence. The energy in the streets felt prosaic; the rushing and bustling centered around the vegetable stalls and meat markets. The alleyways nestled near Luxor Street, the fiefdom of the militants in the early 1990s, were crowded with children playing soccer and swinging in garbage-strewn playgrounds. The melodramatic weddings once staged in the streets for all to scrutinize and for the militants to break up, had retreated indoors into private clubs. The streets that once reeked of sewage were paved.

"Why does the West think such terrible things about Imbaba?" Sayyed Mursi Abbas, the owner of a spare parts store, asked me as I strolled along Buhi Street, once the heart of the militant's domain.

"The West doesn't know about Imbaba," I tried to explain. "The only thing people on the outside knew about Imbaba was that it was once home to the militants. So, you see, it is not Imbaba itself that had a bad reputation, but some of the people who lived here."

Abbas's neighbor, a tailor who was sewing from a stand he had arranged in the middle of the sidewalk, overheard our conversation and chimed in. "The West fixed our streets because when the police came to arrest Sheikh Gaber, they couldn't drive through the sewage and the unpaved roads. They had talked about improving the neighborhood for a long time, but they finally did it after Gaber," explained the tailor, an unshaven, middle-aged man with brown teeth.

If the West's response to Sheikh Gaber was to pave the streets, the state's reaction was to close the mosques. I noticed that the mosques were locked for most of the day, except during prayer times, on orders from the state to discourage meetings aimed at undermining its authority. The Assyuti mosque, the base for *Jihad* where I had tried unsuccessfully to make contact four years ago, was in transition. I returned hoping this time around I would have more luck talking to the *sheikh* or the worshippers themselves. I met a man there who identified himself as Sheikh Mahmud. He had a small frame and a thin beard and worked at a tiny grocery behind the mosque. He was overly polite in the kind of courteous way I knew meant he would never talk. "On Friday, the state will put in its own *sheikh* at the mosque," he said. "It's part of the new program to get rid of people like me."

"Who are you exactly?" I asked. "Have you been a *sheikh* here for years?"

"I've been here about three years, long enough for them to decide to replace me. I can't talk anymore," he said suddenly, before disappearing behind large heaps of garbage that obstructed my view as he darted north along the street.

The long arm of the Egyptian government was about to end the private life of the Assyuti mosque, bringing it under state control as it had so many other unofficial places of worship. It was, I thought, an appropriate finish for this popular Imbaba holy place, capping a story that mirrored the modern social history of the district and of Egypt itself.

For years the mosque, built by Mohammed Assyuti, a local follower of mystical Sufi Islam with veterans' benefits he received for wounds in the 1967 war against Israel, had offered the neighbors a place to worship and brought honor to its benefactor. When Mohammed died in the late 1980s, however, he left the family vulnerable to one strong-willed son. Sharawi Assyuti was an avid reader in primary school and finished first in his class. In secondary school he began reading the writings of Sayyid Qutb, and by the time he reached seventeen he had become an active member in the *Jihad* organization. Sharawi was arrested once in the early 1990s; police thought, mistakenly, that he was involved in the burning of a video shop, a favorite target of the militants. When he was released thirteen days later, he turned his talents and his hatred on the secular state. He took over the Assyuti mosque upon the death of his father and converted it into a base for the militants. He partitioned the mosque, creating restricted areas off-limits to certain worshippers.

The separation in the mosque prompted division at home, as well. Sharawi's brother, Hamdi, a staunch secularist, was using the mosque to teach poor children to read. Sharawi kicked Hamdi out of the building to make room for his radical peers. At the family home, he forced his mother, three sisters, and four brothers to comply with his definition of a proper Islamic lifestyle. He broke the family television set, a source of Western decadence in his mind, and ordered his sisters to wear the veil. He continued on in this way until the Imbaba raid. Sharawi was arrested one day before Sheikh Gaber and remains in prison.

But the religious values he imposed by force on his family, with the exception of Hamdi, soon became second-nature. His sisters joined the militant movement and, on the instructions of *Jihad* leaders, took on new names after figures in the Koran. When one sister, Dawlat, decided to marry, she was approached by two suitors. One had a university degree and offered a way out of the Imbaba ghetto. But he knew little about Islam, and could not recite from the Koran. The second suitor was poor, lacked a university education, but knew the Muslim holy book well. Dawlat chose the latter, sacrificing the only chance she may have had to rise out of poverty.

As I listened to Hamdi recite this tale, I realized that the saga of the Assyuti family, in many ways, was the story of the Imbaba slums, the city and nation beyond. Like tens of thousands of others, the patriarch brought to the slums of Cairo the deep-set attachment to religious values and traditional mores common to much of Upper Egypt. The construction of the mosque brought his family a measure of social standing for its piety and generosity. Later, it provided Sharawi with the base he needed to spread the message of *Jihad*.

Members of the family, meanwhile, fell increasingly under the sway of the militants, turning their backs on the few material options available and eventually cutting themselves off from the secularist Hamdi, the only one who rebelled. Even with the arrest of Sharawi, and the later seizure of their mosque by the state, the remaining members of the Assyuti clan and their followers retained their loyalties to the Islamic cause.

"A few years ago, I felt something was wrong all over Egypt," Hamdi Assyuti said, as we sat in his dark law office hidden in one of Imbaba's many alleyways. "I felt this problem in every house. For every ten families, four had fundamentalists in them. And the effect has remained here. Women wear the *hijab* and the *niqab* (the face veil that covers all but the eyes). People get married according to the kinds of ceremonies the militants once promoted, and everyone's life is ruled by religion."

Religious teachings, increasingly the determinant of every aspect of daily life, varied immensely, however, depending on the messenger. Just as Imbaba was a laboratory for Egypt's religious transformation, it was also a miniature of the span of religious interpretation that had evolved over time unfettered by official doctrine. To move from mosque to mosque across Imbaba was to receive diverse opinions concerning marriage ceremonies, veiling, divorce, and the general duties of keeping up the Muslim faith.

Sheikh Mahmud Abu Azzam, who preaches at the Gamiyya Shariyya religious center, explained the proper Islamic rituals from courtship to marriage. In between customers at the crowded furniture shop he runs down the street from the mosque, Sheikh Azzam, a menacing figure with a long straggly beard and fuzzy hair, reads the Koran from a desk at the back of the store. "A man must see a woman three times wearing a *khimar* (a veil extending to the waist) in the presence of her family during the courtship. If he is satisfied, he then asks God to help him make a decision. If he feels he needs personal details about the woman, such as the texture and color of her hair or her scent, he has the right to ask her mother or sister to answer his questions." I told Sheikh Azzam I had heard about many courting rituals, but never the one he described. Nor was it recognizable to readers of the Koran and the *hadith*s. Likewise, I suggested, it would take the scholars of Al-Azhar, repository of official Islam for centuries, by surprise. But Sheikh Azzam would not be moved.

"This isn't common just in Imbaba; it happens all over Egypt," he said, before returning to his Koran.

3

THE FOUNT OF ISLAM

On March 4, 1994, Sheikh Adawy prepared to deliver the noon sermon at al-Azhar mosque in central Cairo as he did on most Fridays. But he knew this afternoon would be different. It was five days after a bloodbath in Hebron, a Palestinian town in the Israeli-occupied West Bank. A Jewish fanatic from Brooklyn, New York, had massacred twenty-nine Palestinian worshippers as they prayed in the Ibrahimi mosque, a sacred Islamic shrine. Muslims across the Arab world wanted revenge, and Egyptians were no exception. The Muslim Brotherhood had called for a demonstration at al-Azhar; the country's premier mosque seemed a suitable place to express public hostility toward the Jews. And Sheikh Adawy, who never made any secret about his contempt for the Israeli occupation of Palestine, was the ideal man to express what everyone was feeling in his heart.

Thousands of protesters wedged inside the mosque in small rows before prayer time and long before bands of riot police standing outside could bar the way. I mingled in a crowd of a few hundred people gathered outside. We contemplated whether we should risk our lives by joining the worshippers. The police, carrying machine guns and tear-gas canisters, were poised for action. As the prayer was about to begin, there was a surprise. Sheikh Adawy had been replaced. The Ministry of Religious Endowments appointed a preacher guaranteed to deliver a benign sermon. During the next hour, I listened to the stand-in *imam* talk about fasting in the holy month of Ramadan. He talked in abstract terms about the Islamic awakening. But he said nothing specific about who was to blame for Hebron. "The way to mourn effectively is not through leaflets and banners but through the return to Islam," the *imam* counseled the crowd.

By the time he finished the sermon, or *khutba*, the crowd boiled with anger.

His words, designed to tame the audience, had the opposite effect. *"Khaibar, khaibar ya yahud! Jaish Mohammed sawf yaoud!* The armies of the Prophet will return to take revenge upon the Jews," the protesters shouted.

Then the young men, many bearded and wearing *gallabiyyas*, burst out of the mosque, ignoring the riot police standing in front of them. They broke through chains blocking the mosque grounds from the main street and stopped traffic along one of Cairo's central thoroughfares.

"With our souls and blood we sacrifice for Islam," they shouted. "There is no God but God and the Jews are the enemies of God . . . Wake up Egyptians, the Jews have killed the Muslims!" The chants of the marchers were a direct challenge to the secular Egyptian leadership, which had broken Arab ranks to make peace with the Jewish state in 1979.

Suddenly, a blast went off and tear gas filled the air. It was so thick the protesters began choking and vomiting. Swept up in the crowd, I ran north along the street, trying not to trip in the stampede. The men's sandals and *gallabiyyas* slowed them down. Tear-gas canisters fell in the courtyard of the mosque, trapping some worshippers in clouds of noxious fumes. Dozens of people collapsed and were later taken to the hospital.

The shots grew louder and closer, and no one knew for sure if the sound was coming from a second volley of tear gas or whether the police were firing live rounds. I hid under a bridge for shelter as the stumbling throng of demonstrators fled in all directions.

"We will not give up," Magdi Hussein, a leading Islamist and the editor of *al-Shaab* newspaper, had told me as we stood outside the mosque before the prayer. Hussein was referring to the protesters' determination to demonstrate in the face of the formidable threat they faced from the police. His words seemed to hold little truth as I watched thousands of frightened men in desperate flight. But, like Hudaiby, the street *sheikh* from Imbaba who answered the Brotherhood's call and boldly turned out for the protest, Hussein's vow was not limited to one afternoon, but for a lifetime.

The state won this particular standoff with the Islamists the way it wins every confrontation in which the disaffected dare to express their political beliefs. Under an emergency law imposed by President Sadat in 1981, public protest is officially banned in Egypt. But what happened that day in March marked a significant turning point in the populist Islamic revival.

The events surrounding Sheikh Adawy's canceled sermon exposed the emerging alliance between leaders of the Islamic revival—the outlawed Muslim Brotherhood and the popular *sheikh*s of Imbaba and other neighborhoods—and powerful elements within the religious establishment. As a member of the official orthodoxy, Adawy had unified the *ulama*, the religious scholars licensed by the state, with the people in the street. There were thousands of Islamists like Sheikh Hudaiby who had looked forward to Adawy's Friday sermon, only to be disappointed when he was banned from preaching. Shortly afterward, Adawy was exiled permanently from the al-Azhar pulpit and relegated to the less prestigious al-Nur mosque in Cairo's Abbasiyya district.

In the eyes of the state, Adawy's sin was not that he would surely have preached a tirade against Israel. For days after the Hebron massacre, state-run newspapers and President Mubarak blamed the Jewish state for creating a political climate that encouraged violence and fanaticism against Arabs. Sheikh Adawy had committed a far greater crime. Through his *khutba*s, he had emerged as an influential voice among ordinary pious Egyptians who had come to lump the state together with foreign infidels as enemies of Islam. Friday sermons at al-Azhar are traditionally reserved for a *sheikh* who is both popular among the people and acceptable to the state. In Adawy's case, once a majority of his followers were members of the banned Muslim Brotherhood and traditional Islamists active in the poor neighborhoods, he had to go.

For centuries the rigid *ulama* class, literally "the one with knowledge," has faithfully served the political interests of the ruling powers by enforcing religious and social customs according to its reading of the Koran and the sayings of the Prophet, the *hadith*s. As a complete, all-embracing prescription for life, Islam makes no distinction between the spiritual and the political spheres; it draws no line between church and state. Thus, the *ulama*'s overt power of social control is a potent one and can never be divorced from its political overtones. When pashas, kings, and presidents wished to declare war on their enemies, they often turned to al-Azhar for a religious stamp of approval.

Traditionalist *sheikh*s like Adawy skillfully exploited this interrelationship, speaking out on explosive political issues—rejecting peace with Israel or spurning U.S. aid to Egypt worth $2.1 billion a year—in order to attract followers on the more fundamental social issues of the day. Their newfound credibility, based on anti-American and anti-Israeli rhetoric, gave them the legitimacy among the masses of believers to advise on social matters, including birth control, female circumcision, divorce, marriage, and veiling. It is this power to transform society's mores and value system, not the high-profile threat of violence at the hands of Islamist militants, that poses the greatest danger to the modern secular state.

In Egypt, as in much of the Sunni Muslim world, al-Azhar mosque serves as the *ulama*'s spiritual home and its highest seat of religious learning. Under its Grand Sheikh, al-Azhar teaches advanced Islamic philosophy, history, Koranic law, and theology, and trains religious authorities from across the Muslim world. Committees and councils within its walls hand down *fatwa*s, or religious orders, governing all aspects of the lives of pious Muslims—from declarations of war to whether women should be veiled or whether books about sex or religion offend Islamic teaching.

For most of the last sixty years, secular intellectuals and the Muslim Brotherhood have criticized the *ulama* for lack of innovation and insight into modern Egyptian life. Al-Azhar was seen as such an apologist for the state that in July 1977, when Islamic extremists wanted to retaliate against the government, they chose an Azhar *sheikh* as their target. Members of a clandestine group kidnapped and killed Mohammed al-Dhahaby, a former minister of religious endowments, justifying their attack on a representative of the official orthodoxy with their own reading of Islam.

Beginning in the 1970s, however, some members of the *ulama* began to change. The elderly *sheikhs* closeted behind the vast brick walls of the Azhar compound, ornamented with calligraphy and centuries-old gold hanging lamps, began to open their minds to the masses and bridge the gap between the *ulama* and the Islamists leading the popular religious revival. By the 1980s, three distinct Islamic groups had developed in Egypt: moderate Islamists, some of whom were new leaders in the Muslim Brotherhood and others who were former Marxists; elements of the *ulama*, who were split into factions of varying degrees in opposition to the state; and the burgeoning militant groups, such as the *Gama'a al-Islamiyya* and *Jihad*.

For some *sheikhs*, the growing strength of the Islamic movement outside al-Azhar allowed them to create an opening inside the institution for discourse that contradicted the mainstream *ulama* and its government patrons. Such rebellion is expressed in different ways, from the language used during Friday sermons in the mosques to *fatwas* issued by committees within al-Azhar. "The men of religion do not offer their unconditional support for the state anymore," wrote French scholar Malika Zeghal in a groundbreaking analysis of the institution. "They oppose it openly by using an Islamist discourse."[1]

Unlike the old Azhari aristocracy that maintained its allegiance to the government, many of the official *sheikhs* challenging the state are the first generation in their families to become clerics. They often come from rural areas, rather than from Cairo, and typically from poor families.[2] More important, they formed relationships with those involved in the political Islamic movement and believed Azhar should not hold a monopoly on religious teachings. In 1993, some members of the *ulama*, including Sheikh Adawy, served as mediators between the government and leaders in militant groups carrying out assassinations and bombings in Cairo and Upper Egypt. By serving as arbiters, the *ulama* created more separation in the public consciousness between their traditional place in the official orthodoxy and their emerging role as leaders in the grassroots Islamic revival.

The public conversion of these *sheikh*s contributed to the spread of Islamic sentiment from a limited movement of militants and the Muslim Brotherhood in the 1970s to a broad-based populist revival twenty years later. By the late 1980s, Azharis such as Omar Abd al-Rahman, the *sheikh* convicted in the United States for his involvement in the World Trade Center bombing, Sheikh Omar Abd al-Kafi, later placed under house arrest for condemning Christianity and encouraging middle-class women to rebel against their bourgeois husbands, and Sheikh Abd al-Hameed Kishk, the "star of Islamic preaching" who advocated radical reform within al-Azhar, had left the institution and attracted millions of followers around the world. So great was Kishk's fame that the Ministry of Religious Endowments, in charge of official mosques, had to build several annexes to the Source of Life mosque in Cairo to accommodate his swelling number of followers.[3] His reach extended across the Middle East and around the world, driven in large part by the same use of tape-recorded sermons that helped Ayatollah Khomeini undermine the Shah of Iran.

The brazen behavior of a few gave inspiration to other *sheikh*s inside al-Azhar to reconquer society through social change, justified through conservative interpretations of the principle Islamic texts, the Koran and the *hadith*s. By changing society at its roots, the Azharis are not only returning to the institution's original role as a source of religious inspiration, but also erasing al-Azhar's reputation of the last several decades as a mere tool of the secular state.

The Fatimid Dynasty built al-Azhar mosque in 970 A.D. in its new capital of Cairo as part of the struggle with the Sunni caliphs in Baghdad for doctrinal control of the expanding Muslim world. The Fatimid caliphate was one branch of the Ismaili underground movement, a splinter group of Shi'ites who aimed to substitute lineal descendants of the Prophet Mohammed for the established Sunni rulers in Iraq. Al-Azhar was a symbol of Shi'ite ideas and served as a congregational mosque. From the outset, it was given a role in society that overtly fused religion with politics.

Historians are uncertain why it was named al-Azhar, Arabic for "most shining." It may derive from the nickname—*al-Zahra*—for the Prophet's favorite daughter Fatima, from whom the dynasty takes its name. Many Fatimid caliphs enriched al-Azhar with gifts and structural improvements. The original roof was soon raised, and between 1009 and 1010 a vast central courtyard surrounded by porticos with Persian arches was built. Surviving bands of Kufic design and rows of pointed arches, however, testify to its Fatimid origins.

Ibn-Killis, one of the great Shi'ite jurists who was influential in the palace, used al-Azhar mosque to promote Fatimid teachings. The young caliph at the time, al-Azeez, was eager to promote a judicial system of his own and gave power to Ibn-Killis to expand al-Azhar's reach. Al-Azeez ordered living quarters to be built for Shi'ite scholars alongside the original mosque. After Friday prayers, they gathered to discuss Islamic law. Soon, classes were created for students and a complete program of study was established, laying the foundation for al-Azhar's current role as the premier institution of Islamic education.

The Fatimids had two main reasons for creating such an institution: to teach jurists the Fatimid system in place of the prevailing Sunni code of Islamic law; and to serve as a podium from which to win converts to their ideology. Several qualities of Fatimid rule distinguish it from Sunni practice. Most important, the head of state, the caliph, must be a direct descendant of the Prophet Mohammed. Claims of direct descent from the Prophet are still used today by Arab leaders, such as King Hassan of Morocco and the late King Hussein of Jordan, to legitimize their rule, particularly when challenged by Islamic groups.

The fall of the Fatimids in 1171 saw the collapse of Shi'ite ideology in Egypt. The new ruler, the great Kurdish warrior Saladin, banished Shi'ite teachings and imposed the Sunni code of law, to this day the prevailing teaching in modern Egypt and the official outlook of Al-Azhar. Saladin, champion of Islam against the Christian crusaders, established the Ayyubid dynasty and set in motion Cairo's gradual emergence as the center of Islamic learning and culture.[4] Copying the *madrasas* of Persia, he built similar Koranic schools in Cairo based on the Sunni system of religious education.

Saladin's innovations, however, saw the eclipse of al-Azhar. Eager to wipe out all traces of heretical Fatimid thinking, the new ruler barred the prestigious Friday prayers at the mosque and closed down its schools. The mosque's religious thinkers were forced to take up common trades or become simple clerks.[5]

It was not until the Mamluk period, almost 100 years later, that al-Azhar began to recapture its former glory. Originally a group of foreign slaves imported into the country to boost the authority of ruling princes and dynasties, the Mamluks eventually routed the Ayyubid royalty from power and built strong armies and a sophisticated warrior caste.[6] They enlisted al-Azhar to help legitimize their rule, preserve the Arabic language—the Mamluks themselves spoke Turkish dialects—and uproot the prevailing trends of superstition and fanaticism.[7] The most famous Mamluk sultan, Baybars, restored al-Azhar structurally and spiritually, reviving Friday prayers, installing an ornate wooden pulpit in the sanctuary, funding the depleted endowment, and returning the mosque to its scholarly mission. Once again, al-Azhar was back in its accustomed role as a pillar of the ruling elite.

By the beginning of the fourteenth century, the domain of the Mamluk beys extended to the Arabian peninsula. Friday prayers in the name of the sultan in Cairo were said as far west as Tripoli and Tunis. Scholars fleeing the Mongol hordes of Asia and later the Christian conquerors of Andalusia, took refuge under Mamluk protection; al-Azhar enjoyed a golden age.

Egypt's three centuries as the undisputed center of Islamic cultural and intellectual life ended in the early sixteenth century when the Ottoman conquest saw the locus of temporal and spiritual power shift to Istanbul. The *ulama* at al-Azhar continued to serve as an arm of the state, but a newfound wealth allowed it to gain popularity in its own right among the Egyptian people. During an eight-month journey in Egypt, Sultan Selim displayed great reverence toward al-Azhar, attending Friday prayers and giving money to support the work of the mosque.[8]

With the *sharia*, or Koranic law, the foundation of Ottoman jurisprudence, the new rulers took advantage of the expertise of the *ulama* and *mufti*s educated at al-Azhar by assigning them to jobs throughout the empire.[9] These *sheikh*s were given wide-ranging power and exposure, strengthening al-Azhar's influence throughout the Muslim world.

At home, al-Azhar cemented its primacy by leading resistance to the French occupation under Napoleon Bonaparte. However, this brief period of French rule, from 1798 to 1801, injected a dose of European rationalism and secularism into an insular Egyptian society, which until that time rejected such thinking and nearly all other forms of European influence. Napoleon made it clear from the outset he had come to rescue the *ulama* from their Mamluk oppressors, not to cleanse the country of its Islamic tradition: "O *Sheikh*s, *qadi*s, *imam*s, and officers of the town, tell your nation that the French are friends of true Muslims, and proof of this is that they went to Rome and destroyed the Papal See which had always urged the Christians to fight Islam."[10]

Despite Napoleon's public campaign to win over the Muslim masses, Egyptians responded to cries from the Ottoman porte in Istanbul to rise up against the infidels.[11] The *sheikh*s of al-Azhar, recognized as natural leaders of the community of believers, established a council for revolution. Abd al-Rahman al-Jabarti, a respected historian who lived from the mid-1700s to 1825, says in his chronicles that Cairenes rebelled specifically over the high taxes the French imposed and the expropriation of property. When Napoleon wrote to the *sheikh*s at al-Azhar and appealed for calm, they refused to comply. He then ordered the bombardment of al-Hussein, the neighborhood surrounding the mosque compound. Jabarti gave this account of the attack: "The (French) troops entered . . . al-Azhar on horseback. They broke the lamps and demolished the chests and books. They tore up the books and copies of the Koran, throwing them on the ground and trampling on them with their feet and boots. They also committed ritual impurity, defecated, urinated, drank."[12]

The uprising against French occupation was the only time in their history when the al-Azhar *sheikh*s openly rebelled against the ruling power. However, it must be noted that a Christian ruler by nature is illegitimate under Islam, and the *ulama*, in theory the religious representative of society, had a sacred duty to overthrow him.

The French departure from Egypt in 1801 left a power vacuum. Mohammed Ali, a young Albanian officer, filled that void with the blessing of the Ottoman Sultan in Istanbul. His rule is commonly credited with the formation of the beginnings of the modern Egyptian state. He laid the foundation for the future nation-state, which would be established only after independence from British rule in the 1950s; he revolutionized education by introducing courses in the sciences and arts; he established a government bureaucracy, installing the country's first ministry of foreign affairs; and he modernized the tradition-bound agricultural sector.

At the same time, Mohammed Ali launched a campaign to weaken al-Azhar. He eliminated the institution's financial independence, making it an arm of the state by confiscating the institution's religious endowments. He dismissed militant *sheikhs* and manipulated elections for the al-Azhar leadership.[13] The result was a passive al-Azhar, subservient to the ruler of the time.

Egyptian resistance to foreign occupation continued through the later British invasion. However, this second colonial period, from 1882 until the 1950s, left its mark on both secular intellectuals and on the *ulama*. Great religious scholars, writers, and philosophers emerged to blend the country's general resistance to foreign influence with a desire to adapt religious thinking to what was clearly a more modern world outside Egypt. Among them was Sheikh Mohammed Abdu, who sought to pull al-Azhar in a new, more modern direction. As an Azhar graduate and a member of the *ulama*, in 1900 during the British occupation Abdu secured a position as Mufti of Egypt, formally in charge of official religious rulings.

In direct conflict with the traditionalists, Abdu believed the *ulama* should move away from strict interpretations of Islamic texts and integrate religious values into a society that was inevitably touched by Western influences. He also challenged al-Azhar's authority, arguing that members of the *ulama* had no religious authority over society except as a source of general guidance and advice.[14] Although Abdu's thinking remained grounded in Islamic teaching, his liberal influence spawned a generation of modernists who relied more on reason and science than religion. These intellectuals of the early 1900s demanded that Egypt turn toward secularism to keep pace with Europe.

The new tendency split society into two camps: the nationalist-secularists, who believed Egypt must rid itself of foreign evils while adapting to the modern world, and religious-nationalists, who believed the *ulama* had failed to keep Islam alive, leading to disunity within the *umma*, or community of believers. In the religious camp, the belief that Egypt had strayed from pure Islam and failed to repel foreign influences helped lead to the formation of the Muslim Brotherhood.

For Hasan al-Banna, the founder of the Muslim Brotherhood, there was a direct link between economic and political intervention by the British and what he saw as religious and moral decay in Egyptian society. Just five years before al-Banna established the Brotherhood, Britain had granted Egypt quasi-independence and permitted formation of a parliament. The attempt to disguise the continued occupation in a cloak of autonomy provoked even more hatred toward foreign intervention.

"Eject imperialism from your souls, and it will leave your lands," al-Banna was fond of saying.[15] From the group's early beginnings in the late 1920s until the 1952 coup that brought President Nasser to power, the Brotherhood presented itself as an alternative to both the state and the *ulama*.

Al-Banna tried publicly to put a positive face on relations between the Brotherhood and the official *sheikhs*. Behind the scenes, however, things were very different. One writer has observed that there were two Islamic groups in Egypt, the officials of al-Azhar and the Islamic societies, and they "do not co-operate."[16] The consensus within the Brotherhood was that the *ulama* had not only come up short in its mission as the intellectual keeper of the faith, but had failed to resist the occupiers and found common ground with the monied class. The Brothers denounced this "civil servant *ulama*" as a tool of the government by which they were paid.[17]

By the time of the 1952 Free Officers' coup that brought Nasser to power, the Muslim Brotherhood was firmly entrenched as a formidable threat to both the state and the *ulama*. A member of the Brotherhood was blamed for an attempt to assassinate Nasser as he addressed a large audience in Alexandria in 1954. This sparked an outright assault on the organization and its temporary suppression by the authorities. For al-Azhar, the conflict was significant: To take the sting out of growing fear across the Muslim world that his socialist government was an enemy of Islam, Nasser began to accommodate the *ulama* even as he cracked down hard on the Muslim Brotherhood. In this way, he sought to change the perception of the new republic as antithetical to Islamic values and traditions.

Nonetheless, Nasser's bid to harness the power of Islam behind his revolution inflicted enormous damage on the influence and prestige of al-Azhar, a blow from which it is only now recovering. One of Nasser's first moves in taking direct control of the *ulama* occurred in 1955, when he abolished the autonomous *sharia* courts in order to unify the judicial system. He then issued orders to bring all mosques under control of the new Ministry of Religious

Endowments, a government body created to administer religious properties. The new ministry also took control of religious contributions, depriving Azhar of the right to manage its own financial affairs.

Even more damaging to the Islamic establishment was Nasser's administrative reform law of 1961, the most significant turn in Azhar's fortunes since the time of Saladin. However, the Azhar *sheikh*s were once again to prove their remarkable resilience in the face of state coercion. In fact, the reforms of 1961 helped create a generation of rejectionists, a neo-*ulama*, inside the institution and laid the foundation for political opposition grounded in religion.[18] More important, key elements of this same *ulama* generation later made common cause with the Muslim Brotherhood—a result precisely opposite to what Nasser had in mind. The groundbreaking reform that aimed to seal al-Azhar as an arm of the state once and for all instead inspired a cadre of traditionalists who would later link up with the informal Islamic revival and work to undermine state policies in the 1990s. Members of this neo-*ulama* were generally opposed to the long-standing idea among their more state-oriented colleagues that al-Azhar held a monopoly on religious interpretation. They believed that Islamists outside the confines of the institution were also qualified to give authoritative advice to the pious. In keeping with this mentality, the neo-*ulama* favored dialogue with moderate Islamic groups, such as the Muslim Brotherhood. This openness allowed the neo-*ulama* in the 1990s to distance itself from the state, while moving closer to its goal of deeper integration with Egyptian society.

Nasser's plan to reform al-Azhar was aired on June 21, 1961, at a tense session of parliament that ran until 3 A.M. The government criticized the *sheikh*s for resisting change and failing to adapt to modern times. Al-Azhar, the ministers said, could no longer hope to attract students from across the Muslim world unless the curriculum were expanded to include sciences and other modern disciplines. Likewise, the university's core religious studies were substandard and dated.

Kamal al-Din Hussein, a member of the Revolutionary Command Council, (the reconstituted group of Free Officers who led the revolution) made this observation at the time: "The fact that al-Azhar has for long years been compelled to stand in the face of all attempts at aggression has made it acquire a sort of reserve which is probably one of the characteristics of the defensive attitude it has adopted all through those centuries. When life revived around it, and the causes that led up to its reserved and rigid attitude no longer existed, it failed to find the proper means of renewed activity that would help it adapt itself to contemporary times while retaining its characteristics and assuming its duties of defending the religion and preserving the heritage of Islam."[19]

The most significant articles of the 1961 law separated al-Azhar University from al-Azhar as a religious institution that set policy for the Muslim world. An "explanatory memorandum" published with the reform law justified the changes on the grounds that religion was not a vocation. Therefore, religious instruction should be separated from courses with practical applications, such as the sciences. It also argued that the *ulama* was ignorant of nonreligious matters and this had created an artificial barrier between al-Azhar and the outside world.[20]

The provisions under the reform law touched all aspects of the institution, from the way al-Azhar was administered to the university's curriculum. For the first time, the Grand Sheik of al-Azhar would be appointed by the president of Egypt, instead of being chosen by members of the *ulama*. Al-Azhar was to consist of five organizations: the Supreme Council, presided over by the Grand Sheikh; the Islamic Research Academy; the Administration of Islamic Culture; the University of al-Azhar; and al-Azhar's primary and secondary educational institutes.

The government also created state agencies and committees, completely independent of al-Azhar, that were charged with interpreting religious codes and served as a counterweight to the institution's powerful *sheikh*s. A young military officer, for example, was made director of the High Committee for Islamic Affairs, under the Ministry of Religious Endowments.[21]

The immediate impact on al-Azhar was devastating, for the reforms threatened its very reason for being. Religious knowledge, the ability to authoritatively interpret and spread the word of the Koran and the *hadith*s, is one of the foundations of Islam. Muslims had always maintained that required classical education can only come from institutions such as al-Azhar. *Sheikh*s across the Muslim world engage in lively debate over who is authorized, and who is not, to issue opinions on matters that affect society. It is common in Egypt for one *sheikh* to dismiss a rival as lacking appropriate "knowledge."

"The one notion that probably summarizes the predominant ideal associated with Islamic authority would be the concept of *'ilm'* or knowledge," wrote Patrick D. Gaffney, a leading expert on the *sheikh*s and their world.[22] In the expansion of the university curriculum, al-Azhar saw its mission as the premier source of religious teaching diluted by the introduction of utilitarian training of graduates for the job market. The change opened the door to criticism from all directions. Modernists seized the moment to dismiss al-Azhar's educational system as archaic. Traditionalists inside the institution blamed the state for tampering with its classical curriculum. And radicals used the changes to confirm what they had been saying since the British occupation: al-Azhar graduates were little more than puppets serving the whims of an irreligious state.[23] Thus, the reform was not only a matter of introducing science or mathematics to al-Azhar University. It called into question the utility of mastering the *sharia* and the Koran as tools for dealing with modern life.

Al-Azhar also lost its privileged position as guardian of the collective conscience. Once the regime fused religion with Arab nationalism, the state emerged as the country's spiritual guide. And Nasser became the defender of the state and the faith.

The government followed up its reform of al-Azhar with an extensive propaganda campaign in the state-run press. "The revolution, the banner of which was raised in al-Azhar University, is the first real upheaval which has taken place in that great institution for the past 1000 years," proclaimed *Akhbar al-Youm* newspaper. "The feeling of increasing isolation which has been suffered by tens of thousands of al-Azhar students and graduates will come to an end."[24]

President Nasser went a step further, trying personally to discredit the *sheikh*s as loafers and deadbeats. In a new government quarterly journal, *Minbar al-Islam*, he declared: "Of course the *sheikh* does not think of anything except the turkey and the food with which he filled his belly. He is no more than a stooge of reaction, feudalism and capitalism.... From the beginning, Islam was a religion of work. The Prophet used to work like everybody else. Islam was never a profession."[25]

For the most part, the al-Azhar *sheikh*s quickly fell in line with the new order, lest they face expulsion from their positions of power and influence. Mohammed Shaltut, then the newly appointed Grand Sheikh, not only supported the new "Islamic" socialism, but neatly found religious justification for it: "The revolution is considered the extension, especially in foreign policy, for Islam's mission itself."[26] After witnessing the application of the reforms at al-Azhar, Shaltut was far less enchanted with the results and submitted his resignation to Nasser in a letter dated August 6, 1963.[27] However, his resignation was not accepted and he remained Grand Sheikh of Azhar until his death.

The *sheikh*s' initial public endorsement of the 1961 reforms was in sharp contrast to earlier positions staked out by the *ulama*. In 1948, for example, the mufti of Egypt, Sheikh Mohammed Makhluf, issued a fatwa in defense of private property and condemned state ownership as a violation of Islamic principles. Al-Azhar's later support for Nasser, who nationalized virtually all private property, represented a 180-degree turn.

The Azharis had little choice. Helpless to fight the state's ever increasing power over religious affairs, they were in no position to challenge Nasser's credibility with the Egyptian people. "Determined to preserve their shrinking yet substantial niches, they have tended to rationalize or at least acquiesce in the views of the government while expressing their misgivings in guarded and often convoluted language," wrote scholar Robert Bianchi. "This combination of collaboration and caution has earned the *ulama* the mistrust of the secular regime as well as the contempt of its religious opponents."[28]

The *ulama* was not only restricted directly by state policies, but its voice in religion and politics was forced into the background by Nasser's domineering public persona. His unprecedented popularity stemmed from his leadership qualities as an Arab nationalist. For the first time in centuries, an Egyptian leader succeeded in introducing an alternative ideology to traditional Islam. Nasser fused elements of Islam with Arab socialism. His success had much to do with his charisma and the historical developments in the Middle East at the time. Nasser was the first native Egyptian to rule the country since the Pharaohs. He was seen by many as the man who would at last unite the Arab world against Israel and the West, which had helped established the Jewish state at the expense of the Palestinian struggle for a homeland.

At the outbreak of the 1967 war with Israel, Nasser was riding high, with al-Azhar functioning like many of the state agencies his government had melded into a Soviet-style bureaucracy. Predictably, the *sheikh*s of al-Azhar sanctioned Nasser's decision to wage war against the Jewish state. The ensuing military disaster, however, forced a humiliated president to offer his resignation on June 7, 1967. More important for the later Islamic movement, the defeat was widely interpreted by the pious as a sign from God that Egyptian society had strayed too far from the path of the Prophet.

The embarrassing defeat only compounded a backlash already simmering underneath the surface from Nasser's decision in August 1966 to hang Sayyid Qutb, one of the leading ideologues of the Muslim Brotherhood, and two of his senior colleagues. Qutb and more than 100 other Brothers had been arrested after security forces uncovered a plot against the regime. His death earned him the highest honor in Islam—designation as *shahid*, or martyr— and his memory still provokes deep passions among millions of admirers, but the death and imprisonment of so many members badly depleted the ranks of the Brotherhood.[29] Public disenchantment with the Nasser government soon boiled over into street protests. Thousands of students demonstrated to demand the prosecution of the military leaders responsible for the 1967 defeat. The Muslim Brotherhood wasted no time in joining the chorus of criticism and soul-searching. This marked the end of Egypt's experiment with a hybrid ideology of Islam and socialism; in its place were planted the seeds of today's Islamic revival.

When Anwar Sadat succeeded Nasser, he deliberately took a different tack. Sadat used religion as the basis for political ideology, instead of the other way around, in what has been called the "Islamization of nationalism."[30] The new president sought to blend the symbols of Islam with the qualities of the nation-state to concoct what he believed was an appropriate response to the political and economic failures of the Nasser period and the rise of religious feeling. "The Arab world cannot function without Egypt and its Azhar," he said, shortly after taking office.

Symbols were important to Sadat. Egyptians today still tell jokes about the president using makeup to apply a mark on his forehead before appearing on national television. "Jihan!" Sadat calls to his wife. "Hand me my *zabeeb*." The mark—the *zabeeb*, or raisin—is the dark callous developed over time by pious men from touching the forehead to the ground in prayer and it is worn as a badge of honor.

During his early years in office, the new president pursued a dual policy regarding religion: As he moved closer and closer toward a risky peace deal with Israel, which virtually every Egyptian saw as the Zionist enemy, he also became more tolerant of the Islamists. But the more room Sadat gave them, the more progress they made toward his undoing. In 1976, he legalized two publications of the Muslim Brotherhood, *al-Dawa* and *al-Itisam*, only to find them used as platforms against his policies of economic liberalization and improved relations with the West.[31] Religious tensions escalated further in the late 1970s when armed clashes erupted in Cairo neighborhoods between Muslims and minority Christian Copts.

Sadat's response was swift and direct. Just as quickly as he had cozied up to the Islamists, he launched a massive crackdown on the movement. Thousands of Islamists were arrested in September 1981. In the months leading up to the arrests, he had moved to diminish the power of the official orthodoxy. He introduced legal sanctions against religious scholars or preachers who discredited government laws and decrees or issued religious advice that contradicted state policies. Sadat's moves against the *ulama* were reflected in one of his most famous slogans: "No politics in religion and no religion in politics."

At the same time that al-Azhar was battling new state-imposed constraints on its authority, it was losing legitimacy in the eyes of society as a whole. Militant Islamic groups were becoming more powerful, and some of them promulgated the belief that Islamic scholars, the official *imam*s and *sheikh*s, should be scorned. This idea was based on a revived notion that individual Muslims should speak to God directly and interpret for themselves the Koran and the *hadith*s without the mediation or interference of the *ulama*. One of the most prominent radicals of the time, Shukri Mustafa, accused the *ulama* of interpreting religious texts solely for the convenience of the authorities.

Shukri Mustafa was a leading member of the radical *al-Takfeer wal-Hijra*, which claimed the right to determine who was an infidel and who was a true Muslim. Ironically, Shukri Mustafa himself was found to be unable to read a single verse of the Koran when he was arrested in 1965.[32] The pretensions among extremists like Shukri Mustafa to hold the key to true Islam were a source of fierce rivalry between the militant groups and the more established Muslim Brotherhood, which maneuvered for decades in and out of official state channels.

"They (the *ulama*) . . . might issue *fatwas* tailored to fit the views of the sovereign—whoever he was, and whatever his views—in order to spread sin, to declare the illicit legal in the name of Islam," Shukri Mustafa told a criminal court in 1977.[33] To support his accusations, he cited Sheikh Sharawi, the most popular preacher within official Islam during Sadat's reign. Sharawi ruled that state Treasury bonds did not contradict Islamic law, even though most devout Muslims consider such interest income illegal.[34]

Shukri Mustafa also singled out Mohammed al-Dhahaby, the former minister of religious endowments, as a leading culprit among the *ulama*. He chose Dhahaby because he held him responsible for portraying the *Takfeer* as a renegade group of terrorists. The group kidnapped Dhahaby, and Shukri Mustafa gave the order to execute him. The murder, which some *sheikh*s blamed on Azhar's reputation as a tool of the state, would prove to be the beginning of a split within al-Azhar between those tied to the regime and a growing group of independent *sheikh*s who derived their legitimacy from the Muslim Brotherhood and the people at large.

While the *ulama* were under attack from the Islamists, who at the time had amassed a large following, the military also blamed al-Azhar indirectly for violent attacks against people like Dhahaby. At the military trial of those charged with Dhahaby's murder, a general used his opening statement to accuse al-Azhar of failing to offer youth a proper religious education, which he claimed was the source of the current evil.[35]

The Sheikh of al-Azhar at the time, Abu al-Haleem Mahmud, angered by the military's campaign against the *ulama*, blamed the violence among Egyptian youth on deficient state leadership. He said young people carried out violent acts in the name of Islam because the rulers' political ideology was not rooted in the religious culture of the country.[36]

Under this barrage of attacks from the military, radical Islamists, and to some extent society in general, al-Azhar began a long journey toward independence that became evident only in the 1990s. Al-Azhar's turn coincided with dramatic changes within the community of believers at large. It is impossible to know whether the *sheikh*s sensed the winds of change and seized the moment to regain legitimacy among the people, or whether they, like the people themselves, experienced an awakening as part of a reaction to the secular trend that dominated the Nasserite period. Nonetheless, by the early 1980s, a majority of Egyptians had shed most of Nasser's nationalist legacy and once again looked to religion as their anchor in life. A decade later, Islam was effectively the prevailing ideology; the first priority for most ordinary Egyptians was to be a good Muslim.

The man at the vanguard of al-Azhar's challenge to the secular state was

Gad al-Haq Ali Gad al-Haq, the mosque's Grand Sheikh from 1982 to 1996. After a lackluster tenure as the Mufti of Egypt, during which he effectively parroted government policy, Gad al-Haq was named Grand Sheikh by President Mubarak, who was certain of his loyalty to the state. But Gad al-Haq exploited the resurgent power of al-Azhar and its growing popular appeal to turn on the very state that had nurtured him. Gad al-Haq and the other senior *sheikh*s of al-Azhar contradicted official policy at every turn, embarrassing the government and exposing its loss of control over many aspects of daily life.

Al-Azhar's purpose, the Grand Sheikh believed, was to preserve and defend the Islamic faith not only in Egypt, but throughout the Muslim world. The whims of the Egyptian state were less important as an influence on opinions issued by al-Azhar, which instead gave religious legitimacy to practices and customs that society already agreed were required for any good Muslim.

Gad al-Haq proclaimed it an Islamic duty for Egyptians to produce large families, while the state's Population Ministry, backed by Western aid donors, urged family planning. He publicly sanctioned the widespread practice of female circumcision—an initiation rite in which parts of the genitalia, including the clitoris, are removed to inhibit a woman's sexual pleasure—and dismissed government attempts to stamp it out. Circumcision has no legal basis in Islam and its origins appear to lie in pre-Muslim African societies. But in countries such as Egypt, Sudan, and parts of Yemen, it has taken on an Islamic meaning, largely as means of controlling female sexuality.

The Grand Sheikh also denounced the payment of bank interest, or *riba* and issued a *fatwa* barring visits to the Muslim holy sites in East Jerusalem under Israeli occupation. Both rulings challenged the policies of the Egyptian state, which was keen to develop Western-style financial markets and sought a leading role in the Middle East peace process.

President Mubarak's decision to host the United Nations Population Conference in September 1994, gave Al-Azhar and its allies in the streets a global forum for their fight. Promoted by the authorities as a showcase for "modern" Egypt, the Cairo conference quickly degenerated into pitched battles over female sexuality and birth control between Islamic traditionalists, backed by newfound allies in the Vatican, and a consortium of Western donors, women's groups, family planning organizations, and development specialists. This outcome should have come as no surprise.

In conservative Islamic societies marriage and procreation are religious duties, the key to perpetuating the faith and ensuring the continued viability of the *umma*. The average Egyptian woman has four to five children in her lifetime, with several more pregnancies typically ending in miscarriage. To be a woman living in Egypt is to fend off daily questions about marital status and the number of children one has. The Western idea that a couple should deliberately limit the number of children in the family is not only an alien concept, but is considered heretical by the pious. Such power must be reserved for God.

Clearly defined sex roles and institutions such as the veil and the segregation of men and women all stem from a need, grounded in traditionalist thinking, to harness human sexuality toward religious ends. The outlook of the Azharis, and of most Egyptians, is summed up in remarks made by the Tunisian *sheikh*, Ibn-Murad, who argued that Islam believes in sexual inequality. "The meaning of marriage is the husband's supremacy.... Marriage is a religious act.... which gives the man a leading power over the woman for the benefit of humanity."[37]

In the West, the status and treatment of women stem largely from an underlying cultural and social assumption that females are physically weaker and intellectually inferior to men. In Islam, however, it is fear of female power that justifies the suppression of women. Women must be controlled to prevent men, who are easily tempted, from being distracted from their social and religious duties. In Islam, women are perceived as active beings; in Western secular societies as passive. Therefore, controlling women, particularly their sexual desires, is essential to controlling men and ensuring order in society.

The Prophet likened the powerful attraction of women to that of Satan. "When the woman comes toward you, it is Satan who is approaching you. When one of you sees a woman and feels attracted to her, hurry to see your wife."[38]

Inside the walls of al-Azhar, the *sheikh*s had no doubts that the Western notions of family planning, women's empowerment, and reproductive health driving much of the Population Conference were a direct threat to the *umma* they were sworn to protect. The Mosque and its powerful Grand Sheik went on the attack.

Months before thousands of card-carrying members of American and European nongovernmental organizations landed at the Cairo airport, their suitcases stuffed with condoms and other birth control devices, al-Azhar rallied Islamists from all corners to demand the conference be canceled. How could the state, they insisted, have the audacity to host a gathering to promote ideas most Egyptians vehemently reject?

Al-Azhar denounced the conference as a plot against Islamic family values and a scheme by Western imperialists to reduce the Muslim population, which multiplies at a much faster rate than the Christian community of believers. Sheikh Mohammed al-Ghazali, a leading scholar, accused "the enemies of Islam of conspiring to bring down Islam and destroy Islamic countries economically and morally." Gad al-Haq and the Scholars' Front, a stronghold of the Azhari traditionalists, also denounced the conference. Their reasons were the same: birth control and abortion violate the *sharia*. Abortion is permitted, according to Azhari traditionalists, only if the mother's life is at risk.

As the conference drew near and the criticism grew louder, the Azharis further challenged the state's credibility. If the underlying reason to limit population growth was to reduce poverty, they argued, why has the state neglected its responsibility for decades by failing to meet the most basic economic needs of the people? Instead of forcing Muslims to limit the size of their families, the state should install electricity and water systems in the countryside and reform the economy in the cities to create more jobs. Government officials appeared helpless to respond.

While the debate raged between al-Azhar and the government, few people in the countryside, where the use of birth control is minimal and big families are the rule, were even aware that a population conference was under way in far-off Cairo. I traveled to the remote village of Izbit Abdullah to learn firsthand of the peasants' views on what some had termed "contraceptive imperialism" being practiced inside the glitzy halls of the capital's convention center.

In Izbit Abdullah, deep in the rushes of the Nile River, the villagers still laugh about an encounter between foreign aid workers who came offering birth control pills and local resident Mohammed Ali Mohammed. And there is no doubt where their sympathies lie. Mohammed, it seems, listened for a bit before driving his visitors away with his cane and chasing them through the towering cornfields and into the safety of their Land Rover.

Only two things determine the size of the family in Izbit Abdullah: God and the donkey. "We don't believe in these ideas foreigners have," Mohammed explained with a grimace, twisting the long strands of his gray handlebar mustache. "God who created the whole world decides and provides enough food for the family. It's forbidden to use birth control."

While the men in Izbit Abdullah rely on the power of God, the women look to the donkey. Gathered around a kerosene stove as they prepared coffee, they explained their homegrown birth control methods. "I don't use contraceptives, but I have only five children," said Gamiya Mohammed, a gaunt woman wearing a paper-thin silk dress of flaming fuchsia. "My sister told me about the donkey method. When a donkey's breast is filled with milk, I leave the door open and I lie on the ground. When the donkey comes and hovers over me, I know I won't have children again."

In the remote villages of Upper Egypt, as in the shantytowns of Cairo, it is the message of al-Azhar and its powerful *sheikh*s, not that of the central government, that reflects popular notions of what is required under Islam. "The foreigners came here and they said, 'Our way is better,'" says Gamiya. "But I don't think so. Taking birth control pills is contrary to nature and to

God. It is like having a plant that begins growing and then suddenly someone comes along and cuts it off."

Questions of female sexuality, long a subject of debate in the vast halls of al-Azhar, became a national preoccupation after CNN broadcast a report, timed to coincide with the Population Conference, showing a young girl's circumcision in all its gory detail. The procedure, known in Arabic as *tahara*, or purification, involves trimming or removing the clitoris and often the labia minora. Viewers around the world were transfixed by the terror of the ten-year-old, her wrists bound to her ankles, as her mother sings and relatives look on. "Why did you do this to me?" she beseeches her father afterwards. International women's groups condemned the government for turning a blind eye to the procedure, often performed at home without anesthetic by super-market butchers or barbers.

President Mubarak, seeking to protect the country's honor, announced to the world in a second CNN report that the state would impose tougher penalties to discourage a ritual practiced by an estimated 97 percent of the population. Egyptians, however, responded to the scandal by defending their right to choose; if parents want to circumcise their daughters it is no business of the state, they argued. CNN's Cairo correspondent at the time claimed that the report served a high moral purpose by exposing the ritual and thus limiting its frequency. In fact, the broadcast only sparked a booming under-ground trade for butchers, nurses, and midwives to sever young girls' genitals in back alleys instead of doctors' clinics.

At al-Azhar, the circumcision controversy brought the traditionalists out of the closet. It contained all the ingredients to stir popular passion: sex and the right of the state to interfere in a highly sensitive religious matter. The debate also pitted Gad al-Haq against his successor as Mufti of Egypt, Mo-hammed Sayyed Tantawi. Like traditionalists before him, the Grand Sheikh encouraged circumcision for adolescent girls as a key to limiting female sex-uality and ensuring social order. Circumcision, he ruled, was a "laudable practice that did honor to women."

Mufti Tantawi, a modernist, issued his own opposing *fatwa* in 1994, ar-guing there was no legal text in Islam making circumcision obligatory for women. The practice, he wrote, would deprive men of the pleasure of having sex with their wives, who would be unable to reach orgasm. "Don't ablate fully, that is better for the woman and more pleasing for the husband," Tantawi wrote in his *fatwa*, citing the Prophet Mohammed.

I wanted to hear the side of the argument the state-run press was trying to keep hidden, so I paid a visit to Sheikh Mohammed al-Berri, an Azhar maverick. Sheikh Berri was a lanky man somewhere in his late fifties, with a dry sense of humor. He had recently acquired notoriety as a leader in the Scholars' Front, a benevolent society founded within al-Azhar in the 1950s that in the 1990s emerged as a haven for the institution's iconoclasts. He was willing to tell a Western journalist what other *sheikh*s who identified with the establishment thought, but would never publicly admit. He denounced the security forces, for example, for the well-documented policy of torture and in some cases murders carried out against suspected Islamic militants. Berri did not condone militancy as a means of overthrowing the state, but he believed the current government had strayed from the Islamic path and it was up to religious scholars like himself to set the record straight.

He lived in a well-appointed house a bit more elaborate than what an Azhar sheikh on a low government salary can typically afford. Instead of the usual dreary furnishings, the living room was decorated with floral prints. Adding to the gay atmosphere was his young daughter, who repeatedly fluttered in and out of the dining room during the hours I spent there. Every thirty minutes or so, she would reappear and hide behind the chair where her father was sitting until he placed a piece of candy in her small hand. Her joy and carefree disposition begged the obvious question. I wondered if this sweet girl, who was about four years old, was one day destined for the butcher's knife.

Berri was reluctant to even mention the word circumcision. By that time, the CNN report had stirred up such heated debate between the Islamists and al-Azhar on one side and state officials on the other that few people were talking. For ordinary Egyptians, the mere sight of a foreign journalist was enough to send them scurrying. They feared if it became known that they circumcised their daughters, they could be sent to jail, given the mounting pressure on state officials to prove to Western critics that they discouraged the practice.

I convinced Berri I was interested in the relationship between the traditionalists' ideas on circumcision and their views on female sexuality. Why must a woman be tamed sexually? And how does this keep order in the family?

"A woman can be aroused at any moment," Berri explained, serving up tea and biscuits at his home in the Cairo suburb of Heliopolis. "Even if a woman is riding in a car, if she hits a few bumps, she can become sexually aroused." This was an invitation to *fitna*, or social chaos, stemming from her unbridled lust.

"Once this happens, a man loses control. So you see, this practice certainly is not meant to punish women. But it is necessary."

Berri also spoke in general about the divisions within the institution that were now out in the open. "Azhar must regain its glory," he said with emphasis. "Recently, we've been smelling the odor of attempts to undermine al-Azhar and tarnish its image because of its positions on issues. But our image cannot be tainted because the people support us."

Berri told me there were competing political persuasions inside al-Azhar. The Scholars' Front, asleep for the last twenty years, had risen to the Islamic awakening and become more active in promoting traditional ideas. He would not say directly that the group aimed to be a counterweight to the *sheikh*s supporting state policies, but he implied as much. In any case, he did not have to. The Front's *sheikh*s were vocal about their socially conservative opinions in the mid-to late 1990s, and were repeatedly given a high profile in the press. No matter the issue, the Front often led religious debate. In the striking case of Nasr Hamed Abu Zeid, a professor at Cairo University who was accused of being an apostate for his writings about Islam, the Front called for Abu Zeid's dismissal from the university. During a lengthy legal battle at the end of which a court finally ruled that Abu Zeid must be divorced from his wife because he was an apostate and a Muslim woman cannot be married to a non-Muslim man, and the Front led the attack against him. In fear for his life, Abu Zeid and his wife fled to Holland, where they now live. The Scholars' Front launched a campaign in 1997 against another Cairo University professor, Hasan Hanafi, who had been invited to speak at al-Azhar. The Front declared Hanafi's philosophic writings about religion a violation of Islamic teaching. The Front then initiated an attack against him in the press. The two cases placed the group at the vanguard of Azhar's conservative wing, provoking a sensational secularist magazine, *Rose al-Yussef*, to label the Front's activities "intellectual terrorism."

"The time has come for this country to come out of darkness and return to the Islamic path," Berri told me, choosing his words with care. "The lions of Islam will not be unleashed unless there are Israeli rockets.... We need the enemy to wake us from our stupor. Islam always wakes up under oppression. There is a lot of oppression today."

After several glasses of soft drinks, tea, and more soft drinks, I told him I had to leave. But Sheikh Berri insisted I stay, so I used the only explanation I knew would meet his approval: I told him I had to rush home to make dinner for my husband.

"Well then, if your husband is waiting, by all means go," Berri said, showing me to the door. Little did he know my husband was living in Istanbul.

Like the Scholars' Front, al-Azhar's Islamic Research Academy serves as another potent counterweight to the state. Its committees of respected *sheikh*s are charged with issuing *fatwa*s, or religious opinions. These clerics are appointed by the Grand Sheikh of al-Azhar, and Gad al-Haq used his tenure to stack the Academy with fellow traditionalists. The Academy's *fatwa*s are not legally binding but they serve to rally public opinion to the traditionalist cause. If the Academy issues a *fatwa* that contradicts one issued by the pro-state Mufti, for example, believers could take comfort in following the advice of leading scholars within al-Azhar.

Gad al-Haq's fourteen-year tenure as Grand Sheikh witnessed a palpable alienation between the institution and the state. Gad al-Haq and his allies within al-Azhar and on the streets came to view the state as an obstacle to the creation of a true religious order that would oversee all aspects of Egyptian social and cultural life. Underscoring this rift was a decade-long feud between Gad al-Haq and Tantawi, then the state-appointed Mufti, over whose *fatwa*s were legitimate and binding on all Muslims. After Gad al-Haq, for example, declared that it was forbidden for Muslims to visit Jerusalem while the Holy City remained under Israeli occupation, Tantawi not only argued that Muslims should be allowed to travel to Jerusalem, but declared he would do it himself, if invited by Palestinian President Yasser Arafat.

Underlying the *fatwa* debate were conflicting philosophies on al-Azhar's responsibility to the state and to the people. Gad al-Haq believed Azharis should play the role of guardians of the faith, shielding society from evil while guiding it toward all that is virtuous. When asked his views on al-Azhar's responsibility in censoring films and books, Gad al-Haq replied: "We have to be cautious and protect the minds of the *umma* from these poisons just as ministry of health officials curb those who circulate poisoned food. If we are protecting people's stomachs . . . isn't it more worthwhile to protect them from intellectual poisons?"[39]

Tantawi, on the other hand, believed Azhar had a duty to support state policies. As Mufti of Egypt, and later Grand Sheikh of Azhar after Gad al-Haq's death, Tantawi rarely deviated from government edicts. He also downplayed reports of any rift with Gad al-Haq, noting that such differences over religious interpretation were inherent to Islam. "These disagreements are true and natural and such discord existed even in the days of the Prophet Mohammed. These are differences over legal matters in Islamic law. . . . but these differences did not undermine the mutual respect and friendship between us."[40]

When asked why there were two sources for *fatwa*s, the Mufti's office and al-Azhar, instead of one, Tantawi replied: "Every legal scholar has the right to issue religious decrees or legal opinions. If he is right, we agree with him. If he is wrong we argue with him. But we cannot take this right away from scholars. . . . The issue of uniting or merging the source of *fatwa*s in Egypt is an organizational matter that concerns the government."[41]

The schism between Tantawi and Gad al-Haq polarized the Azharis and contributed to the formation of a conservative alliance that firmly backed traditionalist policies. While members of this alliance were content to work behind the scenes, allowing Gad al-Haq to serve as their point man, after he died in office they became less complacent. When Tantawi became the Grand Sheikh, he quickly discovered that the Gad al-Haq loyalists, whom the *sheikh* had promoted over fourteen years, remained committed to the traditionalist cause. Tantawi faced opposition at every turn. Conservatives boycotted early meetings he held at al-Azhar—unprecedented protests that received only a few paragraphs in the Egyptian press. Even Tantawi's seemingly mundane deeds did not escape the conservatives' critical notice. In May 1996, shortly after Tantawi took office, the Scholar's Front lashed out at him for attending a luncheon hosted by the Lions Club, a Western-based social and charity organization. The Lions Club, the Front said in reprimanding Tantawi, was known to be "Masonic and run by Jewish networks that aim at dominating the world and exterminating religions and spreading immoral chaos and recruiting locals for spying against their country."[42]

Outrage over Tantawi's appointment as Grand Sheikh reached such a feverish pitch that *sheikhs* within Azhar's mosque and university complex who had previously sought to remain inconspicuous began to speak out against his policies. As Tantawi worked diligently to dismantle the traditionalists' gains within the institution, the simmering conflict became even more acute. Nonetheless, the disgruntled scholars were reluctant to overtly challenge Tantawi's legitimacy as Grand Sheikh. It was one thing to criticize his actions in the press, but quite another to question his authority to direct the institution, particularly when speaking to an outsider.

Only through the intervention of the son of a high-ranking Azhari did I manage to penetrate this wall of secrecy. A pair of rare meetings with two influential *sheikhs*, including the deputy head of the Islamic Research Academy, Sayyed Askar, provided an illuminating glimpse of the competing trends of thought at work behind the imposing walls of al-Azhar. When I met him, Askar had recently been forced out as head of another Azhari committee in a purge by Tantawi. Seated with him was a fellow conservative, Sheikh Gamal Qutb. The two scholars had no doubt the new Grand Sheikh was seeking to reverse the gains made by traditionalists in the last decade under Gad al-Haq.

"Tantawi is getting rid of the people who do not share his opinions. We are in a period in which al-Azhar's role is being undermined at home and abroad," Sheikh Askar confided.

"Al-Azhar's influence became so powerful under Gad al-Haq. A bond was created between the *ulama* and those who sympathize with the Islamic awakening. Before him, there was a gap between al-Azhar and the masses, but this gap was bridged under Gad al-Haq. The Sheikh wanted to reach the street."

Now, the *sheikhs* told me, true Muslims everywhere had been thrown into a state of confusion by moves under Tantawi to ally al-Azhar more closely with the state. "The government and the people are facing a most serious crisis. This results from government interference in al-Azhar. This crisis threatens the government," said Sheikh Qutb. "The community of believers is lost. They don't know whom to believe. Now they doubt the opinions of the Grand Sheik, the Mufti and the Minister of Religious Endowments.

"Islamic groups such as the *Gama'a*, all these groups formed in reaction to the government's transgressions against al-Azhar's role. These groups exist because of the people's lack of trust in the government. The government has imposed constraints on al-Azhar. When al-Azhar has a relationship with the state, it too loses credibility."

In that case, I asked Sheikh Qutb, doesn't the solution lie in eliminating the secular state altogether?

"No, Islam is not a style of ruling. We don't want the president of the republic to be a *sheikh*, only to have the *sharia* as the law of the land. It has not yet been implemented in Egypt, even though it was written into the constitution under Sadat."

The Grand Sheikh's battle with his conservative critics boiled over in December 1997, when Tantawi hosted an unprecedented meeting at al-Azhar with chief rabbi Yisrael Meir Lau, leader of Israel's Ashkenazi Jews. Held just before the Islamic holy month of Ramadan, and amid growing outrage in the Arab world toward Israeli intransigence in the stalled Oslo peace process, Tantawi's meeting was nothing short of explosive. Ordinary Egyptians had never accepted the Camp David peace accords, or for that matter any attempt to normalize relations with Israel. Most Muslims saw the invitation of the chief rabbi into the very citadel of Sunni Islam as a complete betrayal of the fifty-year effort against the Jewish state.

Egypt's most respected Islamic thinker, Seleem al-Awa, spoke for many when he bitterly denounced the visit on the front page of the Islamist daily *al-Shaab* and wrote a letter of protest to the Research Academy. "I did not believe my eyes when I read that the Grand Sheikh met the Zionist rabbi in Cairo. . . . It is as if the Zionists want to declare before the whole world that they have achieved normalization with the symbol of Sunni Islam and the entire Islamic world, and with the Sheikh of al-Azhar himself."

"Why did your headquarters become the site of normalization with the Zionists? How are we going to welcome Ramadan with the biggest spiritual defeat of the modern age?" al-Awa asked.

Tantawi was filled with consternation. He had never expected that such a meeting would outrage the Muslim world. Shaken and tense, he defended himself in a long interview with a Qatari satellite television channel that was broadcast in Egypt and across the Middle East. The interviewer asked Tantawi why he had decided to meet the rabbi, when his predecessor, Gad al-Haq, had refused.

"I followed in the footsteps of our Prophet, peace be upon him. He met Jews and had a dialogue with them. . . . Was I supposed to refuse to meet him, so he'll go to his country and say the Sheikh of al-Azhar was unable to meet me?"

"What is your answer to Dr. Seleem al-Awa who said this meeting is more dangerous than any form of normalization?" the interviewer asked.

"This is the logic of cowards and pacifists," Tantawi replied. "Can Dr. al-Awa deny that the Prophet and his companion Abu Bakr met with the Jews? And after that, they say 'normalization.' What normalization?"

Tantawi's response did little to pacify his critics within al-Azhar. In fact, the controversy handed the traditionalists the evidence they needed to challenge his suitability to hold Sunni Islam's highest position. "What we read about the meeting between the Sheikh of al-Azhar and the Israeli rabbi shocked us all," commented Yahya Ismail, the general-secretary of the Azhar's Scholars' Front. "We must abide by *fatwa*s issued by senior scholars since 1936, which are official *fatwa*s that forbid dealing with the occupying Jews with any weapon other than *jihad* (holy struggle) until they evacuate from our lands."

Undeterred by Tantawi's efforts to diminish their influence, today's conservative *sheikh*s remain committed to changing al-Azhar from within. Other rebels before them, however, parted ways with the institution altogether and took their message directly to the masses. Some of these maverick *sheikh*s left profound impressions on Islamic revivalism, not only in Egypt, but throughout the Arab world. Sheikh Abd al-Hameed Kishk, who studied in the *usul al-din*, or principles of religion, faculty at al-Azhar University, amassed such a following from the early 1970s that a Saudi-funded magazine dubbed him "the star of Islamic preaching."[43] Kishk was an iconoclast within al-Azhar from the start of his career. In 1966, he was one of thousands of suspected Muslim Brothers imprisoned as part of Nasser's campaign to purify society of its Islamic influence. He was released in 1968, having been held without charge.[44]

Kishk's rise to stardom was aided by the wide distribution of his recorded sermons. On street corners from Cairo to Jeddah, Kishk's voice could be heard booming from cassette players as he ridiculed al-Azhar for siding with the state and mocked infidel Arab regimes. The great majority of Kishk's followers were young, bearded members of Islamic groups. Kishk condemned the official *ulama* for failing in its responsibility to provide a proper religious education for Egypt's youth. The result, according to the *sheikh*, was the creation of a breed of "pubescent thinkers," such as those extremists who masterminded Sadat's assassination.

When I met him in November 1996, the last interview he would give before his death months later, Kishk was visibly exhausted. The powerful voice that had made him famous was now raspy and distant. Yet his judgment of al-Azhar that evening was just as strident as it had been during his heyday as a media star. Kishk, blind since childhood, called one of his students into the dingy sitting room of his house where we drank tea together, perched on hard wooden benches that served as a sofa. He asked the student to read stories from an old text that demonstrated how brave the Azharis had been during certain periods in Egyptian history. The reading went on for nearly a half-hour before Kishk delivered the moral of the story. "Azhar is not fulfilling its mission. It must reassert itself and decrease its dependency on the state. The Grand Sheikh should be elected. And the university should never have expanded its curriculum to offer courses outside religion."

The day after Kishk died, a short obituary appeared in the Egyptian press. The "star of Islamic preaching," the man who attracted hundreds of thousands of followers across the Arab world, received only a slight acknowledgment from the state that had imprisoned him and eventually barred him from his beloved pulpit.

As with the most intimate aspects of social life—sex, marriage, and family—the *sheikh*s of al-Azhar have expanded their control over the Egyptian mind, trespassing on the state's historical role in controlling freedom of expression. In recent years, al-Azhar has successfully invoked its religious authority to ban films, books, and other materials that it deems un-Islamic. This power is no longer restricted to purely religious questions, representing a significant enlargement of its mandate. At the same time, the Mosque has exerted more and more influence over state television programming, ensuring that traditionalists dominate the public airways. On occasion, this power has even reached beyond the confines of mainstream society, spilling over into the militant Islamic movement to influence extremists who generally find spiritual guidance elsewhere. In the early 1990s, al-Azhar used the militant threat to the state to become a power in its own right. In effect, the message Gad al-Haq conveyed to the authorities was this: Al-Azhar would serve as the voice of reason on Islamic matters on behalf of the state, if the authorities would agree to expand the institution's legal authority.

The authorities, increasingly charged with being un-Islamic, decided that cooperating more closely with al-Azhar could boost their own image. Al-Azhar, therefore, was allowed to expand its control over Egyptian culture by broadening the influence of the Islamic Research Academy. The Academy traditionally reviewed books and films that pertained to religion, leaving all other decisions, such as those relating to secular art and literature, to the state ministries of culture and education. In July 1993, Gad al-Haq asked the General Assembly of the Board of Fatwa and Legislation, the state body in charge of safeguarding civil society, to clearly define al-Azhar's role in censoring films, music, and video cassettes, and to clarify the division of responsibility for such matters between the institution and the state. Gad al-

Haq capitalized on the state's fear that literature and other media were provoking the militant movement. "Some magazines and newspapers intentionally insult religion and religious scholars. Their writers, editors and columnists interpret religion wrongly. . . . If we accept that these newspapers' and magazines' actions are merely extremism, not the demolition of a religious society, should we not expect reactions to it?"[45]

The General Assembly's response, issued in February 1994, was a victory for al-Azhar and a blow to Egypt's secular intellectuals. The Assembly ruled that the Islamic Research Academy must protect public order and morality in general, thereby extending its authority beyond the traditional confines of religious issues. But the Assembly went even further, declaring that al-Azhar's opinions were "binding" and could not be overturned by the Ministry of Culture. The opinion was written by Tariq al-Bishri, one of Egypt's most respected jurists and Islamic intellectuals.

Legal experts viewed the expansion of al-Azhar's censorship powers as an attempt by the state to use al-Azhar to enhance its own religious legitimacy at a time when Mubarak's Islamic credentials were being seriously questioned. Evidence of the state's intentions came from the Minister of Culture, Faruq Hosni, the man secular intellectuals thought they could rely on to defend their freedoms against al-Azhar. When Islamists attacked Hosni in the national parliament for allowing risqué publications, he argued that al-Azhar had approved the contents, and thus issued a religious seal of approval. "Al-Azhar is a higher authority; when al-Azhar speaks all must fall silent," Hosni said.[46]

By ceding additional powers to the *sheikh*s, Al-Bishri's decision built on a long history of censorship by the guardians of al-Azhar. In perhaps the most famous case this century, influential writer and critic Taha Hussein was attacked in 1926 for a study of pre-Islamic Arabic poetry that asserted that all extant verses were actually fabricated after the arrival of Islam. Azhari *sheikh*s led angry demonstrations, which culminated in public book burnings, and Hussein was hounded from his university post and deprived of all employment for a number of years.

Egyptian novelist Naguib Mahfouz also felt the wrath of the *sheikh*s. His novel *The Children of Gebelawi*, critically acclaimed around the world, was serialized in 1959 by the government daily *al-Ahram*, angering al-Azhar for what it said were insults to the prophets of Islam. Street demonstrations ensued. The book was banned in Egypt, although available from discreet booksellers; Mahfouz went on to win the Nobel Prize for literature in 1988. The prestige of being the Arab world's first such laureate, however, could not shield the novelist of secular daily life from the growing Islamic tide. In fact, it only appeared to provoke the extremists.

On October 14, 1994, the elderly Mahfouz, now nearly deaf and blind, was stabbed outside his house and gravely wounded. One of two young men later executed for the attempted murder, electrical appliance repairman Mohammed Nagui Mustafa, said he was fulfilling an order from radical Sheikh Omar Abd al-Rahman, convicted of the New York World Trade Center bombing. While doubts remain to this day whether the state executed the right men— the announcement of impending arrests by the notoriously inefficient police came within 24 hours of the attack—it is clear that Rahman had condemned Mahfouz for committing blasphemy. In reviving the 1959 charges against the novelist, Rahman was apparently following the lead of the Iranian Ayatollah Khomeini, whose 1989 death sentence against author Salman Rushdie remains in effect to this day. That Mahfouz, then eighty-three and suffering from diabetes and heart trouble, survived the attack and subsequent surgery was nothing short of miraculous.

In an earlier case, fellow writer Farag Foda was not so lucky, paying with his life for the secularists' growing vulnerability. Al-Azhar's Academy of Islamic Research declared Foda's writings blasphemous and set in motion a tragic escalation of charges and countercharges. The scholar then provoked the *sheikhs*' wrath further by defending secularism and claiming that al-Azhar University was infiltrated by members of the outlawed Muslim Brotherhood. Sheikh al-Ghazali, a leading member of the Academy, declared that anyone opposing the full implementation of the *sharia*, as Foda did, was guilty of apostasy. In a religious ruling reminiscent of the Iranian *fatwa* against Rushdie, Ghazali sealed Foda's fate by adding that anyone killing such a person was not liable for punishment under Islamic law.

Taking their cue from al-Ghazali, Islamic radicals gunned down Foda in a Cairo street in June 1992. "Yes, we killed him," the *Gama'a al-Islamiyya* announced. "Al-Azhar issued the sentence and we carried out the execution."

The spectacular assaults on Foda and Mahfouz deeply alarmed the government and captured headlines around the world, but the court's decision in 1994 to enlarge the *sheikhs*' legal power over the pen was to have more lasting consequences for the broader Islamic revival. The move angered Egyptian human rights activists and many intellectuals and artists, all of whom viewed it as subordination of the rights of civil society to the men of religion. In the ensuing months, al-Azhar used its increased authority to great effect. Among the most heated debates between the institution and secularists involved the film, *The Emigrant*, directed by Egypt's leading filmmaker, Yussef Chahine. Azhar ruled that the film gave an "anti-Islamic" depiction of the prophet Joseph and should be withdrawn from cinemas. Eventually, al-Azhar won the battle and *The Emigrant* was dropped from Egyptian movie theaters.

The conservative *sheikhs* have so far banned more than 100 books, censored dozens of films, and restricted television programming. One case that received extensive attention was the Research Academy's decision to ban a book by

Sayyed al-Qimany, a prominent Egyptian writer. The *sheikh*s declared that Qimany described central figures in the book, the prophet Joseph, the third caliph Uthman, and contemporary scholars in "a manner inappropriate to their status." Azhar ordered the Artistic Productions Police to confiscate the book, *God of Time*, from one of Cairo's most popular bookshops. Qimany said he intended to "rewrite Islamic tradition" by reexamining the history of the Prophet Mohammed, the caliphs, and the origin of the *sharia*. This desire, shared by many intellectuals, to force a degree of reformation within Islam gets to the heart of one of the major challenges Islamists have confronted this century. To question the basis of belief is to engage in a process of examination in which the outcome is unpredictable. Although many Islamic scholars in Egypt are open to a reinterpretation of religious doctrine, particularly on social matters, most oppose questioning the essence of their religion.

Qimany and other secularist intellectuals vehemently oppose this absolutist tendency rapidly gaining ground within the Islamic movement. "Each one of us has become his own dictator, because we say God is omnipotent and will have his will over my mind and life.... We have this false feeling of completeness because we own the absolute truth in the Holy Book.... So another drawback to this methodology is that it has taught us to be dictators, and now most of us do not know the meaning of freedom."[47]

Once the *sheikh*s' new power had become institutionalized, calls to curb their influence grew louder. Secularist intellectuals, who felt their freedom of expression was being seriously curtailed, and in some cases their livelihoods threatened, demanded immediate action. But having allowed the *sheikh*s to grasp more power over the pen, the state could not retreat; another tactic was in order. When the Minister of Endowments issued his decree in January 1996 to place mosques under state control, the authorities hoped this would limit the influence of conservative *sheikh*s, such as those in the Azhar Scholars' Front. The *sheikh*s were incensed: "No sultan has authority over the house of God," said Yahya Ismail, the Front's spokesman. "The people should choose the preacher from the one who is most knowledgeable about the Holy Koran, and if they are equal, the most knowledgeable about the sayings of the Prophet."[48]

As the mavericks at al-Azhar were tangling more and more often with Grand Sheikh Tantawi, I set out to find Sheikh Adawy. I wanted to know what he thought al-Azhar had become, and as a supporter of Gad al-Haq, the former grand sheikh, what he thought of Tantawi. Since I had seen him last, Adawy had undergone major heart surgery in the United States. I learned of his illness when I looked for him at his office at al-Azhar. Later, in the autumn of 1996, his wife answered the telephone when I called him at home. He would see me, she said, but I had to consider his frail health and restrict my visit to a few minutes.

One November evening I arrived at his flat, which was located in a modern building on a side street, tucked amid a maze of fast-food restaurants in the Cairo suburb of Nasser City. The bright neon screaming out from Burger King, Pizza Hut, Arby's, and Jack-in-the-Box gave me a headache before I found his apartment. When I rang the bell, I was ushered into an equally head-spinning atmosphere. Adawy's salon was covered from floor to ceiling with photographs of Mecca and of worshippers making the annual pilgrimage to the Islamic holy sites. Verses from the Koran, the letters trimmed in fake gold, lined the walls of his vestibule. At least twenty friends and relatives sat in chairs arranged in an L shape along the walls of the sitting room. They all stood and stared at me, wondering why a foreigner was interrupting such an intimate moment. Sheikh Adawy sat in the middle of the line of chairs, his legs crossed in front of him. He was tired, withered, and could barely speak. I felt embarrassed that I had insisted on seeing him, given his condition.

After a few minutes of small talk, I tried to ask him about the current state of affairs at al-Azhar. But Sheikh Adawy motioned in sign language to his wife that he did not want to discuss it. Instead, his wife, a cheerful woman at least twenty years his junior, disappeared and returned a few minutes later with newspaper clippings about the *sheikh*'s glory days: his popular sermons in the mosques, and his photograph in newsletters published by Islamic organizations. When I finally slipped in a question about the *ulama*, Sheikh Adawy refused to acknowledge the current political turmoil surrounding Tantawi. He talked about the greatness of al-Azhar, its historical role in the Islamic world, and the unified message it sought to convey to its followers.

This was how Sheikh Adawy wanted to remember the Islamic community, where he had built his life. In his waning days, he wanted to believe the *ulama* had built a utopia in Egypt. He wanted to forget the conflict of which he was so much a part when he inspired thousands of activists from his pulpit before his banishment. He wanted to be rehabilitated. But it was too late. Adawy's legacy would live on among the younger mavericks determined to disseminate their conservative reading of Islam to the Egyptian masses.

4

THE PROFESSIONALS

E sam al-Eryan, a charismatic doctor and lawyer with university degrees ranging from art to science and religion, had known that one day he would face the men in police uniform at his front door. As a prominent leader in the Muslim Brotherhood, he had been closely monitored throughout twenty years of ups and downs with the authorities. In the volatile days of the early 1990s, when Islamic militants appeared to threaten the integrity of the state, killing policemen and tourists in Upper Egypt and taking shots at cabinet ministers on the streets of Cairo, Eryan emerged as something of a media star. His caustic criticism of the regime, delivered in near perfect English, was a frequent feature in radio dispatches from the British Broadcasting Corporation. His fame rankled a government obsessed with trying to monopolize the flow of information and carving out its own image in the West.

Like most Muslim Brothers, Eryan was not involved with *al-Gama'a al-Islamiyya* or any other armed group. In fact, the Brotherhood, the Middle East's most influential Islamist organization, had long ago renounced the use of force to concentrate on building an Islamic state through political and social change. But in many ways Eryan posed a far greater danger than militant violence. As deputy secretary-general of the doctors' syndicate, a powerful union with hundreds of thousands of members, Eryan had become a potent and articulate voice of the simmering disaffection within Egypt's growing professional middle class.

Nurtured by successive regimes as the engines of westernization, Egypt's middle-class professionals were turning their backs on the government's secular vision. They had grown up on Nasser's dream of upward mobility for all. They studied hard and went to college, often at great expense to their families. But by the time they graduated, most had to face the truth: Nasser's dream had been buried along with his corpse. Sadat's idea of progress was an "Open Door" policy that helped the business elite prosper. And Mubarak was too cautious by nature to instigate radical change.

The middle class was left with little more than prestigious degrees from law schools and higher engineering institutes. But the diplomas, proudly displayed in gold-edged frames in their parents' homes, could not produce enough money for a simple wedding, or put meat on the family dinner table, or cover a short holiday at the beach in Alexandria. At the same time, many of the shared ethical and moral values of Egyptian society—values of social justice as spelled out in the Koran—were undermined by the winner-take-all ethos that first took root under Sadat's "Open Door" reforms and was later perfected under his successor.

Men like Esam al-Eryan appeared to offer a way out. They were searching for the chance to marry the demands of the modern world with the traditional values of their Islamic faith; their goal was *not* to modernize Islam, but to stamp the authority of their Islamic faith on modernity. Eryan and other like-minded Muslim Brothers at the head of the doctors', engineers', and lawyers' syndicates were prepared to prove to middle-class professionals that they did not have to settle for what little the state had to offer. Nor did they have to compromise their ethical standards to meet an idealized vision of "westernization."

Over the course of a decade, the struggle for control of the professional union movement shaped up as a contest the government simply could not win. In contrast to an indifferent state, the Islamists were able to give hope to the lost generation of professionals by taking into account both their temporal and spiritual needs. They parlayed their first foothold in the union movement into a sweeping range of services that sheltered the membership from the worst depredations of the government's failed social and economic policies. No aspect of daily life was too mundane for the unions' helping hands, from increased maternity benefits, to a marriage fund, better pensions, housing assistance, help with consumer purchases, and affordable holidays.

All these services were packaged with an "Islamic" label, a way of governing that emphasized the welfare and needs of ordinary Egyptians. Some reflected a more overt religious character. These included subsidized pilgrimages to the holy city of Mecca, one of the five obligations of any pious Muslim, and a revolving loan fund that respected traditional readings of the Koran's ban on bank interest.

By contesting and winning seats on the union boards in free and fair elections, the Islamists showed the middle class that democracy was possible even under the existing authoritarian regime. In contrast to the sham elections to the national parliament, or worse, the presidential polls in which Mubarak consistently won at least 95 percent of the vote, the Muslim Brothers and their allies triumphed by keeping their promises on bread-and-butter issues. Once in office, they generally proved honest and competent managers, building up huge surpluses in the syndicate coffers and respecting democratic norms and traditions.

By the mid-1990s, the state found itself increasingly unable to compete for influence among the same professionals it had once groomed to lead the country's economic and political development. The authorities knew they would eventually win the war with Islamic militants, no matter how many cabinet ministers or tourists might be injured or killed in the process. With moral backing from their patron, the United States, the security forces were always destined to triumph through brute force. But could this same regime, its aging leaders slouched in gilded "Louis Faruq" sofas inside fortified palaces, win a war of ideas against the new generation of young Muslim Brothers? Mubarak did not wait to find out.

The knock at Esam al-Eryan's door came on January 22, 1995. His wife woke him and said the intelligence police had come to call. Eryan dressed quickly and greeted six men, three of whom were dressed in military uniforms and carrying light automatic weapons. Two were state security officers and one was an informant he had met many times before. The men methodically worked through the rooms, searching first the desk drawers in Eryan's study, then the stacks of papers and books. As they collected the bits and pieces of his life strewn inside the house, Eryan packed a suitcase, drank a cup of tea, and prayed. When the men signaled it was time to go, Eryan kissed his children who lay sleeping, said farewell to his wife, and began a journey that would land him in a crowded cell in Mazraet Tora prison.

With Eryan's arrest and that of dozens of other prominent Brotherhood leaders months later, the state signaled a profound change in strategy. Those close to Mubarak had concluded it was time to rein in the Brotherhood, which until that point was officially illegal but generally allowed to carry out its activities in the open. Eryan's arrest came ten months before parliamentary elections in which he was poised for reelection to a seat he held in the Majlis al-Shaab, the national parliament. The only way to deprive the Islamists of one of their most effective candidates was to throw him in jail before the vote.

Eryan and the other Brothers were charged with criminal offenses, but the underlying motivation was clearly political. They were accused of organizing an illegal group, holding unauthorized gatherings, and preparing anti-government leaflets, all time-honored Brotherhood activities since the organization's creation in 1928 and all largely tolerated by the authorities for decades.

"I consider myself at the moment imprisoned without any legal basis,"

Eryan complained to prosecutors during a court hearing. "It is clear from my intellectual and political activity over twenty years and through my work at the syndicate that I denounce violence and do not see any reason for practicing it."

At another hearing, Eryan made a direct plea to Mubarak: "I ask the president . . . despite my disagreement with him . . . to open a new page that would stop the stream of blood that is still flowing from our youth and from the police. . . . I tell him that the country is going through a very difficult period."

But Mubarak had already turned to a different page, one that betrayed a change of heart toward the long-tolerated Brothers. There was no one event involving the Brotherhood that had invited such harsh action. Rather, the suppression of the organization happened the way most change occurs in contemporary Egypt—slowly, indirectly, and subtly, until a sledgehammer suddenly comes down.

Under Mubarak's predecessors, the Brotherhood had seen periods of un-official tolerance interrupted by periodic waves of mass arrests, the worst occurring under Nasser and later, in 1981, during the months leading up to Sadat's assassination. At first, Mubarak had taken a different approach. On taking power after Sadat's death, he adopted a conciliatory tone and released dozens of political prisoners, including senior Islamist leaders. The Brother-hood's growing influence in the syndicates seemed to escape Mubarak's at-tention. He sought to avoid a head-on confrontation with the unions for the first twelve years of his presidency. He had expected the different factions within the professional unions to devour one another, dividing the syndicates and leaving the organizations politically supine.

It was as if he suddenly awoke one day and noticed what should have been patently obvious for years. By the time Eryan was arrested in early 1995, the Brotherhood had already infiltrated the universities, the courts, and the syndicates. By the time officialdom noticed the religious awakening within the middle class, the bedrock of the society it hoped to construct, the Islamic transformation was essentially irreversible.

The state's true opponents were no longer the Islamist establishment of the Muslim Brothers, largely content to chip away solemnly at Egypt's sec-ularist institutions, but the young generation of ambitious leaders such as Esam al-Eryan. These younger Islamists, many of whom were in their thirties and forties, were markedly different from the Brotherhood's Old Guard. Where the established Islamists still saw the world from the perspective of founder Hasan al-Banna, Sayyid Qutb, and other Brotherhood luminaries of the 1920s and 1930s, the younger leaders were products of a thoroughly mod-ern age. Where the Old Guard took refuge in membership in a semisecret society and papered over many of the problems of contemporary Egyptian society, the new Islamists openly sought to embue modern life with an Islamic value system. This meant tackling such problems as economic development, human rights, foreign affairs, and the role of women and minorities. These men demanded the creation of a modern welfare state, guided by a traditionalist yet flexible reading of Islam. They prided themselves on being more in harmony with their fellow citizens than the state or their mentors among the Old Guard Islamists.

By the mid-1990s, the Brotherhood was merely the most convenient vehicle through which the new generation of Islamists, and ordinary Egyptians, could carve out the Islamic civil society they desired. The organization's long-stated aim was the implementation of the *sharia*, or Koranic law, as the principal source of law in Egypt, rather than one of several sources. If most contemporary Islamists were unwilling or unable to fully articulate their vision of the future, the general outlines were clear nonetheless: creation of an "Islamic order" as determined by the supremacy, in all questions of law, politics, and society, of the *sharia*; rejection of corrupt Western ideologies; unity of "Mosque and State"; and an emphasis on social justice. Economic relations would take on a strong moral component and stress the needs of individuals at the expense of traditional commercial elites and foreign interests. Externally, Egypt would likely move away from its Western allies, in particular the United States, reject its earlier pact with Israel, and focus instead on ties to fellow Islamic countries.

The final configuration of the state was not central to the thinking of Egypt's new Islamists. Nor, as critics of the modern Islamist movement maintain, does it require any return to an imagined order of medieval Arabia. The existing parliamentary democracy in Egypt, however imperfect under Mubarak and his predecessors, could be made to coexist comfortably with Islamic principles. The goal was the creation of an "Islamic order," not a theocratic "religious state."

This vision was inspired by a commitment to democracy that found full expression in the Islamist-controlled professional unions. Leaders such as Esam al-Eryan never lost this faith in fundamental freedoms, even in the confines of a narrow, overcrowded cell at Mazraet Tora prison, where the authorities tried to isolate him from society at large.

Eryan was allowed no visitors, except his lawyer and members of his immediate family, but that did not deter him from continuing his religious studies, closely monitoring current events in the press and on the radio, or engaging fellow prisoners in political debate. After several false starts, including an aborted plan to smuggle myself into the prison as a veiled member of his family, I managed to open a line of communication to his cell.

"The real prison is inside the soul, and not the one behind bars," Eryan told me once we began our secret correspondence. "I do not feel that I am in prison, because most of the nation are prisoners by the same laws that are limiting our freedoms. And I really wonder a lot what is the use of getting out of jail if we cannot change the situation for the better with more freedom.

"The time has not yet come to write my feelings, but in brief, my thoughts, my analysis and my persistence to walk in the same path have not changed. My will has become strengthened to reform things in my country and it may take a long time. But it is an inevitable path."

For their part, Mubarak and his secularist circle had come to represent an ossified and isolated central government, in essence little changed from the days of Nasser and Sadat. Aging cabinet ministers rotated among government agencies but kept their personal grip on power and patronage for decades. The regime in the 1990s had no goals for the future beyond its own survival, no demonstrable interest in improving the standard of living for the average Egyptian, and no plans for pursuing policies that reflected the increasing importance of society's religious values.

Against this backdrop, the fight for the professional unions and its middle-class membership shaped up as a crucial match in the political war between the state and the Islamists. Mubarak launched his attack on the Brothers once he felt confident the militant threat was largely behind him, with leading militants either dead at the hands of his security forces or in prison. The president and his circle had come to realize, albeit belatedly, that control of the nation rested in winning back the average Egyptian. To this end, they sought to imprison the heroes of the middle class and brand the widely respected Muslim Brotherhood a terrorist organization no different from the despised *Gama'a* or *Jihad*.

To any astute observer, the regime's characterization of the Brotherhood's new rising stars as firebrand, Iranian-style revolutionaries rang hollow. Like Esam al-Eryan, the young Islamists were well educated, with some holding advanced degrees from universities in the United States and Europe. In contrast to their secular counterparts who obtained high-level government jobs through family connections, the Islamists had used their education to develop a more sophisticated understanding of the world and where Egypt fit into this complicated universe. Mohammed Abd al-Qaddus was one such Islamic figure. Unlike Eryan, Qaddus made his mark behind the scenes and out of the limelight. When I telephoned him for an interview, he suggested we meet at his home in Zamalek. I looked forward to such a rare opportunity. Most religious men felt more comfortable inviting me to a less intimate setting, and it was difficult to gather any sense of their personal side.

Qaddus explained he was a busy man, and answered my questions directly, making it apparent he had contemplated the issues for years. "The government knows the Brotherhood has nothing to do with violence," Qaddus said, as we drank coffee in his palatial apartment overlooking the Nile. "They decided to arrest members of the Brotherhood and they focused on the younger generation and the leaders in the syndicates. They fear the Brotherhood has become a parallel power to the government."

It was easy enough for the state to make the case to the outside world that all Muslim Brothers were terrorists. Western correspondents who began reporting on the movement in the 1980s applied a limited vocabulary in their reports on the subject of Islam. The word "fundamentalist" was used to label any Islamist opposed to the state. Unwilling or unable to distinguish the methods and motivations of one Islamist from the next, the Western media frequently referred to the Brotherhood simply as a "terrorist organization," even though the last proven militant act the group committed was in 1949, when a twenty-three-year-old gunman assassinated Egyptian Prime Minister Mahmud Fahmi al-Nuqrashi. Hasan al-Banna publicly condemned the murder, but it proved his death warrant all the same. The founder of the Muslim Brotherhood was gunned down in February 1949 in a state-sponsored plot to avenge Nuqrashi.[1]

That the Brotherhood had clean hands made little difference to Mubarak. A powerful faction within his intelligence service, the *mabahith amn al-dawla*, had a particular aversion to the Islamic movement and set out to discredit the Brothers and imprison their leaders. Ahmed al-Adl, the *mabahith* chief, led the campaign. He wove a tale of complex conspiracies and plots to overthrow the state. Eventually, al-Adl, whose name could be translated from the Arabic as Ahmed the Just, was discredited and expelled from the administration. But by that time Mubarak's mind was made up.

Mild criticism directed at the Islamist "opposition" gave way to raving polemic. The Brotherhood, argued the president, was part of an international terrorist network. It was not only Egypt's responsibility to penetrate this web of Islamic extremism, but the duty of the Western world to back the crackdown. Islamist leaders told me that when Mubarak learned that the U.S. embassy in Cairo, well-known for its fears of militancy, was conducting discreet meetings with influential figures in the nonviolent movement, the president demanded an immediate halt to any such dialogue.

"Your government is in contact with these terrorists from the Muslim Brotherhood," Mubarak told the *New Yorker* magazine in 1995. "This has been done very secretly, without our knowledge at first. You think you can correct the mistakes you made in Iran, where you had no contact with the Ayatollah Khomeini and his fanatic groups before they seized power. But I assure you, these groups will never take over this country, and they will never be on good terms with the United States." Mubarak's public outrage achieved the desired effect: the Islamists later told me that the Americans abruptly ended their brief contacts with the Brotherhood.

The fear that Egypt might turn into another Algeria haunted Mubarak.

On numerous occasions he went so far as to compare the Brotherhood's potential to incite unrest with that of Algeria's Islamic Salvation Front. The Front, or FIS, was allowed to run candidates in national elections in 1992. But when the party was headed for victory at the polls, the secularist government and its supporters in the army decided democracy was not such a good idea and canceled the elections, unleashing a savage civil war that continues today.

"Look at Algeria, what has happened there?" Mubarak said in an interview in April 1994 with the German magazine *Der Spiegel*. "I advised the Algerian president not to allow religious parties but he did not take my advice and Algeria (as a result) is facing problems now. . . . I know well what it means to mix religion with politics and all the Islamists care about is power, influence and money. But as long as I am president, religion and state will remain separate. We know well the activities of the Islamist politicians since 1928 [the year the Brotherhood was founded]."

On November 23, 1995, one week before Egypt's parliamentary elections, Esam al-Eryan was tried before a military court along with fifty-three other Muslim Brothers. It was the first time civilians were brought before a military tribunal for charges other than Islamic "terrorism." Until that moment, the state had reserved such courts for armed militants of the *Gama'a* and *Jihad*, a practice widely condemned by human rights groups at home and abroad. The evening before his scheduled appearance, Eryan learned of the state's decision to try him before a military court, in which he knew he had no chance for appeal. The Islamists received three to five years in prison at hard labor.

Within hours of the verdicts, interior ministry troops burst into the Brotherhood's headquarters in Tawfiqiyya, a small neighborhood crammed with vegetable and fruit stalls in downtown Cairo. The troops seized files, a fax machine and other equipment, and expelled the staff. Offices in the same building where the Brothers' magazine *al-Dawa*, or "The Call", was printed were also shut down. Despite its "outlaw" status, the headquarters had been allowed to operate, unmolested by the authorities, since the 1970s.

The raids signaled the start of one of the most dramatic clampdowns on the Brotherhood in years. Not since late in 1954, when Nasser blamed the Brotherhood for a failed attempt on his life, had the state's hand come down with such force. A number of historians now believe the attack on Nasser was staged by the government as part of an attempt to crush the organization once and for all. Six Brothers were hanged, thousands of others were imprisoned, the group's headquarters was set ablaze, and a two-month campaign was launched in the press detailing "the conspiracy" against the president.[2]

At the time of Mubarak's own crackdown, the popularity of the Islamic movement was surging. Many Egyptians saw the Brotherhood as a welcome antidote to the militants, an instrument of change without violence. The syndicates themselves served as a symbol of what the Islamists could accomplish if given enough freedom. They had molded the unions into self-sufficient, democratically run institutions and displaced many of the traditional functions of a government too incompetent, too callous or simply too corrupt to serve the people. These achievements on the part of the revitalized syndicates represented a challenge to the legitimacy of the state; as such, they had to be stopped.

In May 1995, police forced their way inside the engineering syndicate headquarters along Ramsis Street, one of Cairo's largest boulevards. Heavily armed officers blocked engineers from entering and confiscated files and office equipment. Dozens of Islamists were arrested. Soon it was the turn of the lawyers' union. The government secured court approval for an order placing the syndicate, together with the engineers' union, under *hirasa*, or state guardianship, which restricted most operations. Islamist board members elected in 1992 were ousted from their posts and state henchmen were installed in their place. Bank accounts owned by the two syndicates were frozen along with most other assets; union social clubs were closed; and meetings among members were banned.

The shutdown would leave the unions in limbo. But the Islamists' new converts within the professional middle class nonetheless proved loyal to the religious revival, distancing themselves further and further from the regime.

The marriage between the Muslim Brotherhood and middle-class professionals, which began in the mid-1980s, was no accident; it just took longer than the Old Guard had expected. From its early days, the Brotherhood had sought to change society from within. "My Brothers, you are not a benevolent society, nor a political party, nor a local organization," Hasan al-Banna wrote in a message to his followers in 1943. "Rather you are a new soul in the heart of this nation to give it life by means of the Koran. . . . If you are told that you are political, answer that Islam admits no distinction. If you are accused of being revolutionaries, say 'We are voices for right and peace in which we dearly believe.' "[3]

As far back as World War II, the Brotherhood saw itself as the champion of Egypt's disenchanted labor force. Unemployment due to the closing down of Allied establishments and high inflation inspired "waves of members" to flock to its headquarters.[4] After the war, the Brotherhood created a labor section, where workers were invited to attend meetings to protest the government's economic policies. The labor section served as a clearinghouse for jobs for the unemployed. Throughout the 1940s, the same department was active in organizing unions among transport and textile workers.[5]

By the 1980s, the professional syndicates had come to offer the young generation of Islamists the best vehicle for changing Egypt's political and social order. The constitution bans religion-based parties, making it impossible for the Muslim Brotherhood to run candidates of its own in parliamentary elections. Instead, Islamists such as Eryan were forced to seek election by running under the banner of one of the legal opposition parties. As a result, their ability to campaign openly for their ideas was restricted and their success limited. Such polls were also subject to widespread vote-rigging and ballot stuffing by agents of the ruling party, according to investigations by the Egyptian Organization of Human Rights and numerous western correspondents. In 1987, candidates affiliated with the Brotherhood won 38 of 444 seats in the Majlis al-Shaab, the People's Assembly, by running under the banners of the Labor party and the Socialist Liberal party. But eight years later, the state ensured that the Brotherhood would not be represented in parliament. Of an estimated 150 Brotherhood candidates who ran as independents or in alliance with the Labor party, not one was elected. Those who came out on top in the first round of voting saw their winning margins evaporate in the final round in what domestic critics and foreign journalists say was blatant vote-rigging and intimidation by government supporters.

In contrast to the government, the new Islamists were quick to recognize that a dramatic shift had occurred in the social composition of the doctors', engineers', and lawyers' syndicates. Historically, these professions had drawn their ranks from Egypt's upper classes, the wealthy few who had access to higher education, and from among privileged military officers and senior state bureaucrats. The syndicate chairmen, once handpicked by the state, often used the position as a stepping-stone to a seat in the cabinet. But by the 1980s, the democratization of higher education that Nasser initiated years earlier had produced a new generation of trained professionals from more diverse socio-economic backgrounds. The new engineer, lawyer, or doctor was far less wealthy or politically well connected and more religious and socially conservative than his older colleagues. At the same time, the system had churned out many more trained professionals than the plodding economy could possibly absorb.

Nasser's aim was to create a socialist system from the remains of King Faruq's paternalistic rule, which had encouraged well-defined divisions within society. Like many of his fellow Free Officers, Nasser came from modest roots and had a particular disdain for the traditional Egyptian elite. In 1961, he kicked off massive waves of nationalization, in which the state took over most large-scale industry, all banking, insurance, and foreign trade, utilities, airlines, and many big retail stores. But one of the fundamental flaws of Nasser's reforms was the state's inability to generate foreign exchange to pay for the imports it needed. A lack of technology and efficiency prevented Egypt's centralized economy from exporting competitive goods to other markets.

When Sadat came to power in 1970, he sought to streamline the bloated public sector and open the economy to Western markets, a policy of *infitah*, or openness. The idea was to stimulate domestic growth and foreign investment and move Egypt away from Nasser's legacy of central planning and toward a free market economy. The result, however, was a hybrid economy with many of the ills of both systems: Too little was invested in agriculture and industry; too much went to the service sector and to purchase imports. At the same time, steady migration from the countryside to Cairo was in full swing, creating an urban population explosion. With the agricultural areas increasingly depleted of labor, per capita food production fell. Egypt was forced to rely on substantial aid from the United States and import more than half of its grain, also largely from America.

Despite criticism of Nasser's policies, the bloated public sector continued to grow throughout the 1970s. Political change was also largely stymied. Sadat introduced a multiparty system, but then stripped it of all meaning by denying any real role to opposition factions. Yet internal and external pressures forced an inevitable degree of economic and political liberalization. Egypt's new-found relationship with the United States and Israel, which produced a huge volume of U.S. aid amounting to 10 percent of Egypt's GDP from 1975 to 1991, gave the United States leverage in encouraging large-scale privatization.

The large migration of Egyptian labor to the Gulf states as a result of the oil boom in the mid 1970s took the pressure off Sadat's government to show immediate benefits from its *infitah* policies. The annual volume of remittances from the Gulf during much of the 1980s was about three times as much as the combined revenues from the Suez Canal and tourism—Egypt's primary sources of cash—and represented an average of 30 percent of Egypt's foreign currency receipts.[6] It is estimated that about 2.1 million households benefited from the remittances of one or more migrant workers during the 1980s—a total of roughly 12.6 million Egyptians, or about 23 percent of the population.[7]

Yet the same oil boom, at the time a welcome safety valve that eased the political and financial pressures on the state, fed resentment among middle-class Egyptians and helped accelerate the religious revival. Tens of thousands of engineers, doctors, and other technocrats were forced to find work in foreign lands, underscoring their own country's inability to meet their needs. Salaries in the oil states were as much as ten times greater than those available back home. Many young men knew that dreams of marriage, family, and a home of their own first meant years of toil overseas to raise the needed cash. Life in the Persian Gulf states also exposed them to a powerful and strict version of Islam that gave many a new idea of what it meant to be a "good Muslim." In Saudi Arabia, unlike Egypt, all alcohol is banned and women are required to be fully veiled in public. Such social policies, given the seal of approval by religious scholars and *sheikh*s, were easily exported back home.

And when the oil bonanza dried up and the good jobs evaporated, Egypt's deep-set social and economic problems were back on full display.

Mubarak attempted to repair the damage by reducing state subsidies, raising agricultural prices, and reforming public sector management. But few real structural changes were implemented. By the mid-1980s, Egypt was caught up in a deep economic crisis. The national debt had reached $40 billion and oil prices had dropped, undermining the value of Egypt's modest exports and causing a shortage of foreign currency. The *nouveaux riches* created by the *infitah* were understandably unwilling to give up their advantages over those left out of the state-sponsored bonanza, and any attempt by the government to take them away outright would risk alienating its primary constituency.

After more than twenty years of economic experimentation, the middle-class professionals who had earned their degrees through Nasser's reform and expansion of higher education were abandoned in midstream. They were unable to create a lifestyle in line with their technical qualifications or their social goals. They held university degrees, but earned salaries that failed to reflect their qualifications and achievements. Government statistics from October 1991, the latest available, show the average monthly salary for a civil engineer at 336 Egyptian pounds, equivalent to less than $100. Average monthly salaries for doctors were put at 332 Egyptian pounds, while lawyers earned 292 Egyptian pounds, about $85.[8] These figures have not changed substantially in recent years.

Wherever I went I encountered the deep disillusionment of Egypt's professionals. Most represented the first generation in their families to be educated, and they had made huge sacrifices to get a university degree. They thought it would make a difference. But what was the point of higher education if you could earn more money driving a taxi cab?

"My father worked in a government refinery," Mohammed Abdullah Shami, an engineer and commentator for the opposition newspaper, *al-Shaab*, recalled one day. "We were poor, from the lower class. We were so poor we didn't have coats. Once, I received a scholarship and was allowed to meet Nasser to receive my award.

"Nasser was so tall and I was so small. Nasser took my hand, and I could see the tears in his eyes. He told the people in his office, 'These boys are undernourished.' The next day the Revolutionary Command Council declared that students in universities be given a monthly stipend. I was given 12 pounds. It was so much money at the time.

"Nasser always said, 'I brought people up from the slums.' But he didn't finish the job. He created a huge workforce that could have become the middle class, but it never happened. This is one reason the Islamists have become powerful. We still haven't given up the dream.'"

The Islamists were able to fill the gap that had opened in the Egyptian economy between the wealthy few and the huge lower classes, now swollen by downward mobility on the part of underemployed professionals. The improved standard of living for the few who had flourished under the *infitah*—dubbed "fat cats" by the opposition press—prompted the majority of mostly impoverished professionals to demand profound changes in their own lives. No longer willing to leave their destiny up to the state, they began to seek a place in the political process. The syndicates proved ideal outlets for such frustrations, and the new Islamists seized the opportunity to cultivate this lost generation whose dreams of upward mobility had fizzled into a poverty-line existence.

"There is no factory within the Islamic movement producing these ideas," said Mohammed Ali Bishr, former secretary-general of the engineers' syndicate, explaining the Islamists' surge in popularity. "All of our ideas stem from what the engineers tell us they want. It's like asking your children what they want. But no one in our government cares what we want and no one asks us. There is a joke in Egypt. If you don't want a person to become a cabinet minister, just tell the people to praise him and the state certainly will not choose him."

The inspiration for the Islamic advance within the professional syndicates may not have been handed down, assembly line fashion, from above. But there is no question that the Brotherhood, committed to implementing Hasan al-Banna's dream of social change from within, had the organization and discipline needed to mold the moribund unions into a potent political force. Among the Brothers themselves, it was the younger generation of Islamists who came to the fore. "The Brotherhood didn't have a specific plan of which institutions to penetrate," explained Abu al-Ela Mady, one of the emerging new breed. "It was a Brotherhood idea, but it was up to the young Islamists to implement it."

The younger activists sought to shake off the lethargy of the more traditional Brothers. "In the mid-80s, we wanted our voices to be heard," explained Saleh Abd al-Kareem, a successful British-educated engineer who later became a syndicate leader. "We wanted Egypt to be more Islamic and the government to become more patriotic. We wanted to set an example for the state, but toward what end? We didn't think about that. No one ever thought we would move from the syndicates to take over Abdeen Palace," the seat of state power.

Under the direction of Abd al-Monem Abd al-Futouh, head of the student union at Cairo University from 1974 to 1977, a plan was created for the young leaders in the Brotherhood to run for election to syndicate boards. Esam al-Eryan was already active in the doctors' union and a well-known name in political and professional circles. Eryan and Futouh were designated as future candidates for leadership in the doctors' syndicate. A young sports enthusiast, Esam Sultan, would organize members in the 200,000-strong lawyers' syndicate. Mukhtar Noah, who in 1984 had become the first openly Islamist candidate to win election in the lawyers' union, was already in place. Noah was the only one in the group who first entered syndicate politics independent of the Brotherhood, only later gravitating into the group's orbit.

In the engineers' syndicate, Mohammed Ali Bishr, a savvy Brotherhood supporter who was educated in the United States, was tapped for election. Abu al-Ela Mady, then in his late twenties, would also run for a seat on the engineers' council. Mady was a rising star in the Brotherhood. A towering figure whose charisma dominates any conversation, Mady had moved to Cairo a few years before from his home in Minya, a large town in Upper Egypt. He was open-minded and eager to learn the ins and outs of city politics. With his bright white teeth and warm smile, Mady is a natural politician. He appears conciliatory and self-deprecating, but his ideas and intellectual curiosity reveal a man who is deeply confident and determined to bring about change.

The young Islamists made up the core of what came to be known as "the list," a string of Brotherhood supporters who would come to dominate the syndicates over the next decade. They experienced success far beyond their imagination. After the turmoil of Nasser's failed socialism, and Sadat's troubled opening toward the West, Egyptians were yearning for a return to the country's more permanent national identity, Islam. More and more middle- and upper-class women were taking the veil, often to the dismay of their westernized husbands and sons; conservative *sheikhs* came to dominate the air waves, broadcasting their austere vision of Islam into millions of homes; mosques were attracting thousands of worshippers to Friday prayers, with the excess overflowing onto Cairo's main boulevards.

One measure of the strength of the contemporary Islamic tide was its success in penetrating the engineering profession, a traditional pillar of the regime and long the beneficiary of state largesse. After winning a single place on the engineering board in 1984, Islamists grabbed enough seats in 1987 to shape syndicate policy. Their triumph marked a radical new direction in the history of engineers in modern Egypt.

As a profession, engineers had enjoyed unrivaled status throughout the twentieth century as the motor that would power Egypt toward industrialization and modern development. Engineers had built many of the national symbols the state looked to for its sense of self-worth: the Ramsis Bridge in central Cairo, later renamed the October 6 Bridge to commemorate the Egyptian army's crossing of the Suez Canal in the face of Israeli defenders in 1973, and the spectacular High Dam at Aswan. Nasser's nationalization campaign of 1956–1964 saw engineers appointed as managers to oversee the factories and enterprises seized from foreigners or the traditional Egyptian elite. By 1967, more than 70 percent of the top 646 administrators and managers in the civil service and public sector had an engineering background.[9] Two engineers even rose to the position of prime minister in the 1960s and 1970s. They earned higher salaries than nearly any other profession. In the 1960s, a district in Cairo was named "Mohandiseen"—Arabic for engineers—as a tribute to their prestige.

Nearly all graduates of engineering schools remain *mohandis* for life, the title of engineer prefixed to their names as "doctor" or "professor" is in many Western countries. In the early 1970s, about three-quarters of engineering graduates were members of the engineers' syndicates. It was a club closed to those without a proper undergraduate engineering degree.[10] Graduates from technical institutes, for example, were excluded. Eventually, all engineers were required to be syndicate members in order to practice their profession.

Just as engineers were offered special comforts in life, they were accorded special treatment in death. As a reward for crossing the Suez Canal in 1973 and destroying the Israeli army's Bar-Lev line, in 1975 the board of the engineering syndicate, packed with state apparatchiks, set aside land for an engineers' cemetery. I first read of the graveyard in a Western textbook, but today's young engineers all laughed at the notion that there was a designated resting place for them. After weeks of chasing one false lead after another, I finally located the small patch of desert tucked away in the outskirts of Medinat Nasr, a Cairo suburb jammed with Western fast-food chains. The lone caretaker, delighted that anyone should take any interest after so many years, gave me a tour that included a glimpse of the one remaining empty vault. The design echoed the Pharaonic tombs in the Valley of the Kings in Luxor, marvels, like the pyramids, of ancient Egyptian engineering prowess. In the distance towered remnants of Nasser's failed experiment to revolutionize the economy: unfinished apartment blocks left abandoned when the money ran out, now little more than stretches of desert dotted with slums.

By the early 1980s, most engineers had been forced into the swollen ranks of the *muwazzafun*, state workers sitting idle in rows of desks in the labyrinth of "socialist Gothic" ministry buildings in central Cairo. In the centralized economic tradition of full employment, the workers pretended to work and the state pretended to pay them. Few engineers were actually working in their chosen field. In 1993, the state still had not found jobs for those who graduated in 1984.[11] In the words of the authoritative Western scholar Clement Henry Moore, they were "engineers in search of industry."

The failed economic policies may have alienated the professional class from an uncaring state, but it was the broader religious revival that transformed the syndicates. As children, this new generation had experienced the wrenching defeat in the 1967 war with Israel, which ordinary Egyptians saw as a warning from God that the country had strayed from its faith. When the young professionals of the mid-1980s entered universities, they found themselves surrounded by active Islamic student unions working to integrate religion into every aspect of public and private life. By the time they joined the workforce and began raising children, they had developed a shared vision of a correct "Islamic" lifestyle. And many aspects of contemporary Egyptian society fell far short of those expectations.

Venture out from the pollution, dirt, and endless streams of humanity in Cairo—a cocoon masking the depth of the country's despair—and it is easy to discover just how disaffected Egyptians truly are. I had heard that the engineers in Dumyat, a town 200 miles from Cairo and known as one of the ugliest in the country, were trying to build a new life. Omar Abdullah, an engineer in Cairo with friends there, urged me to visit the Dumyat syndicate. "If you want to see outrage, real anger, activity, go to Dumyat," Abdullah advised me. "The rule of holy law is what is suitable for the Egyptian people. But we are being governed now not by the rule of God, but the law of Caesar."

It was easy to identify the syndicate headquarters in Dumyat, where I was scheduled to meet a few of Abdullah's colleagues one morning in June 1997. The white stucco building, framed in dark brown wood carved in the Arabic *mashrabiyya* style with balconies overlooking the Nile, resembled a rich man's holiday retreat. Otherwise, Dumyat was a classic, provincial Egyptian town: mud huts served as housing and stretches of gravel passed for streets. Women shopping at sidewalk kiosks were dressed in long headscarves and heavy ankle-length skirts, despite blistering temperatures.

When I entered the building, Towfeek Qawima, the syndicate *naqeeb*, or director, had yet to arrive. One of his assistants assured me he was on his way *Inshallah*, "God willing." I groaned under my breath. In this context, *Inshallah* is a common Egyptian expression that means thirty minutes, an hour, two hours, or anyone's guess. I cringed to think I had driven three hours in a taxi to find no one at home, so I decided to strike up a conversation with the young man. But the only information he offered was about Dumyat's special geography. "It's the only town in the country where the Mediterranean meets the Nile," he noted proudly.

Qawima arrived about two cups of tea later, and was anxious to get down to business. He was a tall, burly man with a clownish face and a loud voice. When he greeted me, with an entourage of men from the syndicate at his side, he was visibly suspicious. At first he carefully skirted politics and offered only the bare facts: "The Cairo headquarters gave us the money, but we created this building ourselves. We designed it and constructed it from scratch. Isn't it beautiful?" he asked, warming to his subject as he showed me around.

"The Islamists began winning elections in the syndicate in 1987. One of the first things they did was ensure fairness in employment. Before the Islamists came, only a handful of engineers with connections got contracts in the private sector. But the Islamists imposed a quota system. Engineers who wanted work got four projects. Only when those projects were completed did they get new ones. By 1989, the Islamists won all fourteen seats on the board. I was selected by the Brotherhood to be the candidate for *naqeeb*, and I won."

Then he stopped in mid-sentence. "Let me ask *you* some questions. Which side are you on? Why do you only ask questions about the Islamists?"

I answered his questions with some of my own: "Do you consider yourself an Islamist? And what does that mean?"

"We believe in honesty. We are against corruption, which controls the political system. This country is a dictatorship. What we want is to implement the *sharia*. It holds the solutions to all our problems. The government is trying to shut us down, hoping we'll go away. But it won't happen."

My travels brought me face-to-face with hundreds of Qawimas throughout Egypt, searching for a way around the central government and eager to integrate their religion with their professional lives. Syndicate leaders like Esam al-Eryan and Abu al-Ela Mady, although invisible to the Western world, were everything to them. If Egypt's notion of democracy had allowed for true opposition parties, al-Eryan and Mady would surely have triumphed in national elections and become part of the mainstream political process. Instead, they were left to find their own way to power.

Abu al-Ela Mady was twelve years old when he marched in his hometown of Minya to mourn the death of Nasser in 1970. Minya was famous for the riverwalk Nasser's engineers had built along the Nile, and Mady felt obliged to participate in the procession as a sign of patriotism. Like many in Upper Egypt, Mady's father held no particular affinity for the late president and his pan-Arab ideology. He admired the local *sheikh*s and religious scholars more than the bureaucrats hundreds of miles away in Cairo. While Egyptian families in the heartland were naming their sons Gamal in honor of the charismatic Egyptian leader, Mady was named after a revered *sheikh*.

For most of Mady's childhood, his daily routine centered around two local mosques and a few pious mentors. The al-Fuli mosque, the most distinctive Islamic monument in Minya, was dedicated to Sheikh Ahmed al-Fuli, a Sufi, or Muslim mystic, who died in 1658. Al-Fuli was buried on the grounds of the mosque and widely revered for performing miracles. Sheikh Abd al-Mageed Asa, a founding member of both the Muslim Brotherhood and Minya's Education and Faith Association, was the principal speaker at the mosque. Mady's father enrolled him in one of the affiliated religious schools, where he studied mathematics, mastered classical Arabic, and learned to read the Koran. Mady's second mentor was the head of *al-Gama'a al-Shariyya*, an Islamic organization that focused on social work rather than politics.

Mady entered the local university in 1976, enrolling in the engineering faculty. "I considered medicine, but my grades weren't high enough," Mady confided. He became a member of *al-Gama'a al-Islamiyya*, a religious association with no links to the militant *Gama'a* that would soon penetrate Upper Egypt. A year later, Mady and the *Gama'a* decided to become involved in the student unions, then hotbeds of leftist activism. When he and his friends entered the union offices, leaflets praising the Nasser revolution still covered the walls.

Within a year, Mady had changed not only the walls but the entire orientation of the student union. With the enthusiastic backing of dozens of engineering students, he won election as head of the student council. The group's mission was to apply Islamic principles to all aspects of university life. Women on campus were encouraged to wear the Islamic headscarf; students were escorted to regular prayers in the mosque; and summer camps were organized for Koranic reading.

Mady mobilized students in Minya for the *dawa*, or Islamic call. His future comrades had already engaged in similar activities in student unions across Egypt. Esam al-Eryan had been hard at work at Cairo University, along with Futouh. Their organizing paid off and Islamist candidates captured eight of thirteen seats in the National Student Union, which represented universities throughout the country. In response, the state disbanded the national union and confiscated its assets. Mady had become such a key force in the movement that Sadat referred to him in his speeches warning of a rising Islamic threat. At the time, Mady was leading student protests against the 1979 Egyptian-Israeli peace agreement, the centerpiece of Sadat's turn toward the West. Mady's fame earned him a brief stint in jail in 1981, where his cellmates included members of the Muslim Brotherhood. "It was a typical arrest," Mady recalled in matter-of-fact tones. "Many of the others who were arrested were tortured, and it hurt me deeply, even though I was not tortured myself."

For Mady and the other Islamists, the student activism in the 1970s was a dress rehearsal for their takeover of the syndicates more than a decade later. In the late 1970s a core group of Islamists, comprising about thirty young leaders, deliberately made their choice, splitting with their more radical contemporaries who wanted to change society by force and who would later emerge at the head of the militant *al-Gama'a al-Islamiyya*. While the future leaders of the *Gama'a* adopted the teachings of Sayyid Qutb as their point of reference, Mady and the new generation of Islamists followed the inspiration of Hasan al-Banna. Qutb advocated the creation of an Islam-based state through violent struggle if necessary, while al-Banna was more interested in a gradual evolution toward this goal by changing society from within.

By the time Mady and his contemporaries moved into the professional unions, they were politically astute. They knew how to win converts, and understood the pulse of Egyptian society. They knew that it was impossible to create an Islamic state through armed revolt or through the sham democracy of traditional politics. Instead, the Islamists turned to *tarbiyya*, a gradual process of education and mental change that would guide the nation's Muslims back to a true interpretation of their religion.

This was the essence of al-Banna's message so many decades before. "Our duty as Muslim Brothers is to work for the reform of selves, of hearts and souls by joining them to God the all powerful, then to organize our society to be fit for the virtuous community which commands good and forbids evil doing, then from the community will arise the good state."[12]

In June 1986, a group of young Islamists visited Murad al-Zayyat, a wealthy engineer and a Muslim Brotherhood veteran, at his home in Heliopolis, a stately Cairo suburb. The Brothers were preparing for upcoming polls in the engineering union. They figured the time was ripe to build on their modest victories in 1984 and get "the list" elected to the syndicate board. But they knew they had to be cautious. They wanted to avoid alarming the union's secularists. Their answer was to run younger Islamists for seats on the board while putting forth as secretary-general a seasoned Islamist from the Brotherhood's Old Guard who had respect among rank-and-file engineers.

"We were young. We wanted someone with white hair," Saleh Abd al-Kareem recalled.

Al-Zayyat seemed like the perfect choice. In his sixties, he was clearly not associated with the new generation of Islamists. With his requisite shock of gray hair, thick glasses, and extra slim cigarettes, which he puffs through a silver holder, al-Zayyat lent the younger Brothers the respectability they felt they lacked on their own.

"They came to me and said they wanted me to run as head of the syndicate," al-Zayyat told me during one of our many conversations in his engineering office. "I accepted the invitation because I thought they were well-intentioned. They were actually Muslims, religious people."

The Islamists knew from past elections that voter turnout would be low. Only about 3,000 of 170,000 members, or 1.7 percent of eligible voters, had participated in the previous poll. Success depended on getting out their supporters, while diluting the numbers of Marxists, Nasserites, and army engineers who were their natural opponents. They decided to leave nothing to chance.

The Islamists first tried to cut a deal with the army engineers, the largest and best-organized secularist bloc. They offered the military men 30 percent of the seats on the syndicate board in exchange for their support for Brotherhood candidates. The military refused. The Brothers then took less tactful measures to ensure victory.

They decided to challenge a Ministry of Defense decision to allow some 8,000 engineers to vote inside their barracks, rather than in the syndicate hall. The Brothers knew the ministry ruling was designed to guarantee that the military engineers would vote against the Islamists. And no matter the actual tally, the military leadership would have plenty of opportunity to tamper with the ballots before turning them over to the syndicate for counting, a tried and true government tactic in national polls.

The Islamists organized a general assembly of all members to decide where army engineers should vote. On the day of the assembly, the Brothers and their supporters arrived at the syndicate headquarters at 6 A.M. They packed the hall, occupying nearly all the space inside. When the military engineers arrived later, they were forced to stand outside. By the time the referendum was held, many army engineers had left or were caught unaware that voting was underway. The Islamist-backed motion was carried and military employees were required to cast their ballots not in the syndicate hall or in their barracks but in a third location to be announced later.

The strategy worked. On election day, many army engineers were confused over where to vote and simply stayed away, while Brotherhood supporters were kept informed and marched to the ballot boxes like soldiers off to battle. Of the 14,000 engineers who did turn out, a majority backed the Islamists. Forty-five Islamists won seats in 1987 out of sixty-one on the syndicate board, with al-Zayyat elected as secretary-general.

The Brotherhood's early successes owed a great deal to Osman Ahmed Osman, an enigmatic millionaire and self-described Islamist who served as engineering syndicate chairman from 1979 to 1990. Osman's devotion to the Brotherhood began as a child in the city of Ismailia, home of Hasan al-Banna, where his mother raised him on a steady diet of Islamic principles and religious texts. He was one of al-Banna's students at the Ismailia primary school and came to know him well because al-Banna often visited the home of Osman's sister, who was married to a *sheikh* at al-Azhar.

"It was my good fortune to be a disciple of Hasan al-Banna who strengthened me for the religious path upon which I was raised at home, until this path became the focal point of my life," Osman wrote in his autobiography.[13]

After graduating from university, Osman said he left behind his official duties as a member of the Brotherhood. But he remained dedicated to the organization's ideals. "My ties to the organization remained, both spiritually and in terms of paying my membership dues."[14]

During the eight years before the Islamists came to power, Osman gave the Muslim Brotherhood a good name in syndicate affairs. He raised money for the organization and publicly sang the group's praises. He bragged about the days when he helped Brotherhood leaders escape Nasser's gallows by giving them jobs in the Kuwaiti and Saudi branch offices of his multimillion dollar construction firm, the Arab Contractors Company.

Muslim Brothers still tell stories about how Osman outsmarted Nasser's intelligence chief. Osman convinced him that the Brothers were more of a menace unemployed in Egypt than they would be earning high salaries with the Arab Contractors Company outside the country. To make sure he was operating on sound footing, he persuaded the intelligence service to issue written authorization for each Muslim Brother who left Egypt for a job in the Gulf. When Nasser realized the leading Brothers he was trying to detain were safely employed overseas in Osman's firm, he was outraged and ordered Osman's arrest. But Osman had the papers to prove the intelligence service had authorized their "escape."

"I remember that (Nasser's) *ancien regime* was very disturbed when they found the Arab Contractors had such a large number of Muslim Brothers. For this reason the *ancien regime* put me on the blacklist, and I was literally asked: 'Is this a contracting company or a den of Muslim Brothers?'[15]

"My close ties to the Brotherhood, and my religious upbringing were the reasons I left the doors of my company open to them. . . . I used to agree with them that we had nothing to do with politics, and that we should focus all of our efforts on our fortunes so that we would be able to raise our children."[16]

Osman ran the syndicate much like a modern corporation. His aim was to make the union turn a profit, integrate it into the business world, and establish a social service network for its members. He promised the syndicate would "change from an institution demanding privileges from the state and burdening it to one in which sons of a profession become a productive power capable of active participation in solving society's problems by work and not talk. . . . Instead of playing backgammon and discussing politics, the engineer now wonders whether a macaroni or a fruit juice company is a better investment."[17]

Although he could not know it at the time, Osman did much to revolutionize the role of syndicates in Egypt by introducing social service programs into the engineering union, which were then emulated by other professional organizations. The Islamists would later build on these programs, inserting an overtly moral and religious content to their campaign to better the lot of the average member. Under Osman, the syndicate built a private hospital and apartments for members. He introduced a system of selling consumer goods at discounted prices, launched a social welfare fund for engineers, offered group life insurance, and established a social club for members in the exclusive Cairo district of Zamalek.

Some of Osman's projects eventually went bankrupt, and critics increasingly charged him with mismanagement and even outright corruption. The Mohandis Bank, for one, incurred huge losses. By the end of 1989, almost half the bank's loan portfolio was tied up in a failing joint venture with a foreign soft drink bottling company. Huge taxes on the bottling company and the high cost of equipment forced the bank to stop paying dividends in 1986. At the end of the year, the bank's loans slightly exceeded the value of its deposits.[18] Even while the bottling venture was losing money, the company rented a factory on a piece of land owned by a charitable foundation that was directed by Jihan Sadat, wife of the Egyptian president. Between 1980 and 1988, the syndicate paid the charity two million pounds rent under a fixed contract. Had the land simply been bought outright, it would have cost the syndicate less than one million pounds.[19]

In his heyday, Osman was a man for all seasons. While he was running the syndicate like a Wall Street tycoon, he was also cozying up to Sadat. His close relationship with the president led to marriage between Osman's son and Sadat's daughter, an invaluable connection under Egypt's spoils system. In 1979, the year Osman became the *naqeeb*, Sadat donated to the syndicate the deed to the land where the headquarters is located along Ramsis Street.

Under Mubarak, the mounting accusations surrounding Osman's financial dealings finally undermined his relations with many syndicate members and his powerful state patrons. The ruling National Democratic Party refused to endorse his second four-year term as chairman of the syndicate. He was accused of giving an unsecured loan through Mohandis Bank to a merchant who sold tainted chickens across the country. Some engineers charged Osman with trying to buy votes to guarantee his victory. Nevertheless, he won a second term by mobilizing army engineers and civilians who worked in his enterprises.

By 1987, when the Islamists won their first significant victory in the engineering syndicate, Osman's star was fading. But they used their new strength as a mandate to build on his achievements. One union publication, issued under the Islamists, described the social programs as "part of the syndicate's goals of nurturing the spirit of brotherhood and cooperation among the members." To the Western eye, the array of services introduced by the Islamists appear unremarkable, but in Egypt benefits such as adequate health insurance and pension plans are extremely rare.

One of the most popular programs involved interest-free loans, made available from the funds generated by annual membership dues. Such loans were designed to help members marry and set up homes—heavy financial burdens for all but the wealthiest Egyptians—buy cars, or meet personal emergencies.

Before the Islamists took control, syndicate dues had been collected more or less at random. Now, new procedures improved collection and ensured that excess funds were made available to members or properly reinvested.

The syndicate introduced a modern pension plan, providing money for engineers when they retired and death benefits for survivors. To increase the engineers' salaries, the union leadership also worked out an arrangement with the state to allow engineers to work in their government jobs in afternoon shifts, freeing the mornings for more lucrative employment in the budding private sector.

By 1994, the syndicate had made significant progress on behalf of its members. Aggregate salaries for the 200,000 engineers had increased fourfold from 1985 to 1994. Deposits in the syndicate accounts climbed from 14 million pounds in 1985 to 170.58 million in 1994. Revenue from a special surcharge on all engineering projects—imposed in 1974 but unevenly applied since—jumped from 15. 3 million pounds in 1985 to 78 million in 1994. And gains from investments increased from 36,000 pounds in 1985 to 20.7 million in 1994.[20]

"Even members who weren't necessarily sympathetic to the Islamic cause supported us," Saleh Abd al-Kareem told me. "We never identified ourselves as Muslim Brothers. We held all of our meetings in public in the syndicate headquarters, as opposed to the Muslim Brotherhood veterans who were accustomed to conducting business underground. And when a member brought up the issue of whether we were Muslim Brothers, we would change the subject, and say, 'We are all engineers.' "

While the Islamists were solidifying their hold on the engineers' syndicate, Esam al-Eryan was making similar headway in the doctors' union, in which Muslim Brothers and their supporters had already gained a solid foothold on the board. With elections looming in 1992, the Islamists hoped to achieve their greatest sweep. As with their engineering brethren, social services opened the hearts and minds of the medical professionals to al-Eryan and his allies.

The 1980s saw sharp increases in the cost of health care, driven in part by the opening of private hospitals and clinics under Sadat's *infitah*. Rising foreign investment in the health care sector improved the availability of medicine and equipment, but at a price few Egyptians could afford. Clearly, one way to demonstrate goodwill toward the rank and file was to create a health care plan for syndicate members and their families.

A group of doctors began studying health care programs in the United States which they used as models for their own plan, modifying them in accordance with Koranic notions of social justice. "We wanted to adapt the plan to our culture and our needs," Ibrahim Mustafa, the leading architect of the program, told me. "In America, there were too many restrictions. We wanted our plan to be more humane, in harmony with our Islamic principles, to look after the welfare of our members. In our program, for example, we offer insurance to all people. We don't deny insurance to people who have preexisting conditions, such as cancer."

The health care program proved enormously popular with the doctors, and won a seal of approval from the U.S. Agency for International Development. Soon it was emulated by many of the other professional unions. In 1990, 62 percent of all doctors were enrolled in the medical insurance plan, while 19 percent of the dentists, 16 percent of the pharmacists, and 12 percent of the veterinarians took part in similar plans.[21]

The doctors' union also became involved in national issues. The syndicate worked to increase state production of medicine and encouraged the government to retain subsidies for drugs. The syndicate also advocated restricting the number of students admitted to medical schools in order to limit the number of physicians in an already overcrowded profession.

The confidence gained from their success soon impelled the Islamists to turn to more overt means of spreading their religious convictions among fellow doctors. They wrote a pledge to be a pious Muslim into the oath required to become a syndicate member. The oath opens with a verse from the Koran, and is filled with religious references: "I observe God in my profession. I promise . . . that I will always be one of God's instruments of mercy."

The new pledge aroused the anger of Egypt's secularist intellectuals, such as Farag Foda. "Those who wrote the oath did not think at all that the only way for a doctor to be superior in his profession is knowing well and mastering the medical sciences and that a qualified doctor can be Muslim or Christian or Jew or Buddhist or atheist, and that a doctor can be a good believer, yet a dumbbell!" Foda wrote in a newspaper commentary.

"The syndicate is not only for Muslim doctors, but for all Egyptian doctors. The domination of Islamists on its board does not mean the Islamization of the profession, because medicine is a profession and a science and an art and not a religion."[22] Foda's criticism helped foster the notion among the extremists that he was an apostate, and he was later gunned down by Islamic militants.

If members of the medical profession shared Foda's concerns, they did not show it at the ballot box. In fact, the new direction of the syndicate under the Islamists was so appealing that Christian doctors defied unprecedented demands by Pope Shenouda, the Coptic patriarch, that they vote against the Islamic list. On April 12, 1990, a Christian holiday, the pope encouraged the estimated 20 percent of union members who are Copts to "consider the matter [voting against the Islamists] a spiritual work which you fulfill, and a national duty no one has the right to ignore." It was the first time the pope had issued a public statement that was overtly political in nature.

The hard work by Eryan and his allies paid off handsomely in the 1992 union elections. Islamist candidates won twenty of twenty-five seats on the board in a poll that brought out the greatest number of voters in syndicate history. An estimated 30,000, or 65 percent of those eligible, cast their ballots.

The Islamic tendency also took root within the lawyers' union. On September 13, 1992, Islamists captured eighteen of twenty-four seats on the board of the syndicate, a virtual citadel of secularism since its creation in 1912. Among the victors was Mukhtar Noah, the pioneering Islamist lawyer who first won a seat back in 1984, and Seif al-Islam al-Banna, whose claim to fame was that his father was Brotherhood founder Hasan al-Banna.

The Islamist victory came as a nasty surprise for the government. Nasserite loyalists, Communists, and the National Democratic and Wafd parties had dominated the syndicate for the last forty years. The Wafdists had led the national struggle against the British and later supported the 1952 Free Officers' coup that brought the arch-secularist Nasser to power. But as lawyers, syndicate members were political by nature, and the different factions within the union, mostly leftists of varying stripes, were often at odds. The syndicate also periodically clashed with the central authorities, prompting a series of temporary closures.

When the Islamists first began making inroads among the lawyers in the mid-1980s, they took advantage of the deep divisions within the union while imprinting the Brotherhood seal on an array of activities and perks available to the rank and file. They soon opened summer camps at beach resorts to educate young members on religious thinking and Brotherhood ideology. They provided office space for young law school graduates who could not possibly afford the rent or brave the struggle required to find a flat suitable for setting up shop in Cairo. Twelve social clubs were created for lawyers across the country, and the syndicate was involved in boosting salaries. The Islamists also began a shuttle bus offering free transportation among the sprawling Cairo courts to lawyers too poor to own cars.

The overwhelming 1992 Islamist victory in the syndicate elections touched off a wild celebration. Thousands of lawyers gathered at the syndicate headquarters in downtown Cairo, shouting, "Yes, We Want It Islamic, Islam Is the Solution." Others prayed, stretching their mats out along Abd al-Khaleq Tharwat Street, near the union offices. "Allahu Akbar, the Islamic Alliance Has Won the Lawyers' Election," screamed the front page of *al-Shaab*.

The Islamists were quick to attribute their success to the great religious awakening sweeping the country. In truth, few lawyers had actually voted. No more than 20 percent of all eligible voters had participated. Years of bickering among the various secularist factions had left a legacy of apathy among most syndicate members. Their absence from the voting was a sign of pure exhaustion. Many also recalled the last election, known as "Bloody Friday," in 1989, when fistfights broke out among members. One lawyer even drew a gun and began firing into the air and the police were called in to restore order.

"We deserve what happened in the syndicate," lawyer Sabir Ammar told me, acknowledging the damage done by decades of squabbling among his fellow leftists who had once controlled the union. "We failed."

During the late 1980s and early 1990s, watershed years in the professional syndicates, the state was feeling increasingly vulnerable in its battle with armed Islamic militants. Gunmen hiding out in the canefields of Upper Egypt were murdering policemen nearly every day in Assyut, Sohag, and Qena. Tourists traveling through Upper Egypt to visit the Pharaonic tombs of Luxor and Aswan were killed or wounded, as militants attacked trains, buses, and Nile cruise ships. The extremists also managed to penetrate Cairo, shattering long-standing feelings of security that the threat was confined to the hinterland. In November 1993, gunmen fired at Prime Minister Atef Sidqi as he walked his daughter to her car from her nursery school in Heliopolis. In the SemiRamis, a five-star hotel near the U.S. embassy, a lone gunman went on a rampage, killing three foreign tourists as they sat in a first-floor coffee shop; a fourth died later in the hospital. State security forces, alarmed by reports that the militants had created a "state within a state," raided the Cairo neighborhood of Imbaba, contributing to the general sense of instability.

To the besieged government, Islamic activity within the syndicates was largely background noise, an annoyance when compared with what appeared to be a formidable militant threat. But the Muslim Brothers also managed to antagonize the increasingly nervous state. In October 1992, a massive earthquake hit Cairo, killing more than 500 people and displacing thousands from their homes. The professional unions shifted into high gear. Doctors in the syndicate's Humanitarian Relief Committee constructed makeshift tents in slums such as Sayyeda Zeinab to provide shelter for those whose houses were demolished. Others delivered food to thousands camped out on sidewalks and streets. They treated the ill and injured and distributed medicine to the needy. The syndicate also donated 200 pounds (two-thirds of the average doctor's monthly wage) to families of those who had died; 50 pounds to the injured; and 100 to those displaced and in need of emergency housing. The families of doctors who were killed received 1,000 pounds, and 500 pounds was given to those doctors hurt in the quake or its aftermath.

The engineers' syndicate organized teams of inspectors to examine houses and apartments of any Egyptian who feared his home was unstable and might collapse if another tremor hit. The syndicate inspected at least 10,000 residences. About 250,000 pounds of syndicate money was donated to repair the homes of earthquake victims.

As the Islamists worked around the clock, state-run relief committees were slow to respond to the catastrophe. Stories of the Islamic relief operations dominated the headlines in the opposition press. There were heartbreaking tales from frustrated victims ignored by state workers. One woman complained in *al-Shaab*, the Islamist daily, that she was denied a permit to move into an apartment set aside for refugees because she could not find her identity card. It was, she said, lost in the rubble of what was once her home.

The foreign press also noted the success of the Islamists' charity network in sharp contrast to the state's inefficiency and seeming lack of concern. Echoing the slogan of the Muslim Brotherhood, an article in the American magazine *Newsweek* was headlined, "Islam Is the Solution." Esam al-Eryan, the doctors' syndicate chief, became a regular feature on the BBC as the white knight who had come to save the downtrodden. After ten days, the authorities had had enough. Troops marched into Sayyeda Zeinab and razed the tents constructed by the doctors of the Muslim Brotherhood. Officials ordered the engineers' syndicate to halt the housing inspections. And the government diverted private donations pouring into syndicate coffers or related charities by ordering all aid be handed over to the state-run Red Crescent Society, the Muslim world's equivalent of the Red Cross. The innocent victims were left to wallow in the mess.

With solid backing inside the syndicates and rising popularity among the people at large, the Islamists turned their attention to foreign affairs. Earlier in 1991, the engineering syndicate had opposed Egypt's participation in the U.S.-led alliance against Iraq during the Persian Gulf War. In January, after the United States launched Desert Storm, the syndicate condemned the bombing raids on Iraq and demanded that Egypt withdraw from the allied coalition.

The syndicates' voice in foreign affairs grew louder still. The Islamic world was outraged by the deportation, torture, and killing of Muslims in Bosnia-Herzegovina. The lawyers,' doctors,' and engineers' syndicates organized committees to raise money for Bosnian refugees and staged protests in support of the Muslims there. At least one demonstration was held at al-Azhar, after Friday noon prayers.

The syndicates also held seminars and conferences condemning the 1993 U.S.-backed Oslo peace accord between Israel and the Palestine Liberation Organization for the clear advantage it gave to the Jewish state at the Palestinians' expense. Their criticism came on the heels of the now famous snapshot of the hesitant handshake between Yasser Arafat and Yitzhak Rabin on the White House lawn. The peace agreement, which at the time appeared to be a monumental step toward resolving the Arab-Israeli conflict, was everything to Mubarak. It was his chance to play the part of chief negotiator in the region. It was a chance for Egypt, fearful that it had lost its traditional leadership of the Arab world, to reenter the stage as a world player in international affairs. In the coming years, Cairo was to be the meeting place for peace negotiations and Mubarak stood at the center of the process as a liaison between the Palestinians and the Israelis.

Too much was at stake for the government to tolerate such high-profile internal criticism of the Oslo peace process. Mubarak's greatest concern was that the syndicates were operating as political parties or, worse, as a rival government. It was enough that his adversaries had won in large numbers in syndicate elections. It was enough that they had gone a step further after the earthquake by extending their hand outside the syndicates to the general public. Now, their ambition seemed to know no bounds; they were becoming a voice in foreign policy and undermining the state's objectives.

For their part, the young Islamists were more confident than ever. Choosing to ignore the rising tensions with the state, they moved to challenge Mubarak where it hurt most—on human rights issues.[23] For years the United States and Europe had turned a blind eye to Egypt's appalling human rights record, preferring to see Mubarak as a useful ally in the Cold War and in the intermittent pursuit of Middle East peace. But changes in the geopolitical landscape, most notably the collapse of the Soviet Union, had placed rights abuses back on the agenda. Cairo was deeply concerned that its coveted role as Washington's favorite could unravel as a result.

The doctors' and engineers' syndicates held seminars on the widespread torture of prisoners in Egyptian jails and called for the release of all political detainees. One conference organized to voice opposition to state torture was forcibly halted by Interior Ministry troops, who surrounded the engineering syndicate offices. The engineers had organized the event amid much fanfare in the days leading up to the conference. Notices were published in the opposition press, inviting the public to attend. Abu al-Ela Mady, then assistant secretary-general of the syndicate, held a press conference to condemn the state's long history of human rights violations.

This time, the Islamists had gone too far. It was up to Murad al-Zayyat, the "man with white hair," to set them straight. "I was on a trip to Pakistan, and they had attached my name as secretary-general to the advertisements endorsing the conference on torture. I came back and asked Abu al-Ela, 'What have you done?'" Murad al-Zayyat told me, expressing exasperation with the younger members' indiscretion. "I told them, 'I'm ready to accept aggression by the state. I am ready, okay. But what is your plan? Do you want revolution? If not, we have to play the game. We have to be polite. These kinds of events have a cumulative effect, and will lead to a state crackdown.'"

Mady and other young Islamic leaders ignored al-Zayyat's warning. They were too eager, too euphoric. Somehow they failed to apply the same political savvy they had used to woo the syndicate rank and file to their relations with the state. They became too impressed with their own success.

It took them years to admit to their cockiness. "We were running the syndicates like political parties," Abu al-Ela Mady confessed four years after the event. "This was never our intention. It just turned out that way."

The victory in the syndicates had come too fast and too easily for the Islamists to fully comprehend the dangerous signals they were sending to the state. "In Egypt, if you give the impression you are challenging the president's position, he won't tolerate it," said Saleh Abd al-Kareem. "But people [the Islamists] didn't think about this at the time. As Muslims we believe in co-existence. We were not looking for confrontation."

It was only a matter of time before al-Zayyat's prophetic warning would come true. While the state held on to political power by stuffing ballot boxes in national elections and banning any real opposition parties from the polls, the Islamists were winning control of the professional unions with more innovative tactics. For many in the middle class the syndicates had become a microcosm of what the country could achieve if the totalitarian state were out of the way. It was predicted that the authorities would sooner or later set out to crush the syndicate movement.

The opening salvo came on February 16, 1993, when the government rammed Associations Law 100 through the docile parliament, spelling out new rules for the professional unions. Introduced as the "Law Concerning the Insurance of Democracy within the Syndicates," the new bill removed union elections from the authority of the syndicates themselves and placed them in the hands of the courts, which the state felt it could better control.

Most significant, Law 100 also specified that at least 50 percent of eligible voters must take part for an election to be valid, although somewhat lower thresholds were set for subsequent rounds. Repeated failure to meet these standards meant a Cairo court would be empowered to appoint the syndicate leadership. These same courts were later authorized to vet candidates for the syndicate leadership and were given veto powers over the time and place of union elections. Police officers and state bureaucrats were delegated to enforce the new regulations. Finally, Law 100 restricted the solicitation of donations and the use of syndicate funds for outside projects, such as the Cairo earthquake relief that had so embarrassed the government or aid to co-religionists in Bosnia.

The authorities were well aware that low voter turnout had worked in the Islamists' favor. Even though they were a minority in some syndicates, the Islamic leaders were well organized, with determined and disciplined followers who voted in large numbers. The legislation was designed precisely to prevent political maneuvering, such as the engineers' victory in 1987, when they packed the assembly hall and voted to change the polling stations, or the lawyers' triumph in 1992.

In Egyptian politics, the truth often lies in the exact opposite of what is stated publicly. The authorities' response to widespread indignation and outrage over Law 100 was just such a case. "The aim of the new legislation is to ensure the broad participation of the grassroots," Mubarak declared.

The state's hypocrisy was transparent. Aside from the fact that elections to parliament and municipal councils are fraught with vote-rigging, the turnout for parliamentary polls had dipped as low as 10 percent in recent years. In municipal elections, voter turnout in some districts did not exceed 5 percent. Yet the state never declared these elections, which Mubarak's National Democratic Party invariably won, invalid.

"The arbitrariness [in elections] was welcome as long as the party in power was loyal to the government," Fahmy Huweidy, a well-known columnist who supports the Islamic point of view, wrote in *al-Shaab* under the headline, "Aborting the Democratic Dream." Huweidy's columns regularly appeared in *al-Ahram*, the official government newspaper. But articles criticizing Law 100 were banned from its pages, and he was restricted to publishing his views in the opposition press.

"When elections brought the opposition to power, the situation became dangerous, alarming the authorities in ways that did not happen even when the earthquake hit Egypt," Huweidy noted.[24]

The change in the election law did little to halt the Islamic march. In the pharmacists' and agronomists' syndicates, Islamic candidates won by large margins, with more than 50 percent of eligible voters taking part.

The Islamists' victory in the pharmacists' syndicate was particularly striking. An estimated 30 percent of its members are Christian Copts, perhaps less inclined than majority Muslims to vote for the Islamists. But by 1993, Brotherhood supporters had made their case and gained widespread support, even among the most skeptical members. The 1994 election saw the pharmacists turn out to vote in numbers far greater than ever, driven in large part by outrage at government meddling in the form of Law 100. Of 21,000 eligible voters, 17,000 went to the ballot box and handed the Islamists their greatest victory since they first won a union seat in 1984. Islamic candidates won seventeen out of twenty-five seats on the syndicate board.

There are no statistics on the voting patterns of the Christian pharmacists, but many told me the programs and campaign promises of their Islamist colleagues had overcome their early doubts. Others set aside their suspicions that the union would be reduced to little more than a front organization. Mohammed Abd al-Gawwad, a wealthy pharmacist, is one such convert.

Gawwad, himself a Muslim, was suspicious of the Brotherhood supporters when they first became politically active in the syndicate.

"I didn't want the syndicate to become a platform for the Muslim Brotherhood. But after a while, you see that they help any member, whether he is a Copt or a Muslim," explained Gawwad, who is deputy secretary-general of the pharmacists' union. "Before the Islamists came, there was no one to meet you at the syndicate. If you had a problem with the tax authority, there was no one. Once the Islamists came, there were people in the syndicate headquarters waiting to help at all hours of the day. My feeling now is that their performance has been excellent. . . . So it's not my business to know what they do at night behind closed doors in their Brotherhood offices."

One needs only to visit Mohammed Maqsud, the secretary-general of the pharmacists' union, to understand the Islamic appeal. A pudgy man with a prominent *zabeeb* on his forehead, Maqsud sits behind a large oak desk in the syndicate headquarters from morning to night, offering personal assistance to union members. On the day I stopped by in September 1997, a dozen pharmacists prayed on green mats outside his office at noon, while others gathered inside to ask about their insurance benefits or the loans the syndicate offers. "Every pharmacist from Alexandria to Aswan knows me and knows my home telephone number," Maqsud told me with a gentle smile. "My door is always open. I am the first secretary-general to sit in the syndicate office all day. And I do this despite the fact that I must pay a druggist to run the pharmacy I own while I sit in the union office."

I asked Maqsud how the Islamists had managed to convince the Christian members to support them. But before he could answer, a Coptic pharmacist happened by, as if on cue. "Why don't you ask this man?" Maqsud advised. So I did.

"Every pharmacist wants a strong syndicate, particularly since we often have problems with the minister of health, who is often a physician," Mohammed Besheer explained, hovering over Maqsud's desk "You know, there is always rivalry between doctors and pharmacists. We can trust the Islamists to work for us, no matter what problems we face. This isn't a syndicate for Muslims. It's a syndicate for all pharmacists."

The failure of Law 100, enacted at further cost to the government's already poor democratic credentials, left Mubarak increasingly exposed to the legitimate political power of elected Islamists heading the professional unions. Already the pharmacists and a handful of smaller unions had gone over to the Islamists despite the hurdles imposed by the new law. There was no reason to expect them to fail to cement their hold on the more powerful syndicates, in particular the big engineering union. The state's efforts to change the rules had proved incapable of stemming the tide. Ending the game altogether appeared the best among limited options.

"The state did not try to negotiate with leaders of the syndicates, but it entered into a failed competition several times through elections," Esam al-Eryan commented in a letter to me from his prison cell. "There was a possibility to reach a compromise. However, the state's decision was to confront us strongly and decisively, even at the expense of the middle class."

On May 2, 1995, police officers invaded the engineering syndicate headquarters along Ramsis Boulevard, in downtown Cairo, to enforce a court order placing the union under official state custodianship, or *hirasa*. Dozens of journalists huddled inside the hall, while a group of Islamists, including Saleh Abd al-Kareem, Abu al-Ela Mady, and Mukhtar Noah, tried to argue the *hirasa* order was illegal. As the lawyer representing the syndicate, Noah telephoned Judge Waddahi al-Wakeel, chief of the north Cairo court, to verify the decision. To his surprise, the judge said the order had in fact been issued. An angry Noah stood before the crowd and described the action as "the execution of a military decision by police who were led by someone getting their instructions from the Ministry of Interior."[25]

"We couldn't believe it was happening," Saleh Abd al-Kareem recalled. "There were so many ways the state could have accomplished its objective. They could have tried to prevent us from winning elections by persuading swing voters in the syndicate. They could have done many things, rather than use force. When I met the security men the day they invaded the syndicate, I told them, 'You did this the *balady* way,'" said Saleh, using a common Egyptian expression meaning "like a country-bumpkin."

Perhaps the Islamists should not have been so surprised. In fact, trouble had been brewing within the syndicate itself for some time, with the board, dominated by the young Islamists, increasingly at odds with its own chairman, Hasaballah al-Kafrawi. In the end, Kafrawi was to prove the instrument of their downfall, driving the imposition of *hirasa* against his former syndicate colleagues.

When I met him in 1997, Kafrawi did little to hide his pleasure with the government takeover of the syndicate. I asked him if Mubarak had encouraged him to pursue court action against the engineers. "He didn't order me to do it, but I can say he was pleased with the outcome," he replied.

The Islamists initially turned to Kafrawi, former minister of housing and development under Sadat and a close friend of Murad al-Zayyat, to lead the engineering syndicate as secretary-general in 1990. They hoped he would use his connections from his ministerial career to act as an effective liaison between the syndicate and the authorities. The Islamists figured they would run the day-to-day affairs, while Kafrawi would wear the face of moderation, calming any fears that the Islamists might use their new power to turn the union into a proselytizing arm of the Muslim Brotherhood.

But Kafrawi was not as compliant as they had hoped. Not only did he later prove allergic to anything with an Islamic approach, he was accustomed to the high degree of deference he once enjoyed as a member of the cabinet. When the Islamists ignored his ideas, his healthy ego was wounded. But the size of his ego should have come as no surprise; it emerges in any encounter with Kafrawi. This was not a man to sit on the sidelines while others make all the decisions.

Along the street where Kafrawi's private office is located in Garden City, a scenic district near downtown Cairo, watchmen in his employ keep an eye out for his visitors and his enemies. They refer to him as "pasha," a grand title from the days of the Ottoman empire: "Did you come to see the pasha? Is the pasha expecting you?"

"I am famous. Everyone knows me all over Egypt," Kafrawi told me numerous times during a brief meeting in his office.

Shortly after his election as *naqeeb*, he began to clash with the Islamists at every turn. In 1993, the syndicate voted him out as chairman, but Kafrawi refused to budge. Instead, he charged the board with financial mismanagement of union monies and helped place the syndicate under the control of the state.

"I was shocked at the Islamists' behavior," Kafrawi told me. "I had to confront them. As a nationalist I had an obligation to express opposition to their behavior. We were supposed to be a syndicate, not a political party."

Whether or not Mubarak played a direct role in the decision to close the syndicate, the move against the union was clearly a political one. In the past, the *hirasa* law had been applied by the state after the 1952 revolution to seize property owned by Egyptian aristocrats. The statute had never before been applied to a syndicate, and many lawyers argued that the action was illegal.

In fact, in 1996 an appellate court ruled that the law could not be used to strip the elected syndicate board of its powers. If the *hirasa* had any validity at all, the court said, it could only be applied to confiscate the syndicate's coffers. The court also ordered the state-designated guardian, the *hiras*, to return some two million Egyptian pounds he took for his personal use from union funds. But the government ignored the ruling, and syndicate leaders say the money has never been returned.

Another guardian the state selected to run the syndicate was jailed in 1997 on corruption charges unrelated to syndicate business. Egypt's High Security Court ordered Abd al-Wahab al-Habbak to pay the largest fine ever issued. Habbak was convicted of amassing a fortune in illegal commissions as the head of the Holding Company for Industrial Engineering, a private firm.

Eight months after the engineering syndicate was closed, *hirasa* was also imposed on the lawyers' union. Tensions with the state had already reached unprecedented levels after the death in custody of a young Islamist lawyer, Abd al-Hareeth Madani, in May 1994. Madani, known to represent suspects accused of Islamic extremism, was arrested in a raid on his law office. After days of official silence on Madani's fate, authorities announced he had died of an asthma attack—a claim ridiculed by government critics and later contradicted by a coroner's report, which indicated he had been tortured. The syndicate called a strike on May 15 that paralyzed the court system.

Two days later, I headed for the syndicate building where lawyers planned a protest in defiance of Egypt's state of emergency laws. Security forces with shields and automatic weapons surrounded the union headquarters in central Cairo, while a recorded recitation from the Koran played in the background. Police soon moved in behind a haze of tear gas, beating the protesters and hauling many off to jail. Before fleeing to safety, I was struck by the curious image of dozens of Egyptian lawyers, their trademark briefcases clutched by their sides, filing into police vans.

The riot and Madani's death brought a chill across the country. The events themselves were not unusual. It was common knowledge that the syndicates were a threat to the state, and it certainly was not news that an Egyptian had been tortured while in police custody. But the dramatic incidents exposed the hypocrisy of the regime. If Egypt ever had any illusions of being a democracy, the clampdown on the very people charged with bringing justice to the land shattered this myth. "Lawyers are enemies of the regime," one Islamist told me the day of the riot. "The government suppresses freedom and the lawyers defend freedom."

As with the engineers, the initiative for the *hirasa* action in the lawyers' syndicate came in part from within the organization. Despite the Islamists' success in improving the personal and professional lives of the members, they too had fallen victim to internal bickering, just as their secularist predecessors before them. A three-year power struggle between Mukhtar Noah and Seif Islam al-Banna, played out in the press ad nauseum, had left the Islamists vulnerable to attack. Their syndicate rivals convinced a court that the Islamists were involved in financial corruption, such as employing only those companies owned by Muslim Brothers for syndicate business. A report by the state Central Auditing Apparatus, issued in March 1996, uncovered what it said were irregularities in syndicate affairs: Companies with whom the syndicate had contracted were identified under false names and checks had been addressed to individuals, rather than to the travel agencies that supposedly arranged syndicate-funded trips. However, the overall findings were inconclusive and fell short of evidence justifying the *hirasa* action.

An international team from the Geneva-based Centre for the Independence of Judges and Lawyers, sent to Cairo in early 1998 to explore the problems of their Egyptian colleagues, found a pattern of abuse by the government and their allies inside the Lawyers' syndicate. They also found that the effective suspension of the union's activities was in violation of United Nations regulations and, arguably, a violation of the Egyptian constitution as well. Rather than sequester the syndicate and deprive its members of the legal right of association, the commission said, police and prosecutors should have been called in to investigate any allegations of corruption. Shutting down the union appeared a political move by the central authorities to avoid creation of alternative centers of power and influence within society. "The Mission was surprised at the apparent complacency of the government to the effective suspension of the (syndicates) as democratic organizations. This is particularly surprising given the role of Bar associations in the administration of justice," the panel's report concluded.[26]

The use of the *hirasa* laws has given Mubarak and his allies some respite from the Islamist onslaught in the syndicates, but only after doing enormous damage to what remained of the legal and political credibility of the government. Court rulings invalidating all or parts of the *hirasa* decisions have been routinely ignored, depriving union members of elected representation and access to syndicate funds. A Cairo court, meanwhile, has refused to sanction new elections to the boards of the engineers' and lawyers' unions, leaving the organizations rudderless. *Hirasa* orders have also been issued against provincial syndicates, including the Alexandria branch of the doctors' union, which was closed down in August 1997. Many expect it is only a matter of time before the physicians' headquarters in Cairo is also seized from those Islamists who remain free from prison.

Despite these setbacks, the syndicate movement under the new Islamists has touched Egyptian society in ways few could have imagined when Abu al-Ela Mady, Esam al-Eryan, and their comrades launched their extraordinary venture. In a society bereft of democracy, they proved that free elections and free debate were in fact possible. In a nation crying out for moral guidance, they successfully married a vision of social justice, rooted in the Koran, with the demands and stresses of modern life.

In practical terms, the brief Islamist tenure within the professional unions must be seen as a success. The new leadership raised living standards for union members, eased pervasive corruption and cronyism, and filled in for an incompetent state that could no longer address the concerns of the middle classes. The syndicates also demonstrated an admirable degree of democracy and pluralism, in stark contrast to the authoritarian Mubarak regime.

It was, however, on the moral and intellectual plane that the young Islamists left their greatest mark, one that will help drive the Islamic revival for years to come. The new syndicate leaders helped map out a new Egyptian identity, no longer subservient to the demands of "westernization" that have little to offer the common man. At the same time, they shattered the corrosive myth that the Islamists were bent on recreating a medieval Arabian "paradise," by violence if necessary. And they broke with the more furtive traditions of the outmoded Muslim Brotherhood, accustomed to operating in the netherworld of Egyptian politics. Indeed, they openly courted modernity, seeking not to banish it but simply to make it more Islamic.

To this day, Esam al-Eryan remains in prison, as committed as ever to the path he has chosen. In our last prison "conversation," I asked him whether Egypt was effectively an Islamic society.

"The official religion in Egypt is Islam and the *sharia* is the main source of legislation. There is a laxity in applying these texts, despite growing Islamic sentiments that are increasing day after day. No one doubts that Egypt's middle and modern history is associated with Islam, and its future will also be associated with how much Egypt is committed to the laws and spirit of Islam."

5

SCHOOL OF REVOLUTION

On a cloudy afternoon in March 1998, I took a creaking train from Cairo to Minya, nearly four hours to the south, to retrace the life of Abu al-Ela Mady, the Islamist who made the kind of history the state hopes will never be repeated. I descended onto the platform and climbed the stairs to a dilapidated bridge. Glancing down to the bustling street crowded with donkeys, vegetable vendors, and carriages, I recalled my first impression of Minya when I last visited in 1994. Downtown Minya is an Islamic version of a small American town, where everyone knows a little too much about everyone else. But there are too few cars in Minya and no real town square.

As I searched patiently for a taxi amid the donkeys and horses with a gusty wind blowing sand and dirt into my face, I remembered there are no taxis either. While I waited, people stared with the penetrating glance that becomes all too familiar to a foreigner in outlying parts of Egypt. In the end, I hired a carriage for what turned out to be a bumpy, thirty-minute ride behind a weary horse who limped reluctantly to the rhythm of his master's whip. Police had closed the main road, so we were forced onto the macadam paths and back alleyways, maneuvering through vegetable stalls, kiosks, crowds of anxious shoppers, and chickens scratching around in the mud. When I arrived at the Nefertiti Hotel along the banks of the Nile, the stares grew more hostile and suspicious. "What are you doing here?" demanded the young woman behind the reception desk. "Don't you know foreigners are a problem for us?"

The problem was Minya itself, known as the last stronghold of the Islamic militants. By 1997 the security forces had cleaned house and most of the militants were either dead or in prison, but sporadic gun battles still occurred there. I did not know it at the time, but a week before my arrival, several policemen had died in a shootout with militants in a nearby village. Over the last two decades the Minya province had been part of a corridor, extending south to Assyut, for militant activities. Through different periods, the venue of the violence shifted between the two towns, and the region gave birth to some of the most notable militant leaders. A handful of key Muslim extremists, among them the second-in-command of the *Gama'a al-Islamiyya*, the core militant group, operated from Minya. Khalid Islambouli, the lead gunman in Sadat's assassination, came from Milawi, a town in Minya province.

At the time I traveled there, the U.S. embassy had just issued a warning for citizens to stay clear of the region, extending from Beni Suef, a town about seventy-five miles north of Minya, to Assyut, about sixty miles to the south. The embassy often gave alarmist advice, exaggerating the threat at hand. But this particular warning came in response to the massacre of sixty-two people in Luxor, the largest such attack in Egyptian history. All of this made the visit by a foreigner a delicate matter. For the dozens of secret policemen lurking conspicuously around town, my presence posed two problems. One was the burden of protecting me. The last thing the government needed was an international scandal stemming from yet another foreigner killed by Muslim extremists. The second task was to ensure that I did not learn anything that might be bad publicity for the Egyptian state.

I did my best to put everyone at ease, first by explaining to the woman at the state-run Nefertiti that I came to Minya not to seek out Muslim militants, but to meet ordinary people. Then I offered the same explanation, in more convincing tones, to the plainclothes policeman slouching on a rickety chair outside the hotel lobby.

"Where are you headed?" he asked, smiling slightly to avoid appearing too intrusive.

"I'm going to Minya University," I replied, knowing the university was far more benign than my other destinations, which included mosques and the homes of influential *sheikh*s.

"Do you have an appointment there?"

"Yes."

"With whom?"

"Professor Ahmed something. I can't remember his full name."

Of course, I was not about to reveal the names of the people I was going to meet, and my answer was clearly unconvincing. Yet it was carefully tailored to meet the requirements of Egypt's prevailing bureaucratic mind-set: the important thing is to always give an answer, something to be registered on paper; never mind whether it is true or not.

The intelligence officer dutifully jotted down "Professor Ahmed" in the notebook he secured under his armpit, smiled, and waved good-bye.

I then set out on my journey. I wanted to find the house where Mady had lived as a child, but I had no clue to its whereabouts. Mady had refused to give me the address. "Don't go to see my family in Minya," he advised when I last saw him in Cairo. "They are simple people. They won't understand why you want to know something about my life. I know it's an American thing. Everyone always goes to Arkansas to understand why Bill Clinton behaves the way he does. But this is Egypt, and we don't do that here. My family will think I'm trying to show off and they won't like it."

Such candor was rare. Mady was certainly not the first person to shy away from revealing personal details about his life. But most of the time, Egyptians create polite excuses for not indulging the Western penchant for psychoanalysis, an alien concept in the Middle East. Questions about one's family background are considered an invasion of privacy.

As it turned out, I found his house shortly after my arrival. It seemed everyone in town knew where he grew up. Mady was famous, not so much for his activity as a syndicate leader in Cairo, but for his years as a student activist at Minya University. When I arrived for what I thought was a meeting with Mady's childhood *sheikh*, Mohammed Abd al-Mageed, I instead met a carpenter who lived with his wife in a mud-brick house beside the local mosque. The *sheikh*, he told me, had left for the day. I thought this man, a lifelong Minya resident in his early forties, could give me a good idea as to just how well known Mady was in his hometown and the impression he had made during the years he helped create a student movement that laid the foundation for today's Islamic revival.

It was obvious Mady was a local hero. "You want to know something about the guy who told Sadat everyone in his government was a hypocrite?" the carpenter asked, when I inquired about the location of the Mady family residence. He was referring to a speech Mady had given twenty years before as a fearless and morally certain student leader.

When I headed along the road toward Mady's house, I passed the al-Fuli mosque, an elegant neoclassical limestone structure that sits facing the Nile. It is considered the most prestigious Islamic monument in the entire province. It is also the place where Mady learned to read the Koran. Al-Fuli, the Sufi saint for whom the mosque is named, was buried on the original site in 1658. Sheikh al-Fuli was such a legend that the city itself was named after him. Local residents told me the full name of the city is actually Minya al-Fuli, even though it is known simply as Minya.

Sheikh al-Fuli was a Sufi mystic, mixing Islamic teachings and traditions with native mysticism and folk religion. Orthodox Islam was seen by many across the Muslim world as too formalistic, and they turned toward mysticism in search of more direct contact with God. Peasants and workers in the underclass were among the most devout followers of Sufism, particularly in Minya and other towns in Upper Egypt. At a typical Sufi gathering, the name of God is repeated to the accompaniment of rhythmic movements and drumming. The purpose is to achieve a state of mind and body that is in union with the divine.

Leading Sufi *sheikh*s held such enormous popular appeal that state officials and the religious scholars of al-Azhar had long searched for ways to undermine their authority. Today, Sufi rituals continue among Egyptians, particularly those from Upper Egypt. Every year, millions honor the birthdays of saints at one of the last vestiges of Sufi piety, an annual festival called a *mawlid*. Although at one time religious rituals were performed at the *mawlid*s, the modern-day version is little more than an amusement park, filled with games for children and food kiosks for adults.

Mady's parents, like many other residents of Minya, were themselves adherents of Sufism. So it was no surprise when I discovered that the Mady family home was in a neighborhood called "the land of the *mawlid*," a narrow, three-story brick structure with a small balcony. The house was situated along Jadid Street, a gravel road running northeast behind the al-Fuli mosque. It had been freshly painted. The doors were still bright blue, and had yet to fade from the steady winds and sand blowing incessantly through the city. When I stopped in front of the house in the large van I had rented, the only vehicle for hire according to the reception clerk back at the Nefertiti Hotel, I created something of a spectacle. The local barber, who had set up shop outside next to Mady's house, turned his head to inspect the new visitors on the road. A young man, who I later learned was Mady's cousin, approached the van to ask who we were and what we wanted. I had promised Mady I would not interview his family, so the driver told the young man we had made a wrong turn and would soon be on our way.

A glimpse of the house and the surrounding neighborhood revealed all the things Mady was too discreet to discuss. He came from modest roots. Local residents told me his father was a manual laborer, and Mady was the first in his family to graduate from the university. "Because he knew poverty, and his father was an ordinary man, Mady became involved in social work organized by religious associations. He always wanted to help other people, because he knew what it meant to struggle," Sheikh Mohammed Abd al-Mageed explained, when I met him one afternoon in the hotel coffee shop.

From everything the townspeople said about Mady it was clear why he was one of the few Islamists in the syndicate movement who has remained out of jail. He was a master at compromise, a man who avoided confrontation and got what he wanted in life by understanding intuitively how to win people over. This was precisely how Mady rose to head the student union at

Minya University from 1977 to 1979, and went on to win election as deputy head of the Egyptian National Student Union from 1978 to 1979.

In 1976, when Mady first arrived at the engineering faculty at Minya University, a 1960s-style pillbox building located around a small courtyard in the rear of the campus, the Marxists, Communists, and socialists were breathing their last gasp. They had been the products of Nasser's flirtation with socialism and pan-Arabism, but the attraction of the old ideology was winding down. The Islamist students, particularly those in science faculties, were steadily attracting support across the country. There were no well-organized groups at the time, except one umbrella organization, the Religious Societies, which had existed since 1972 and focused entirely on Islamic principles and teachings, not politics.

The religious revival at the universities was influenced to some extent by leaders of the Muslim Brotherhood. In the 1970s, Sadat released many of the Brothers who had been imprisoned under Nasser a decade earlier. Once again they focused their efforts on the universities, as they had done so effectively in the 1940s. Mosques became the favored venue for regular meetings, attended by tens of thousands of students. Prominent *sheikh*s from al-Azhar such as Mohammed Ghazali were frequent speakers on campuses, and the Koran, supplemented by the writings of Hasan al-Banna and Sayyid Qutb, fed a growing religious appetite.

The Islamists organized summer youth camps as training grounds for their emerging ideology. The camps taught students how to lead a proper Islamic lifestyle, how to eat, sleep, and pray in accordance with the Koran and the *hadith*s. The regimen was strict, much like military training. Students rose before dawn for the first prayer of the day. They prayed five times a day, and studied the Koran in between their devotions. The camps gathered students together from universities across the country and created a spiritual bond that would facilitate a rapid spread of the movement. "Such camps will produce a generation of serious youth with integrity which our *umma* (community of believers) needs nowadays," preached *al-Dawa*, a publication issued at the time by the Muslim Brotherhood. "Our *umma* is surrounded by conspiracies from every side."[1]

The new trend was billed not only as a way to reclaim religious legitimacy, but as an alternative to leftist student activism that had permeated university campuses under Nasser. Islam was a vote for a more virtuous lifestyle, where good would overcome evil. It was an endorsement of a different value system, a rejection of what was perceived as the decadent and ultimately futile socialism and pan-Arabism of the Nasser era.

The Islamists took full advantage of the backlash under way against atheism, women's liberation, rock music, and casual sex. They condemned parties on the campuses, encouraged women to give up their miniskirts for the veil, and men to grow beards. Women were segregated from men in the classrooms. Students were offered a cut-rate fare of 35 pounds, the equivalent of about $20 at the time, for the annual pilgrimage to Mecca.

In many ways the new generation of Islamists saw themselves under siege from foreign influences that undermined traditional social and religious values. Nasser's prescription for what ailed Egypt was, they argued, itself part of the problem. "The propaganda surrounding the youth today is all incorrect," Esam al-Eryan, one day destined to lead the doctors' syndicate, wrote in 1977. "Many of the writers and intellectuals are agents of the intellectual invasion, both eastern and western. They are spokesmen who were trained and influenced by Freud, Marx, and Nietzsche. So is there any good to be expected from them?"[2]

The Islamists proceeded methodically, almost as if they had been handed a guidebook charting the course of the movement. Yet there is no evidence of a coordinated effort at this early stage. Mady did not know Eryan at the time. Nor did he know Abd al-Monem Abu al-Futouh, the powerful student leader at Cairo University or Ibrahim Zafrani at Alexandria University, with whom he would later apply the skills he learned as a student activist to the Islamic takeover of the syndicates. But the geography that separated them proved no obstacle; their common faith provided the language and bond that would link student activists for years to come. On every major campus, Islamists were involved in similar activities and promoted similar ideas—all without a centralized group leading the way.

"Sometimes we went on field trips out of town. Mady conducted quizzes on the bus," recalled Adel Abd al-Mageed, one of Mady's former classmates at Minya University. "He asked questions relating to religion and gave prizes to the winners. This is what made him popular. He didn't proselytize, but he got the results he wanted. More and more students became religious."

For Mady, his religious activities at Minya University were not part of a personal awakening. Nor did he jump on the bandwagon, once Islamism was in vogue. "He was never a slave to slogans," Sheikh al-Megeed told me about the boy he had seen grow into a man. Mady's activism was instead the logical extension of beliefs he had developed as a child, growing up in a devout home. His three sisters wore the veil, he told me, even when Nasser's popularity was at a peak in the early 1960s and secularism held sway. While most other children across Egypt spent their afternoons playing soccer in the streets and playgrounds, Mady's mother encouraged him to read the Koran.

Mady was ahead of his time, partly because Minya had remained behind the times. Nasserism and its secularist ethos never penetrated Upper Egypt the way it did less remote parts of the country. Mady's life was a single, uninterrupted continuum. When he left his hometown in 1982 for Cairo, his ideas were as solid as his religious upbringing. He simply refined his technique. "I used to be a *saidi*," Mady often jokes, using an unflattering term for Egyptians born in Upper Egypt. "But I was cured of that. Now, I'm a city person."

Twenty years later, students all over Egypt are seeking to emulate Mady, Esam Eryan, and other Islamist icons of the late 1970s and early 1980s. Their generation had transformed the universities into the laboratories in which ideas about religion were increasingly applied to real life. Then they turned their skills and ideas directly to society, as leaders in the professional syndicates, as members in the national parliament and professors in universities. But in trying to follow in their footsteps, the students of the 1990s faced serious obstacles. Just as the Islamists had benefited from twenty years of trial and error, so had the state.

On October 24, 1997, a clanky minibus carried Mohammed Mahmud al-Kurdi, a twenty-one-year-old student at Helwan University, to Ramsis central station. It was seven o'clock at night and Mohammed and his friend, Mohammed Abd al-Kareem Hasan, were headed home for dinner with a great sense of accomplishment and relief. After several trips to a nearby printshop over the previous days, after numerous trivial conversations about paper quality, paper size, and the usual hassles involved in doing most things in Egypt, they carried in their hands the fruits of their labor. A lengthy handbook, filled with sample examinations, would be distributed to students at Helwan the next day to help them prepare for upcoming tests. It was also somewhat of a gimmick: The young men were running as candidates in annual university elections, and the handbook was a clever campaign tool.

The two students told me they had worked assiduously, first to collect old exams and then to compile the handbook, which included selected religious sayings, some from Muslim Brotherhood ideologue Sayyid Qutb. "Who are we and what do we want?" read a page between two sample tests. "We are your brothers who believe that Islam is the only solution for the problems and defeats our society faces." At the bottom of the page was a word of advice: "Go to pray as soon as you hear the call to prayer."

As the minibus approached a roundabout at the station, the Mohammeds clambered out, elbowing their way through an aggressive mob already trying to climb aboard. But before the boys' feet could touch the pavement, a group of men nabbed them and began beating them. The crowd tried to intervene, but the men flashed badges of the state security forces. One brief glance was enough to send the crowd into rapid retreat. The men then hurled the two youths in a car and sped away.

"The first thing they did was blindfold us," Mohammed al-Kurdi recalled a few months later. "They ripped off the white T-shirt I was wearing and tied it around my eyes."

Everyone knows that you never mess with Egypt's security forces. Whether it is at a rare street protest or a demonstration at a university, you have to be willing to endure the consequences. To put up a fight only guarantees more suffering. As student activists, the two Mohammeds knew this well, and as they traveled to an unknown fate, they did not ask questions. They simply tried to figure out their destination based on the noise and traffic patterns in the streets, the volume of horns blowing, the bumps in the road, the few, brief glimpses of light peeking through their blindfolds. When the car finally stopped, they soon learned the reason for their abduction.

"We were taken inside a building. They put me in a room and began punching me, and they asked me to take off my clothes. Then they put one electric wire in my foot and another down there," Mohammed al-Kurdi explained with such a grimace on his face I resisted asking if he meant his penis or his rectum, the favored targets of police torturers.

"They laid me out flat on the floor and wanted to know the names of people who were in our Islamic group at the university, why they were running for election, and where we got money for the campaign."

"Did you give them the names?" I asked.

"I gave them only obvious names, the ones I thought they already knew."

"Did this satisfy them?'

"No. They knew I was lying. Mainly, they wanted to know what was the link between the Islamists inside the university and the Islamic trend outside. They asked, 'Who is telling you to run in the election?'

"Then they tortured me for about four hours, until after midnight."

The experience terrified Mohammed to such an extent that he never told his parents the full details. When a human rights lawyer tried to encourage him to file a case against the security forces for maltreatment, he refused. Fear of retribution overwhelmed him. He was afraid that somehow it would backfire, and he would revisit the torture chamber.

For the security forces, however, it was a routine night. Hundreds of students were arrested, according to lawyers and human rights organizations, and some tortured across Egypt in the days leading up to the university elections. The objective was to prevent students affiliated with Islamic organizations, such as the Muslim Brotherhood or the Islamic-influenced Labor party, from winning seats in student unions. Those perceived as a serious threat were kept in jail until after the polls were held. Others who were considered a mere nuisance were struck from the election rolls by university administrators, under orders from intelligence agents working undercover on the campuses, one day before the vote.

The state's national drive against the Islamist students included a disinformation campaign. Students who were either coopted by undercover informants on campus or affiliated with the ruling National Democratic party conveyed one message to university voters: Those who call themselves Islamists are terrorists in disguise. One leaflet entitled "Humiliated Oppressors" blanketed Helwan University with depictions of the Islamists as criminals and murderers: "The Islamic voices in the university ... are illegal organizations who call themselves Muslim Brothers and are trying to falsely raise the banner of Islam and the Koran. ... Under this holy flag they commit the worst sins. They have been revealed to the Egyptian security and they are the terrorists. ... They are united to destroy security in Egypt and tarnish its bright image in front of the world."

The state's tactics sealed the defeat of the Islamist candidates and victory for students allied with Mubarak's Democratic National party. The Islamists were either in jail or banned from running as candidates. But such strongarm methods could do little to derail the broader religious movement. In fact, as one former university administrator admitted, today's anti-Islamist campaign helped turn many on campus against the authorities, fueling the very religious revival it was meant to suppress.

"The problem with this approach is that the result is the opposite of what the state wants," said Sufi Abu Taleb, a former president of Cairo University in the 1970s who now teaches in the law school. "They do not distinguish between the moderates and the militants. It has been going on for many years. We have tried to explain this to them. But they say, 'We will take them all, and then later we decide whom to keep in jail and whom to release.'

"But if the state continues to take action against those who are simply religious, it will continue to lead to more religious sentiment. We already see the results. Ten years ago, you didn't find the number of veiled female students that you see now. The Islamic moderates are on the increase, and arresting students who are believed to be militants will not change this."

The course of modern Egyptian history has been shaped, in large part, by the course of student activism. The Revolution of 1919, when armed revolts and strikes swept the country in protest at Britain's rejection of complete independence for Egypt, was touched off at the Law School of Cairo University. The Wafd Party, which spearheaded the revolutionary drive against the British, relied on students to carry out its directives. "It is upon you, students, that your nation and the Wafd depend," said Abd al-Rahman, the secretary of the Wafd's Central Committee.[3] Students remained one of the driving forces of the Wafd Party until after World War II, when Hasan al-Banna began an aggressive recruitment campaign of students into the Muslim Brotherhood. He considered them "the striking force" of his organization.[4]

The immediate postrevolutionary period, from 1952 until the humiliating defeat in the 1967 war, was the only time in which Egyptian students generally supported the central authorities. This newfound loyalty was largely due to the charismatic personality of President Nasser, widely seen as a father figure and nationalist leader who would satisfy Egyptians' craving for a sense of dignity.

Once he had pacified the student population with the compelling power of his personality and diverted attention to soccer, Nasser introduced a series of repressive measures to curtail political activity and ensure full loyalty to the regime. Demonstrations were banned, as were the distribution of political leaflets and the use of wall magazines—a collage of political slogans painted or hung on the walls of universities. Troops were stationed at the campus gates in 1954, and University Guards, uniformed police under the control of the Interior Ministry, became a permanent fixture on campuses, persisting to this day.

All this cleared the universities of political activism until the 1967 war. The scale of the defeat at the hands of the Israelis cast doubt over the legitimacy of Nasser's pan-Arabist ambitions. On the domestic front, there was by now enough evidence to point up the failures of his economic agenda. The explosion in the number of university graduates, fueled by the government's populist policies, could not be absorbed effectively into the economy.

In the academic year beginning in 1952, for example, there were 42,485 students in higher education institutions, with 14 percent of the general education budget allocated to the universities. By the 1962 academic year, the number of students had jumped to 98,537, with 21 percent of the budget earmarked for higher education.[5] With the end of the war, the dreams of a generation had evaporated and Egypt's youth were abandoned somewhere between Nasser's ill-conceived socialist utopia and the traditionalist past they thought had been left behind. What were they to do?

Students broke the enforced silence in February 1968, seven months after the defeat by Israel, when they staged a series of demonstrations at universities in Cairo and Alexandria that then spilled out into the streets. The protests occurred after a court handed down light sentences to senior officers in the Egyptian air force who were held responsible for the 1967 debacle. The government attempted to explain away the demonstrations by saying the unrest was related only to the court verdict. But the students' demands, issued in a declaration, reflected their national political concerns. They called for freedom of the press, an investigation into police intrusion in the universities and police brutality against students, a full explanation of the air force commanders' culpability in the war, and the withdrawal of secret police from university campuses.[6]

The protests continued sporadically for days, with students shouting slogans condemning Nasser's regime. "Down with the intelligence state!" "Nasser there are limits to patience. . . . On the ninth of June (before the war) we supported you. . . . Today we oppose you!"[7] Students from engineering faculties were the most vocal critics. They were supposed to be the key beneficiaries of Nasser's mass education. They were the ones being groomed to lead Egypt into an industrial, high-tech era. Instead, they were the vanguard of the student protests in the early 1970s, and later became the backbone of the Islamic movement of the 1980s.

Nasser was forced to make concessions to the students. He ordered a retrial in the case of the air force officers and formed a new cabinet, including several university professors, to demonstrate a public commitment to political reform. At the universities, guards were forbidden from interfering in student activities, and censorship of wall magazines was lifted.

The stage was set for Sadat to inherit a generation of self-confident students, poised for confrontation with the state. Campus activists wasted no time after Nasser's death and Sadat's rise to power in 1970. Students formed a number of independent societies, focused on issues such as the Palestinian cause for a homeland. Public meetings were held to criticize government policy, and wall magazines, which had replaced newspapers and journals as the primary means of communication, covered the campuses.

Not long after he became president, Sadat initiated a new approach to a generation of students starved of political activity, a response characterized by a mixture of accommodation, restraint, and manipulation. He reversed a number of Nasser's polices, suspending the University Guards and reviving the banned student unions. Sadat's early reforms coincided with increasing religious activity on Egyptian campuses, in particular at Cairo University, a center of social and political ferment. These first stirrings of religious revival, haphazard and virtually devoid of political content, could not fail to catch the eye of Egypt's new leader as he sought ways to neutralize the leftists whom he considered a threat to his own hold on power.

The man Sadat appointed to keep tabs on the Islamist students was Mohammed Osman Ismail. For much of 1997 I tried to find Ismail, who for years has remained a shadowy figure. At the peak of the militant violence in the early 1990s, a sensationalist leftist magazine repeatedly blamed Ismail for the rise of armed Islamic extremism. When militants killed foreign tourists or shot at cabinet ministers, the fingerpointing often targeted Ismail, so it was no wonder he kept a low profile. When I finally reached him, I repeatedly pleaded my case for an interview. At last he agreed.

I knew I was near Number 14, Mahmoud Basyouni Street, when as I saw a cadre of men parked outside a brown brick building near the Groppi cafe, a Cairo landmark. Ismail had told me his office was near Groppi, and like many men who once held government positions, he had his own watchmen on alert outside his building. When I entered the office, he was sitting behind a large oak desk. The deep wrinkles in his colorless face made him look waxen and weary. His diminutive frame appeared smaller still juxtaposed with the massive desk. He asked me to be seated in a chair facing him.

Sitting to his left was a younger man, whose job I quickly figured out was to stare at me long enough and hard enough until I became so intimidated I left, or so nervous I would be pacified with mindless chit-chat.

"We need to get something straight," Ismail snarled with a leathery voice that became even more scratchy with each new cigarette. "I'm not going to talk about the Islamists and Sadat."

I was flabbergasted. Why then had he agreed to the interview? What else did he think I wanted to talk about?

Before I could give an answer, a male voice interrupted. "Why does American policy support the Jews?" I turned and followed the sound to discover a half dozen men sitting on a long sofa against the wall behind my chair. They stared at me, whispering and laughing among themselves.

Then Ismail began talking about himself and his achievements when he served in Sadat's administration. "I was a lawyer, not just a government employee," he declared.

As Ismail continued, I tried to ignore the icy stares of the young man on his left. A boy came in to serve coffee, a required ritual when visiting anyone in the Middle East. But this hospitable gesture seemed inappropriate, considering the hostile atmosphere.

Ismail suddenly blurted out, "For my own personal reasons I don't want to discuss details about the Islamists. But I admit I am the one who created the Islamic groups in the universities. I have always been against Marxist thought."

With his admission out in the open, Ismail followed up with his self-defense. "There is no relationship between the Islamists in 1972 and the militant groups now. Now, the militants shouldn't be associated with religion. In the 1970s, they were true Muslims, their ideas were based on religion."

"Did the leftists truly threaten Sadat's presidency?" I asked.

"No, they didn't pose a real threat. By their very nature, they would never be a lasting movement in Egypt. This is a religious country. But Sadat hated Marxist ideas, and the leftists pushed him too far. They insulted his wife. It became personal. It was impossible to have a dialogue with these people. They had to be dealt with. They had to be stopped before they spread."

Ismail realized he had revealed more than he planned, and he abruptly ended the interview. "Now, drink your coffee and be on your way."

Perhaps only in hindsight is it apparent that the leftists were merely a passing phase without any permanent roots in Egyptian society. But a wave of spontaneous student rebellions at the time was reason to think otherwise. Sadat had promised that 1971 would be a decisive year. He would declare war against Israel over the occupation of the Sinai, land Israel had seized from Egypt in the 1967 war. The issue was important to the leftists, who took the Israeli occupation of Palestine as their battle cry. But in a January

13, 1972, speech Sadat explained that the time was not yet right for war. A "political fog" had been created by the Indo-Pakistan war, Sadat argued, and the Soviet Union, which was involved in that conflict and was then Egypt's military anchor, could not be drawn into two battles at once.

When students read about the speech in the newspapers, they immediately began organizing at Cairo University's engineering faculty, where a group called the Society of the Supporters of the Palestinian Revolution was particularly active. Two days after the speech, they held a four-day sit-in, focused on Sadat's justification for delaying the war. The sit-in at Cairo University and later at Ain Shams University, also in Cairo, continued as the controversy deepened into a political crisis. A delegation of students met members of the Egyptian parliament, and students later demanded a meeting with Sadat himself.

On January 24, the state decided to take action. The Interior Minister gave orders to storm Cairo University and arrest the students.[8] The action only enraged the campuses, and about 20,000 irate students marched to central Cairo, staging the first street protests of Sadat's presidency. They held a sit-in at Tahrir Square in central downtown. Eventually, police broke up the demonstration and arrested hundreds of students.

Kamal Abu-Magd, a sophisticated, Western-educated lawyer who was Sadat's youth minister at the time, recalled the students' intransigence and his failed efforts to negotiate with them, before demonstrations broke out. "Sadat was one hundred percent justified in what he did," Abu-Magd told me, referring to the president's decision to delay the declaration of war against Israel. "It was not possible to start the war sooner. I know because I was familiar with our arms capability. . . . Our air defense was not yet completed and the range of their [Israeli] firepower was greater than ours."

They may have been politically naive, but the leftist students could hardly be ignored. They had gained widespread support among Egypt's middle class, searching for a way to reestablish the country's self-esteem after the 1967 defeat and longing for a civil society as an antidote to the highly controlled, highly centralized political system bequeathed by Nasser. "We were so arrogant then. It was a time of big dreams," recalled Hani Shukrallah, a leading leftist at the time at Cairo University and today the managing editor of the official English-language newspaper, *Ahram Weekly*. "We felt we were running the university, and we thought we could run the country. When we went to the parliament to meet the deputies, we addressed them as *inta*," the informal form of address in Arabic, he recalled with astonishment.

In the end, the leftists got their wish. Sadat went to war against Israel in October 1973, regained much of the Sinai, and declared victory. The war lifted the ennui gripping the nation. Yet whatever political boost Sadat might have gained was soon obliterated by his foreign policy shift toward the United

States and a peace agreement with Israel. His domestic reforms, centered on a free-market economy, also provoked discontent among students and the middle class who correctly predicted that only the elite would benefit. In the aftermath of the war, four political tendencies generally existed in the universities: the radical, Marxist left; the Nasserite left; the Islamists; and the right, which supported Sadat's new policies.

Wael Osman, the son of an Azhar scholar who worked as a judge in the *sharia* courts, was a student in the engineering faculty at Cairo University when the 1973 war ended. He believed the euphoria then spreading across the country would at last lift all the pain and despair—the remnants of Nasser's legacy. He wanted freedom and justice, and he believed Islam was the solution. He hoped to convince his fellow students that religion was not limited to rituals, but could become a comprehensive system for modern life.

Osman had never met Esam al-Ghazali, another engineering student, but they had much in common. Ghazali was also the son of an Azhar scholar, and, like Osman, he knew far more about religion than most students. While Ghazali was an aspiring poet, Osman thought of himself as a writer. Even before the war began, Ghazali had decided to form the first Islamic group in an Egyptian university. The idea emerged from a student conference in September 1972 in Mansura, a large city in the Nile Delta.

The plan was to establish Islamic groups in various university faculties, beginning with engineering. The groups would educate students about religion through social activities and prayer sessions. The activities would be coordinated through Cairo University's state-sponsored student union. But the Islamic groups would raise independent funding. The groups would be called the Gamiyat al-Shabab al-Islami, the Societies of Islamic Youth, and build on the loosely formed Religious Societies. Unlike the latter, however, the new Islamic groups would combine rising religious sentiment with the fervid nationalism that emerged after the war. Sheikh Mohammed Ghazali, one of the most influential Azharis, gave the idea his blessing at another conference a few months later, in November 1972.

Esam al-Ghazali was slow to follow through with the plan. He was still testing out his ideas in the poetry he wrote and distributed in the engineering faculty at Cairo University: "The prayers are calling you. Don't let the silk thread slip from you. The *Gama'a* is waiting for you . . . sitting on the carpets. They are not just extending their lips indifferently, gathering at mosques. Go towards them, and when you arrive the big gathering will say, 'God is Great.' We are behind you. . . . Our love will lead us all."

Meanwhile, Osman was baring his soul in the popular wall magazines he wrote at the university. "When I hear someone say, 'What is Egypt?' I say, 'Egypt is my nation.' But I wonder what is a nation? Is it a piece of land where an individual is born to suffer? Is it the society that makes him lose his respect and humanity?"

With the release from prison of key leaders of the Muslim Brotherhood in 1971, the organization expanded its influence in the universities, where it sought to use the campuses as a platform for reintegration into Egyptian society. Officials who were once in Sadat's administration told me that the president held secret meetings with key Brotherhood players to gain their cooperation. As his liaison with the Brotherhood, Sadat called on influential members from among his own circle of friends, including Osman Ahmed Osman, the founder of Arab Contractors Company.

In the early 1970s, the Brotherhood's activities within the universities were nearly invisible. The organization worked through known contacts to establish a semblance of influence. Students who were the sons of prominent families in the Brotherhood, for example, were designated to begin activity on campus. The group generated interest among students by sending some of its most inspiring leaders, such as Omar al-Tilmisani, to give lectures at the campus. After seeing the welcoming response to the Brotherhood's overtures, Wael Osman and Esam al-Ghazali, who were never members of the organization, began to form Islamic groups in university faculties. They soon discovered there was a third player, whom, until that moment, they had never suspected.

"When we became visible in the university, the state tried to co-opt us," Wael Osman told me. "We were called to a meeting with Mohammed Osman [Ismail] and he offered us 10,000 pounds, and he said, 'Take this money to spend on your activities, and we will organize a summer camp for all the Islamic groups in all universities in Egypt and you will be the leader.' "

"Of course we knew this was too much money for our activities. The implication was that it was a bribe. He was offering us a lot of money so we could keep a large part for ourselves. We told him we didn't want his help and we turned him down."

Ismail, who was then secretary-general of the ruling Arab Socialist Union, had a theory that if the Islamists had enough money to fund their activities, they could replace the leftist troublemakers opposed to Sadat. At this critical stage, he knew the balance must be tipped among the four political trends in the universities. All the Islamists needed was a slight push. Wael Osman claimed that Ismail at one point offered 1.5 million Egyptian pounds to him and other Islamic sympathizers to undermine the leftists at Cairo University. When Wael Osman refused to participate in Ismail's scheme, Ismail held the youth camp at a site outside Alexandria, and he continued his efforts to generate Islamic activism by recruiting students from politically benign campus organizations, such the Boy Scouts and theater clubs.

To this day, Ismail's involvement and influence continues to be a matter of heated debate. The conventional wisdom, widely repeated in books and articles, is that Ismail encouraged the Islamists on Sadat's behalf and planted the roots of a movement that blossomed into the militant groups Egypt contends with today. The Islamists, however, claim Ismail's activities had only a marginal influence. Students were hungry for religious instruction and guidance, they say. The Islamists were able to establish groups that met the needs of students, and attracted a massive following in their own right.

"The state absolutely did not create the Islamists," explained Kamal Sayyed al-Habib, a leader of the militant *Jihad* group in the 1980s who served ten years in prison for plotting Sadat's assassination. "I was in the economics faculty at Cairo University in the 1970s. I was involved in telling students the importance of going back to Islam. . . . My generation was raised on Nasser and Nasserite thinking. What we found out in reality was different from what we were told, and we needed another solution.

"The university was simply the institution in which the change in society was expressed so clearly. When the state discovered the Islamic revival, they tried to use us to counter the leftists who were responsible for the 1972 demonstrations."

Even if Ismail's activities helped swell the ranks of Islamist students, their numbers inevitably would have grown simply because the universities, and society itself, were returning to Islam. In the early 1970s, the spirit of the religious revival at the universities was guiding mainstream society. As one student leader from Assyut explained, "In small communities in Upper Egypt, the society was the *Gamaat* [the Islamic groups] and the *Gamaat* was society. There was no distinction between the two." Sadat's contribution to the rise of the Islamists was indirect, rather than direct; he simply did not stand in their way. The difference between his approach, for example, and that of Mubarak is illustrated in the student experiences of Mady and al-Kurdi. While Sadat sought accommodation, Mubarak sought eradication. Where Sadat tried to court allies for his government, Mubarak confronted directly what he perceived as the Islamist challenge to his authority.

The fact that students from all social classes had access to higher education for the first time ever was largely responsible for the fusion of the university and the street. Their sheer numbers enhanced their power. Between 1970 and 1977, the number of students enrolled in public universities rose from 200,000 to about half a million.[9] By giving the middle and lower classes access to the Ivory Tower, the state inadvertently encouraged political activists who brought the burdens of their deprived lives to the classroom, where they consoled their peers and searched idealistically for wide-reaching solutions.

The conditions at the universities added to the students' urgent desire for change. In lecture halls, jammed in by the hundreds, two or three students were forced to share one seat. The student–teacher ratio in the mid- to late 1970s swelled drastically, as many qualified university professors fled Egypt for the rich oil-producing countries in the Persian Gulf, where wages were up to ten times higher.

Most students could not afford required textbooks, the sole source of instruction in most courses. Living quarters in the university hostels were often worse than in the students' homes back in their villages and towns. Small, unkempt rooms housed two or three students at one time. And even before students living in major cities reached the university each morning, they tolerated packed buses, so crowded that passengers typically hung from the doors and windows on the way to their destinations. In a prudish society such as Egypt, the lack of private space in public places is considered a violation of sexual mores. The constant pushing, smashing, and rubbing of women and men on a bus can be a great source of anxiety. One psychiatrist who was a student activist in the 1980s has argued that one of the greatest attractions of students to the Islamists was hope for more public space. With the state behaving like an absentee parent who provides basic shelter but no other means for survival, students were driven to take charge of their own destiny.

In the background, while organized religious activities on university campuses and discontent with university conditions increased, and Sadat displayed his leanings toward the West, were the first stirrings of armed Islamic militancy. As moderate Islamists formed groups in the universities, a radical and violent fringe was evolving behind the scenes. In 1974, the first Islamic violence of the period broke out at a military academy in the Cairo suburb of Heliopolis. A shadowy group of cadets led by a Palestinian named Saleh Sirriya tried to foment an uprising. Their goal was to stage a *coup d'etat* and kill Sadat in order to establish Islamic rule. Although the attempt was unsuccessful, it was apparently a dress rehearsal for the assassination of the president in 1981 and marked the debut of a new armed political struggle such as the country had not experienced for almost twenty years.

Sirriya was believed to belong to the pan-Arab Islamic Liberation party, formed in 1950 as a reaction to the defeat of the Arab armies in the 1948 war, which led to the creation of the state of Israel. Sirriya had been in Egypt only three years, but he had amassed a following all the same. The credo of the Liberation party centered on the need for radical action in order to Islamicize society. Moderate Islamists, such as the Muslim Brotherhood, by contrast, believed in establishing an Islamic society first and then changing the political order. The plot at the Military Academy was foiled when guards opened fire on the aspiring putchists.

Back at the universities, Islamist students generally opposed Sirriya's violent approach and condemned the Academy attack. But the incident proved a landmark in the development of the student movement; it offered another approach to the grievances students were beginning to voice. Violence against the state was certainly not a new phenomenon in the history of the Islamic movement in Egypt. However, the Academy episode was the first exposure students of the 1970s generation had to the violent alternative. Eventually, extremists such as Sirriya indirectly inspired some religious students to decide that violence, rather than the gradual Islamicization of society, was the most effective avenue to achieve their goals.

The Islamist students in major universities, meanwhile, had by the end of 1973 officially formed the *Gama'a al-Islamiyya*. Student leaders such as Esam al-Eryan, Abd al-Monem Abu al-Futouh, and Ibrahim al-Zafrani, who had been active in the Religious Societies in Cairo and Alexandria, joined forces to formally establish the new group. Until then, they had been reluctant to declare the existence of an Islamic-oriented, nationwide organization. But by that time, Sadat's government had made it clear that the state would not stand in the way of the Islamists. The president, in fact, promised in 1974 to make the student unions more democratic and more in tune with society's prevailing values. That promise became law in 1976, with the formal declaration that the unions' objective was "to deepen religious values among the students." With the state's implicit endorsement and secure support on the campuses through their prior work in the Religious Societies, the young Islamists were poised to put forth all their energy into persuading millions of students to return to Islam.

The first objective of the *Gama'a al-Islamiyya* was to prepare candidates to run in student unions elections in 1975. The student unions, funded by the state's Supreme Council of Youth and Sports, had been run by leftists who focused their efforts on social events. The Islamists opposed these activities, which included mixed parties between the sexes at which alcohol was served. They believed the unions should abandon such events and instead develop religious and political life on the campuses.

Al-Gama'a al-Islamiyya candidates won control in eight of twelve student unions in universities across the country in 1976. "Last year, when the university chose Islamic elements to guide the union, it was announcing its return to its origins," Abu al-Futouh wrote in 1977, explaining how the Islamists interpreted their electoral landslide.[10] They quickly capitalized on their impressive victory and began carving out a role that combined the duties of a moral police force and a religious guide or mentor. In an attempt to impose an acceptable code of behavior between the sexes, a bus system was established for female students to shield them from the overcrowding and unwanted attention of men on public transport. At first, the Islamists rented the buses. They then went a step further by raising enough cash to buy them outright.

The Islamists also worked to separate men from women in the classrooms, a policy that was eventually adopted sporadically in some colleges in Upper Egypt. One religious student expressed the reason for segregation of the sexes: "We don't object to teaching girls, but do they have to be indecent and wear the latest fashions? Is she a model or a student? How can male students concentrate on what the professor is saying while sitting beside an immodest girl? How can we mix oil and fire and not expect an explosion?"[11]

Modest clothes and religious garments for women, such as ankle-length skirts and *khimar*, the long veil that frames the face and extends to the waist, were sold to students. Marriages were even arranged according to "Islamic" norms. Any activity that the Islamists perceived as immoral was banned: films were canceled and evening dances were stopped. In 1977, the dean in the college of agriculture at Assyut University ordered that classes stop for the noon prayers in response to the demands of Islamist students.[12]

In the field of education, the Islamists held book fairs and sold textbooks, normally too expensive for the average student, at cut-rate prices. They also offered cheap tutorials, a necessity for passing many courses in which poor classroom instruction was common. The appeal of the Islamist message, in sharp contrast to the callous, uncaring state, was clear to all, even the sons and daughters of the Egyptian elite.

"I remember the Islamists as serious people, who sincerely wanted to help students," recalled Sameeh Sarag el-Din, scion of the family that founded the pro-independence Wafd party and a student at Cairo University in the late 1970s. "I was not really that religious but I went to their meetings," he said years later. "They were the only ones doing anything on the campuses."

The *Gama'a* organized educational camps during summer holidays for teaching the Koran and the *hadith*s. These gatherings were held on university campuses, where students were indoctrinated on the tenets of Islam. Summer camps, funded by the state, were also held in the countryside each year. The camps were modeled after those organized by the Muslim Brotherhood in the 1950s, but the Islamist program of the 1970s differed in that it offered not only religious studies but also sports activities.[13]

Specially designated "Islamic weeks" were used to inform students of the *Gama'a* position on women's issues, the national struggle for a Palestinian homeland, and Muslim minorities across the world. They also organized massive prayer sessions with famous preachers in Cairo's downtown Abdeen Square on Muslim holy days, attracting hundreds of thousands of worshippers.

"The vision and the ideas at that time were simple and superficial," Esam al-Eryan told me in 1997 while he was in prison. "They deepened with time, with a lot of activity and getting in contact and listening to lectures by senior preachers from the Muslim Brotherhood. In the camps where we used to spend two or more weeks, we practiced pure Islamic life in praying and reading the Koran. . . . All of this had a big influence in shaping our ideas, which crystalized in the mid-70s."

By 1977, the *Gama'a al-Islamiyya* and the Muslim Brotherhood were firmly in control of student unions, and the groups' message and symbols grew more radical. They were at the zenith of their power—all with the state's blessing. Some Islamists I interviewed denied that the *Gama'a* accepted substantial funding from the state, other than monies redistributed from student dues to which student unions were legally entitled. It was difficult to distinguish members of the *Gama'a* from those of the Brotherhood. In general, the two groups cooperated for the common aim of preparing the ground for an Islamic state.

Outward signs of the influence of Islamic groups were visible everywhere. Male students grew beards and donned gallabiyyas to show their allegiance to the *Gama'a*; women wore veils and flowing skirts to demonstrate their loyalty and piety. The Islamists constructed kiosks to sell an array of prayer rugs and *siwak*, sticks of sweet-smelling wood with horse hair, used at the time of the Prophet for cleaning teeth.

Gama'a publications reveal the Islamists' leaning toward the radical ideas of Sayyid Qutb. At that time, Qutb was the ideologue of preference over Hasan al-Banna, in part because his ideas were less cerebral and easier to absorb. Qutb's proposed remedy was also more tangible. It invited direct action and could be propagated with a lexicon of familiar terms. "They (students) are rebelling against our life that is full of *jahiliyya* (ignorance and immorality). They don't trust the media because they consider it a tool of intellectual invasion. . . . They consider the television particularly to be a hammer that is destroying the Egyptian family by the kind of programs they show," explained *al-Dawa*, a magazine published by the Muslim Brotherhood.[14]

Sadat's provocative actions also served to turn up the heat within the student movement. In November 1977, he made a visit to Jerusalem in preparation for Egypt's peace with Israel. Sadat's trip occurred at a critical juncture in the development of the student movement. At the time radical students within the *Gama'a* were contemplating a violent turn and parting ways with moderates, such as Esam al-Eryan and Abd al-Monem Abu al-Futouh, who by then were firmly aligned with the Muslim Brotherhood. Sadat's visit to Israel outraged many in Egypt and provided credibility to the radical position. It was indefensible, as far as any student within the *Gama'a al-Islamiyya* was concerned. How could the self-styled "believer president" visit the Zionist entity when Egyptians were embracing their religion and rallying around the Palestinian cause?

Sadat's visit not only was viewed as an affront to the Islamic revival on the face of it, but it held deeper consequences for the Muslim community of believers, the *umma*. In the minds of Islamic leaders in and outside the universities, there was a link between liberating Palestine from Israeli occupation and achieving their goal of unifying Muslims in Egypt and across the Islamic world. The wars of 1967 and 1973 provided a case in point. The Arabs were defeated in 1967, the Islamists argued, because they lacked piety. Israel won, on the other hand, because it claimed to be fighting on behalf of Jews around the world. But in 1973, when *Allahu Akbar* was the rallying cry among Arab armies, the Muslims defeated the Jews. The Islamists have embraced this logic from the 1970s until today. The Muslim Brotherhood organized conferences dedicated to finding a strategy to liberate Jerusalem from Israeli occupation. The *Gama'a*, likewise, called for political unity among Muslims and a return to the days when the Caliph ruled most of the Arab world through the application of the Koran. Any Muslim ruler, therefore, who failed to work toward unifying all Muslims and liberating Palestine was considered a traitor to the Islamic cause.

The "believer president" was seen to betray the Islamic call not only in his deeds but in his words. Under growing pressure from a society increasingly opposed to many of his policies, including the separate peace with Israel and an alliance with the West, Sadat felt compelled to recapture some of the power he had relinquished to the Islamic movement. In 1979, he called for separation between religion and politics—an imported Western concept that contradicts the most fundamental principle of Islam. "Those who wish to practice Islam can go to the mosques, and those who wish to engage in politics may do so through legal institutions," Sadat declared.

The *Gama'a* conveyed the opposite message. Islam is a comprehensive system for life, and therefore there can be no separation between religion and politics. "There is nothing called religion and politics. We only know religion," Abu Ala Mady, then president of the Minya University Student Union and deputy president of Egypt's General Student Union, declared.[15]

It became apparent in 1977 that the state's honeymoon with the Islamists was nearing an end. As Sadat moved closer to making peace with Israel, the Islamists felt emboldened to challenge the government even over trivial matters. The first confrontation between Islamist students and the state took place that year, when police blocked students at Cairo University from holding an Islamic camp on the campus, as they had done regularly since 1973. The students refused to yield and moved the meeting to the Salah al-Din mosque in Maniel, a working-class district near the university. The students held seminars and occupied the mosque for eight days. Esam al-Fuli, a student who was asked to act as a liaison between the state and the Islamists, recalled the standoff. "A representative from the (ruling) National Democratic party telephoned me and asked if I would approach Esam al-Eryan and tell him to close the camp. I told him, 'Esam al-Eryan can't do this. The students want this.'

"I went to the mosque with the NDP representative and he said, 'I'm afraid. I don't want to go in there.' But I met Esam al-Eryan and he said the security officer from the NDP was welcome. But this security guy was still afraid to go inside. . . . The importance of this incident was that the Islamist students realized they had political power. They felt they were so important the state was confronting them directly."

Relations continued to deteriorate. During the 1978 student union elections, the government launched the first direct assault on the Islamists with a number of tactics that, honed and refined over time, became unofficial state policy that continues today. University administrators, under orders from the state security, tried to deprive the Islamists of victories in the student unions by striking from the election rolls the names of known members in the *Gama'a* on leading campuses, such as Ain Shams in Cairo and Zagazig University, one hour from the capital and a bastion of Islamic activism. "The justification of officials for these cancellations of members of the *Gama'a* is that they didn't participate in different activities and therefore were not eligible for nomination. But this is completely untrue," Helmi Gazar, a *Gama'a* leader at the time, wrote in *al-Dawa*.

The state's efforts, however, failed to match the overwhelming influence of the *Gama'a* and the Muslim Brotherhood, which never had an overt representation in the universities but retained enormous power in the late 1970s. For Islamists like Esam al-Eryan, leaders in the Brotherhood served as father figures who provided guidance and inspiration. "When Sadat released many of the Muslim Brothers from jail in the early 1970s, we began to meet with them and discuss our ideas," explained Mohammed Abd al-Talat, an Islamist who was vice president of the student union in the medical faculty at Cairo University from 1976 to 1977. "We realized our ideas were similar to theirs, so we eventually decided to cooperate."

The Muslim Brotherhood's increasing power was a factor in the split that occurred within the *Gama'a* in 1978 and 1979, when some adopted a strategy they called "change by force" and others secretly joined the moderate Brotherhood. The Brotherhood's leadership believed the organization should attract a young generation of activists, and they made it their mission to persuade those among the Islamist students who were the best and the brightest. By the late 1970s, the Brotherhood controlled main branches of the *Gama'a al-Islamiyya* in universities in Cairo, northern Egypt and some minor colleges in Upper Egypt.[16] In some universities in Upper Egypt, violent struggles broke out between students in the Brotherhood and those who split and joined more radical organizations.

Some *Gama'a* leaders were from Upper Egypt and advocated a revolutionary, rather than gradual, approach. The *Jihad* organization, for example, believed Sadat's government was leading society toward decadence and heresy. The Brotherhood, by contrast, believed change should come about through "the *dawa*"—a process of education and gradual social transformation. Unless the radicals parted ways with the Brotherhood and formed a new identity to achieve their aims, they knew they could never compete for the leadership of the Islamic movement against the Brotherhood's seasoned godfathers who had earned respect for their years in prison. The only logical alternative for some Islamist students was to split the movement—a schism that saw the emergence of the armed militant groups that live on today in Egypt under the name *al-Gama'a al-Islamiyya*. From this armed *Gama'a*, students formed other splinter groups in the 1980s, such as "Survivors of Fire," which eventually attempted to assassinate government officials. "There was no conscious decision to adopt violence. It was more subtle than that," Kamal Habib, the former *Jihad* leader, told me. "In my view, my generation [born in the 1950s and 1960s] was raised on Nasser's ideas—idealism, the liberation of Palestine. But what we found out in reality was different from what we were told, and we needed another solution."

By their own admission, the radical Islamists had no clear strategy attached to their slogan, "change by force." Their primary objective was to uproot the regime and create an Islamic society, through the ideology of Sayyid Qutb and the philosopher Ibn Taymiyya. Without a well-thought out plan to actively change the status quo, the radicals quickly became solely a resistance movement that placed nearly full blame on Sadat as a heretical leader, nudging society further along the path of *jahiliyya*. "Sadat was pushing society closer and closer to the brink, so he had to go," Kamal Habib told me.

Sadat's fatal error was his failure to realize that the Islamist movement on campuses, driven by religious passion and disenchantment with the state, did not exist in a vacuum. His response to the food riots in January 1977, the worst social upheaval in Egypt in recent history, exemplified his miscalculation. Students played no direct role in the riots, yet Sadat placed the blame on them nonetheless.

The economic malaise had reached a crisis in 1977 due to Sadat's failed *infitah* policies. Under pressure from the International Monetary Fund and the United States, the president was forced to take drastic action to counter the soaring deficit, which had reached 1.25 billion Egyptian pounds by the second half of 1976.[17] Large state subsidies for staple foods proved a heavy drain on the budget. A wide gap existed between the price of commodities in the shops, heavily subsidized by the state, and the price the government paid on the international market. To close this gap, the state was forced either to end the subsidies or bleed the well-to-do by imposing high taxes on personal income. The bourgeoisie, a key constituency, was too important to Sadat, so the state opted to cut in half subsidies worth 553 million Egyptian pounds. Millions of poor Egyptians depended on the subsidies for their daily bread, and the cuts sparked street riots on January 18 and 19, in which tens of thousands rampaged against the symbols of the state. Police stations were attacked, and casinos were looted along the Pyramids Road, for years a strip of decadent excess on the outskirts of Cairo. Security forces moved in to halt the unrest. About eighty people were killed and more than 800 injured.

The government immediately blamed the leftist movement, which was believed to have powerful leaders in the universities, for what Sadat dubbed the "uprising of thieves." But many officials in the regime were skeptical of the charges, as they admitted to students years later. The leftist movement in Egypt was by then too weak to organize public protests on such a massive scale. Sadat, however, chose to lash out at the students. At a meeting with the Higher Council for the Universities held shortly after the disturbances, the president warned: "I am saying that strikes, sit-ins, disruption of studies, and gangster actions on campuses are forbidden. The incendiary kindling of youth must not be manipulated. It should not happen at universities."[18]

During a meeting with the Student Union at Cairo University in 1979, Sadat offered still more harsh words for the students' political participation. But he said that limits on students' political activity, backed up by the security forces, were preferable to a wholesale crackdown. "Restrictions, security, and the use of law can be enforced one hundred percent better than using prisons and oppressing opinions and imposing the 'visitor of the dawn,'" Sadat told the students, referring to the dawn police raids of citizens' houses and massive illegal arrests that generally followed.[19]

Abu al-Futouh was in the audience at the time. He confronted the president in a manner so disrespectful in the Egyptian context that it spoke volumes about the power the students now believed was in their hands. "Sir, I have a question and I want a frank answer. Let's speak frankly. As a young man, I don't know what the country or the political leadership in Egypt wants me to believe in. Do they want me to be a communist? Or a Muslim? Or an atheist, or a cow worshipper, or what? . . . I don't understand."

Sadat replied: "Look, to make it short son, because your (Muslim) Brothers have repeated this talk before. Look, my son, from the year 1971, I have declared it a state of science and belief."

Futouh, attempting to interrupt the president many times, finally answered back: "But we as youth see behavior that contradicts this. I will give you an example. At the same time that we trust your excellency when you say this is a state of science and belief, we find Sheikh Ghazali [a popular Islamist scholar] removed from Amr mosque. . . . Only the scholars who are hypocrites for the authority and hypocrites for your policies remain in Egypt."

Sadat lost his composure and began shouting, "Watch your limits. . . . Islam taught you manners before anything else. . . . Religion does not say that you can talk like this in front of the head of the family or the president of the country, who allowed you to voice your opinion openly."

With Egyptian society in an uncharacteristically rebellious mood and the Islamists moving full speed ahead to solidify their hold on the universities and discredit the regime, the state reversed course and restored the food subsidies. The regime appeared to be backpedaling, but in fact the president had simply taken a new tack. The economic crisis, brought to a breaking point by the riots, pushed Sadat to strengthen his ties with the outside world, where he secured economic support and political capital from the United States by making peace with Israel and demonstrating through his *infitah* that Egypt had abandoned the statist policies of the Nasser era.

Preoccupied with the myth of a leftist conspiracy hatched on university campuses, Sadat overlooked the broader social and religious forces at work in Egyptian society. He was unable to appreciate the danger posed by his new course of alignment with the conservative Arab monarchies and the United States, who raced in with aid and grants to prop up a government seemingly on the verge of radical revolution.

For the young generation of Islamists, the West, in particular the United States, was a spiritual wasteland, driven to impose its immoral value system on the Islamic world. In his manifesto, *The Missing Duty*, Mohammed Abd al-Salam Farag, the leader of *Jihad*, wrote that modern leaders were corrupted by foreign influences. "Sheikh al-Islam Ibn Taymiyya says that those who follow rulers that are not based on the teachings of Islam are considered non-believers. Today's rulers were brought up by colonizers—Christians and Jews—and the only Islamic things about them are their names. Their attack and murder is justified."[20]

In another guidebook issued by a branch of the *Jihad* organization, one of the group's leaders offered a prescription for dealing with the growing American influence in Egypt. "The Islamic movement, in confronting the United States, should offer more blood and martyrs, try to destroy all that is American, increase awareness of the importance of breaking all ties, and tell people that the real role of [Egyptian] rulers is as servants to the United States and Christian interests. Hence, these rulers must be fought against."[21]

When Sadat realized the power of the Islamists had reached the point of threatening his survival, he groped for a solution. But what was he to do? The new generation he hoped to groom to build a nation based on "science and belief" had turned on him. The groups they formed in the universities created the nucleus of a national movement clearly at odds with his domestic and foreign policies. And instead of carrying on some pretense of accommodation with the regime, the young Islamists appeared willing to confront the state, if necessary.

Sadat returned to the path of his predecessor. Before classes began in the autumn of 1979, he issued a decree banning religious groups and political organizations in universities and other educational institutions. All meetings concerning politics were prohibited. To halt the Islamists in the student unions, university presidents were ordered to freeze state money used to fund most union activities.

When students returned to the universities that autumn, they immediately declared the new laws illegal, citing Article 56 in the Egyptian constitution, which allows the formation of syndicates and unions through a democratic process. They were enraged at the implication of the presidential decree that all students in the unions were engaged in violence. By depriving students of political activity, the state was imposing collective punishment; there was no distinction made between the militants and the moderates. "We fear the motive behind the presidential decree stems from accusations aimed at the *Gama'a Islamiyya*. They are blamed for incidents which the student unions reject," wrote the executive committee of the national student union. "The students have published letters rejecting all violent activities and are combating extremist and deviant ideas."[22]

The Islamist rise in the universities would never be eliminated simply by a restrictive presidential decree. The state's blunders over several decades combined with the historical, social, and economic conditions had laid the groundwork for society's return to religion. Esam al-Eryan at the time explained the reasons for the powerful student movement: "Young people believe Islam is the solution to the ills in society after the failure of Western democracy, socialism and communism to address the political and socioeconomic difficulties. Another reason according to the martyr Hasan al-Banna is that young people have the capacity to sacrifice. They are daring and dedicated to any cause they champion. The third reason is the emergence of the Muslim Brotherhood in this century, which attracted a devoted and large following among young people, and its call for the establishment of an Islamic state was a significant factor in the rise of Islamists in universities. The steadfastness of the Brothers in the face of arrests and detention was an inspiration to young Muslims."[23]

There were few tears shed after Khalid Islambouli fired several rounds of automatic gunfire into Sadat's body as he attended a military parade on October 6, 1981. The young officer had burst from a passing military truck, while his accomplices laid down a barrage of covering fire and tossed hand grenades. The Western world was shocked at the loss of a loyal ally, but most Egyptians simply looked the other way. Society breathed a collective sigh of relief and tried not to think too hard about the horror of it all. The transgressions Sadat had committed in the few years before his death made the assassination seem to many like the only rational recourse.

Sadat had recently ordered the arrest of more than 1,320 Egyptians, mostly Islamists, who were perceived as opponents to the regime. He had made peace with Israel, an act Egyptians regarded as a complete betrayal of the country's national identity. After the 1979 Iranian revolution, he had provided shelter to the ailing Shah of Iran, who at the time was demonized across the Islamic world as a creation of Western imperialism and the primary enemy of pious Muslims. Sadat had led the Muslim Brotherhood and other moderate Islamists to believe they could realize their political aspirations, only to change direction and crack down on the Islamic movement. Promises of political liberalization never materialized; political parties were permitted, but their limitations made their role in the political process nearly irrelevant. Sadat promised economic rewards to farmers and other sectors of the underclass, but his *infitah* policies primarily helped the new bourgeoisie.

The fact that almost half of the primary conspirators implicated in the assassination were students revealed that Sadat had literally committed political suicide. Of the 101 accomplices identified by the authorities, forty-five were university students, the majority of whom were either midway or near completion of their studies.[24] In other words, by accommodating the religious tendencies of Egypt's young, educated generation, who Sadat hoped would form one of the pillars of his regime, he indirectly spawned a radical fringe. However, the goal of Sadat's assassins did not end with the killing of the president. The plan, according to the defendants, was to take control of strategic centers of power, such as the state television, telephone exchange, and central security headquarters while the attack was under way. An announcement would be made on national radio and television that the Islamic revolution was in progress.[25] Two bodies, the Council of Men of Religion and a Consultative Council, would be established to run the country. But the security forces managed to take control almost immediately, foiling the plot.[26] "Sadat wanted to show he could establish an Islamic society peacefully. That was in 1978. But it was too late. From that point, the seeds of terrorism were firmly planted, the terrorism that changed society for good," said Sufi Abu Taleb, the former president of Cairo University.

The bitter stalemate that characterizes today's relationship between the state and the Islamist movement on university campuses can trace its roots to the Sadat era and its alternating cycle of freedom and repression, leavened by deep misunderstanding and miscalculation by the authorities. In retrospect, the spectacular death of the self-proclaimed "believer president" masked the underlying weakness of the militant movement and marked a brief "time-out" in the rise of the moderate Islamist activists in the universities. The

1970s generation went on to find practical application in Egyptian society for the religious values and beliefs they learned from Abu al-Ela Mady, Esam al-Eryan, and Abd al-Monem Abu al-Futouh.

"Before I went to Cairo University, I didn't know much about religion. I grew up in Maadi," explained Mohammed Samman, an Islamist who attended Cairo University in the 1970s, referring to a Cairo suburb that is home to wealthy Egyptians and so many foreign corporate executives that it is often called an American ghetto. "The *Gama'a* taught me how to pray and to perform the duties of Islam. There was an advantage to learning religion in a respectable way. My friends followed these people [Esam al-Eryan and other student leaders] and we didn't go astray. We didn't become extremists. Instead, I joined the Muslim Brotherhood and became active in the syndicate in 1991." While activists like Samman turned their attention to Egyptian society at large, with some winning seats in the national parliament and in the syndicates later in the 1980s, the next generation of Islamist students again turned to campus politics.

When I sat with large groups of students in 1997 during several sessions at the offices of the Islamist-oriented newspaper *al-Shaab*, it was clear that the fundamental dynamic between the universities and the state had changed little in twenty years. Their stories were carbon copies of all the horrors experienced by Islamist students since the Sadat era: Some had been arrested and tortured; one young woman who wears a long *khimar* was interrogated for holding a banner with Islamic slogans; another was arrested for reading the Koran each day before classes began. "I was kicked out of the dormitory, after I gave speeches in the (university) mosque about the story of the Prophet Mohammed. I told students that, based on what the Prophet said, it is clear Muslims around the world are not doing enough to liberate Jerusalem from the Jews," explained Rabia Ibrahim Sukur, the twenty-three-year-old head of the Islamist-led Labor party at Cairo University. "I have been known to the security forces because of my political activity. After I was elected to the student union in Dar al-Ulum faculty in 1995, the next year they canceled my name from the list. I didn't try to fight it, because other Islamists won who were unknown to the state intelligence."

Rabia Sukur, a small-framed, young man lived in Sharqiya, about a ninety-minute drive from Cairo. When he was expelled from the university dormitory, he faced the dilemma of either quitting the university, commuting each day to Cairo, or trying to gather enough money to rent a flat. But these inconveniences were the least of his concerns. Like many of his contemporaries, he was willing to endure any hardship in order to promote his Islamic beliefs: "I don't care what happens to me. . . . It would be an honor to go to jail," he remarked.

The journey from Sadat's murder, when a major state crackdown eliminated virtually all activity in the universities, to the Islamists' return to positions of influence spanned about seven years. In 1984, they entered the first polls and won in seven out of twelve student unions in Egyptian universities. The law of 1979 had banned the nationwide student union, but individual unions were permitted. Protests were held across the country, demanding an end to the law, which also mandated the return of state guards to the campuses. By 1988, the students and the regime were as firmly entrenched as they had been before Sadat's murder. Fearing an Islamic landslide in student polls, the interior ministry issued a "preventative plan during student elections." Candidates were monitored, the distribution of campaign leaflets was banned, and university guards were instructed to supervise elections and count the ballots. Students assumed that the polls would be rigged to produce an outcome acceptable to the state.[27]

Demonstrations broke out on campuses across the country after hundreds of candidates were prevented from running for seats. But the Islamists succeeded, despite the obstacles, in winning control of at least eight major universities, including Cairo, al-Azhar, Alexandria, and Mansura. At Assyut University, all nominees were canceled except those from the pro-government National Democratic party.[28]

By the autumn of 1988, the state and the Islamists were back in the exact positions in which they had been in the 1970s: The Islamic groups were at full strength and the state was poised for maximum retaliation. Candidates from Islamic groups achieved sweeping victories in student elections that year, even after the authorities struck hundreds of candidates from election rolls. Students identified as troublemakers were expelled from dormitories; young women were banned from wearing the *niqab*, the veil covering the face; and men were told to shave their beards.

University professors joined the chorus in support of the Islamic movement against the state. Many were from the 1970s generation of students who matured under the powerful influence of the *Gama'a al-Islamiyya*. Some publicized their endorsement in Islamist journals and newspapers. "The youth of *al-Gama'a al-Islamiyya* in the universities are the conscience and the heart of the *umma*. They have put into action the destiny determined by God to this *umma*, and they will be the tool of its development and rescue, God willing," wrote Badr al-Din Ghazi Attiyya, a chemistry professor at Cairo University.[29]

The professors, angered by the increasingly harsh measures on campus, also took collective action. At a national conference in Mansura University in October 1988, they charged the police with bursting into mosques with tear gas and disturbing worshippers while ostensibly hunting for suspected militants. The security forces, they said, were conducting violent and illegal searches for suspects by raiding villages at night and arbitrarily destroying the personal property of innocent civilians. In a declaration issued after the Mansura conference, the professors called on the Minister of Education to freeze the law of 1979.

In addition to those professors who were working openly to strengthen the Islamic cause, numerous others were returning in the early 1990s from universities in the Persian Gulf, where they had retreated a decade earlier seeking higher-paying jobs. As with their fellow professionals the engineers, Egyptian professors returned home from Saudi Arabia, Kuwait, and other Gulf states, shaped profoundly by the overwhelming role of religion in the conservative societies they had come to know abroad. They felt a need to make Egyptian universities more Islamic and to apply the social and political beliefs they had learned in the Gulf.

But the state was quick to try to minimize their influence, the same tactic it had used against the students. The ruling councils of faculty clubs sympathetic to the Islamic cause were dissolved, and some professors were arrested. The authorities believed that professors were responsible for steering students toward the Islamic trend; their solution was to eliminate teachers from influential positions within the universities. In 1994, the Egyptian parliament passed a law, backed enthusiastically by Education Minister Hussein Kamal Baha al-Din, to change the selection process of university deans. The new rules gave university chancellors, who were appointed personally by the Egyptian president, the power to select deans. In the past, the deans had been chosen by a committee of professors in each faculty. The new legislation also handed the education minister power to micromanage university affairs, giving him authority over all matters on campuses.

The state's crackdown within the universities during the early 1990s coincided with the worst street violence from militant groups the country had seen in several decades. The militants who bombed cafes, attacked tourist sites, shot at cabinet ministers, and vowed to overthrow the infidel state, however, represented but a small, isolated fraction of the wider Islamist movement that had its roots in Egypt's universities and institutes. Those armed militants who did emerge in the early 1990s appear quantitatively different from their 1970s counterparts; for the most part, they were poorer, less educated and generally came from rural rather than urban areas. One of the few studies carried out on the makeup of the militant movement shows 79 percent of a sample from the 1970s attended college, while only 20 percent of those from the 1990s did so.[30]

By the late 1990s the militant movement itself had been largely contained, reduced for the most part to scattered clashes with the security forces in remote rural areas, far from the political centers of power in Cairo. Heavy-handed police tactics, abetted by the average Egyptian's aversion to violence in the name of Islam, had ensured the armed movement had only a limited impact on society at large. Even the horrific slaughter of foreign tourists at Luxor, in which students again played a significant role, must be viewed more as the endgame of the militant threat rather than the start of an effective *jihad* against an unbelieving state. Despite its obvious threat to the regime in terms of lost domestic and international credibility in general and lost tourist revenue in particular, the Luxor attack appears more of a passing sideshow to the main event.

The danger posed by the peaceful Islamist movement on campus, contained only by the state's interference and outright repression of leading activists, is of far greater significance to the survival of Mubarak and the secularist elite he represents. The history of the last thirty years makes clear that any loosening of the ties that keep the universities in thrall is certain to end in further, perhaps fatal, pressures on the state for implementation of an Islamic social and legal system. Likewise, history also demonstrates that efforts by the regime to manipulate the Islamist student movement for its own ends are doomed to failure. The result is a nationwide university system in a frozen state of rebellion.

6

TAKING THE VEIL

The young men and women greeted one another cordially as they entered the spacious brick villa, with its gilded furniture, European antiques, and floral Oriental carpets. They were students at the American University in Cairo, the daughters and sons of prominent doctors, lawyers, and government officials. Their fresh adolescent faces, their laughter, and the confidence with which they carried themselves were proof of their elite status. They would never endure the heavy burdens that afflicted millions of other Egyptians in their late teens or early twenties. Their lives were mapped out for them by their mere existence. As the offspring of Egypt's most well-connected families, the men were guaranteed high-paying jobs if they wanted them. The women could all find rich husbands if they chose not to work.

Everyone seemed to know his place, even though most had never been to the villa before. The young men gathered in the living room of the house and were seated on chairs and sofas, while the women sat on the floor in an adjacent room closer to the door. Most of the women wore headscarves and designer jeans or other tight-fitting trousers. Mona, the daughter of the hostess, was covered in a black *niqab*. She sat elegantly on the floor near the foyer of the house, her dark, provocative eyes closely monitoring those who entered. When men were about to pass near her, she pulled the outer layer of the *niqab* over her head, completely covering her face.

"Come into the bedroom so we can talk freely," Mona instructed, after I had introduced myself. She closed the door and began explaining why she and a few hundred students from the American University, once a monolithic pillar of secularism, had gathered in her parents' villa that evening in November 1997. The students were about to attend a *dars*, or religious lesson.

For many Egyptians this would pass as an unremarkable event. But for Mona, the daughter of a member of the Egyptian parliament, the *dars* verged on being classified as an illicit affair. The child of an official from the ruling Democratic National party was hardly expected to participate in what many in government considered "fundamentalist activity."

"I've worn the *niqab* for three years," Mona explained. "In the beginning no one in my family was religious. My father told us, 'You have to pray.' But he didn't practice Islam. My mother wore bathing suits, and my father drank. We had everything in life. I traveled to Europe. I went shopping, but I didn't have happiness.

"After I got married, I felt shy. I started wearing tights underneath my bathing suit. After I had my first baby, I went to a *dars* and I felt I wanted to be a better Muslim. Then I promised God I wouldn't go out of the house without a *hijab*. Then, gradually, I began wearing the *niqab*. My *niqab* is my freedom, because it lets me choose who does and who doesn't see me."

The appeal of popular Islam among educated, privileged women like Mona and her friends poses an insidious threat to the regime and a seemingly overwhelming intellectual challenge to secularists at home and abroad. The elite's attraction to religion goes straight to the heart of the struggle between Islam and modernity and the effort by today's Islamists to forge a workable compromise between the two, this time within the highly charged world of male-female relations. And it highlights the important role of women across a broad social spectrum—to the consternation of critics in Egypt and the West—within the Islamic revival as a whole.

Like their sisters in Imbaba, on university campuses and in the professions, women among the Egyptian elite are responding increasingly to the Islamic call. They, too, have linked up with the newly assertive members of the *ulama* in the elusive desire to become "better Muslims." Many are using their considerable economic resources and social standing to further the movement, setting in motion a trickle-down effect that reaches into society at large. Some have gone a step further, moving beyond being devout followers to emerge as informal preachers. They hold religious lessons and spread their own, unorthodox brand of Islam to friends and followers within their elevated social circles.

For decades the role of women in Muslim society has provided one of the primary battlegrounds in the cultural war between East and West, between the colonized and their colonizers. Egypt's early modernists demanded the liberation of Muslim women in order to better compete with the West. In the 1920s, educated Egyptian women—the same elites who today have been drawn to the Islamic revival—removed their veils as a gesture symbolic of their turn toward westernization. Their opponents, meanwhile, sought anti-

Western "authenticity" in maintaining what were seen as traditional sex roles in the face of foreign domination.

Despite shifting alliances and unsteady battlelines, the struggle began anew in the 1970s, at the outset of contemporary Islamic activism. During my periodic travels to the West, I was struck how editors, publishers, literary agents, and friends wanted to discuss virtually nothing but my impressions of the status of women under Islam. Most of their questions were based on the assumption that Islamic practices were forced on women, too helpless and too powerless in male-dominated societies to control their own destinies. No topic aroused as much interest and visceral emotion as veiling. When I explained that veiling was practiced voluntarily by an increasing number of Muslim women, Westerners often offered a counterexplanation—if veiling was in fact by choice, then women certainly were being brainwashed by Muslim extremists. Such views are little removed from the prevailing attitudes of the late nineteenth and early twentieth centuries among colonial officials, missionaries, and Western feminists in the Arab and Islamic world. The veil was seen as a prime symbol of all that was backward, underdeveloped—in short, non-Western. The attack on the covering or seclusion of Muslim women, often justified in the name of modernization and the cultural superiority of European ways, supported a broader assault on native society in general. The *hijab* was fair game for Western critics of all stripes and persuasions and it remains so to this day.

Nor could I escape the obsession with the veil among Easterners. When I left Egypt and moved to Iran in the summer of 1998, I took along a severe, Egyptian-tailored black *chador*. Mona and her fellow believers had recommended their dressmaker, a woman who designs *niqabs* and veils of all models and for all seasons for Cairo's upper crust, working from a large apartment near the pyramids that she has turned into an Islamic fashion house. She presented several patterns, and I chose a style that completely hid my hair and tightly framed my face before billowing out to the floor. To add a bit of style, I asked her to sew black brocade on the sleeves.

When I arrived in Iran, my *chador* puzzled Iranians and foreigners alike. Most Iranians were accustomed to foreign women wearing loose fitting headscarves, exposing their hair, and knee-length raincoats—an outfit that technically violates the Islamic dress code and is known in Iran as "bad hijab." I chose the most conservative style of Islamic dress for a few practical reasons. I knew I would visit ayatollahs and other mullahs who might feel more at ease if I wore a *chador*. And I planned to interview government officials working in state offices, where signs are posted showing a female model demonstrating the fine points of what is considered appropriate attire. The sketch shows a woman wearing a long veil and a coat extending to her ankles.

A coat was certainly too hot for the blistering Iranian summer, so a loose-fitting *chador* seemed to be the most comfortable alternative.

It never occurred to me that my veil would excite impassioned debate among secular and pious Iranians. "You are more Islamic than the pope," quipped one acquaintance after he got over the initial shock. Another friend, highly Europeanized, declined to give his traditional farewell peck on the cheek after a dinner party: "You look too Islamic," he explained, as a squeamish look came over his face. The women at an upscale health club in North Tehran were horrified that any women, let alone a Western one, would adopt the dress more common within Iran's underclass. Each day in the locker room, as they stripped down to designer workout suits that were skimpier than anything I had ever observed in athletic clubs in the West, the same women glared at me each time as I took off my *chador*. They were so offended by my choice in Islamic fashion that a few offered to take me shopping to search for something they would find more acceptable. Perhaps a crepe manteau would do, with a sheer chiffon headscarf.

The doorman at a Tehran high-rise refused to let me enter the building where I had been invited to attend a dinner party. He had been instructed not to admit religious partisans, or *Hezbollahis*, who might disrupt the illicit dancing and drinking going on upstairs. I was eventually rescued by some neighbors, who pointed to my feet, arguing that no strict Shi'ite woman would wear open-toed, turquoise sandals. Even a Grand Ayatollah in the holy city of Qom, where four years earlier the religious scholars had refused to see me unless I was fully veiled, proposed I trade in my *chador-e arabi* for the raincoat and scarf favored by the more secular Iranian women of means. "You don't have to wear all that, you know," the ayatollah advised.

Contemporary Islamic fashion for women is designed to discourage sexual temptation or attraction between men and women who are not husband and wife. By hiding the contours of the body, women seek to move in and out of the public arena and maintain freedom from being seen as sexual objects. For many Islamists, anonymity within this space—the street, the office, the bank—is a form of liberation and a way of achieving morality and piety.

The source of contemporary veiling practices lies in a response to interpretations of the *sharia*, giving women a specific set of garments referred to as "lawful dress." Many Islamists and their adherents cite a verse in the Koran as proof that veiling is required. The verse instructs Muslims to speak to the Prophet's wives from behind a curtain, or screen: "And when you ask his wives for anything you want, ask them from before a screen: that makes for greater purity for your hearts and theirs" (33:53). Islamic scholars also argue over particular *hadith*s in support of veiling, although many jurists assert that these have not been authenticated because of their less than sound connection to the Prophet.

What is referred to as "lawful dress" in Egypt is primarily an urban, middle-class phenomenon and differs from the traditional forms of veiling still worn in the village—the *tarha*, or headscarf. Within the broad category of "lawful dress" are various gradations. The head veil, or *hijab*, which literally means "curtain," is essentially a headscarf. The *khimar*, a step up in the veiling process, is a headscarf that covers the hair completely and extends down to the waist, fully disguising the breasts. And the *niqab*, usually a black wrap that resembles a cape, extending from the head to the floor and covering everything except the eyes, is the final stage. The *hijab* is considered by many Islamists to be obligatory for Muslim women, while those who wear or advocate the *niqab* tend to exist outside mainstream Egyptian society.

But such generalizations are unreliable. A woman like Mona was clearly part of the Egyptian mainstream, despite her *niqab*. She was living proof that the Islamic resurgence transcended social class. She was a contradiction to conventional Western theory that veiling confines, restricts, and traps women in a mental prison. As a model of the new Islamist woman who has combined tradition, culture, religion, and modernity into one lifestyle, Mona intrigued me. As I inched closer to the edge of the bed, poised to launch my next line of inquiry, we heard a commotion in the living room. Mona opened the bedroom door and we watched the star attraction strut into the house as the students rushed to take their places in anticipation of the upcoming performance.

Sheikh Omar Abd al-Kafi took a seat among the young men gathered in the living room. Silence fell on the house, and all eyes were focused on him. Kafi was not an ordinary *sheikh*; he was a legend for most of the students gathered at the *dars*. He was known as the "sheikh of the stars" for the dozens of actresses he had converted, women who gave up their careers on the silver screen and took the veil. He was also called the "women's *sheikh*" for the large female following he had cultivated among upper-class professionals and housewives who transformed their lives after attending his religious lessons.

Kafi was infamous for his outrageous decrees. Muslims should not address Christians with Islamic greetings, Kafi once declared. He also endorsed the religious death sentence proclaimed by Ayatollah Khomeini against British author Salman Rushdie for blasphemy in his book *The Satanic Verses*. In fact, said Kafi, he himself was prepared to carry out the *fatwa* and kill the author if given the opportunity.

Yet, despite the controversy surrounding Kafi, there was something else about him everyone knew but shied away from discussing openly in the company of the country's power elite. The *sheikh* was officially banned from preaching; the state had placed him in the category of "extremists." He was no longer seen in public, and to contact him required access to the number to a confidential telephone line in his house, one he maintained was free from the listening devices of the state intelligence service.

In the early 1990s his Friday sermons in Dokki, an upscale district not far from my home in Zamalek, attracted so many worshippers that police re-routed traffic to accommodate the tens of thousands who listened to him from the streets surrounding the Asad Ibn al-Furat mosque. As far as the state was concerned, his influence had gotten out of control; it was reaching into the very centers of power. A former interior minister was among his loyalists; the wives of high-ranking officials could not get enough of him; female celebrities proclaimed their devotion to him in tabloid newspapers and magazines as if he were a cult leader or a rock star.

The spell he had cast on the respectable was trumpeted for much of 1993 by the country's most sensational left-wing tabloid magazine until finally the hysteria cried out for action. The magazine dubbed him the "smiling star of terrorism," and likened him to Sheikh Omar Abd al-Rahman, the spiritual leader of the *Gama'a al-Islamiyya* who was convicted in the bombing of the World Trade Center. After fourteen issues of Kafi bashing, the magazine finally got results. In April 1994, under pressure to silence public debate, the state banned the *sheikh* from preaching in mosques and on television.

Here he was in the flesh, a bit more serene and slightly more pragmatic than in his heyday, when his tirades ignited the street crowds of Dokki. "What is the problem that frightens the youth, both males and females, from religion?" Kafi asked the audience. "They say religion contains constraints. Don't look at your female colleague. Don't shake hands with her. Don't go on mixed trips. . . . If we believe religion is freedom and not restraints, it won't be difficult to follow."

Kafi spoke for more than two hours, until his listeners were sated. Then he left the house as swiftly as he had entered. His aloofness was clearly part of his mystique. To linger on and drink tea with his followers and engage in prosaic conversation was not his style.

I asked a few women what they thought of his lesson and why they were so drawn to his words. "He is the only *sheikh* who relates religion to modern life," replied one young woman who had followed Kafi since his days in Dokki. "I asked him once if I could continue to go to the pub and drink. He told me, 'I won't tell you what to do. But if the Prophet saw you in a pub, would he be happy?' I knew what the answer was, even though it is difficult not to go to the pub."

The only woman who agreed to give me her name was DelJane, a chic fashion model and the daughter of a Sorbonne-educated Kurdish diplomat. DelJane gave up modeling a year before and became committed to a religious life after she discovered Kafi through a circle of wealthy women who invited him into their homes for clandestine religious lessons. Her faith, and in particular her veil, had given her new freedom.

"My friends act like I'm dying because I put on the veil," DelJane confided. "But I've had four marriage proposals in the last year. More and more young girls are putting on the veil now, despite objections from their parents. They are doing it for the same reason I did: When I put on the veil, I put on my brain as well."

When the authorities banned Kafi, they hoped his influence would quickly recede. Out of sight, out of mind, they thought. But Kafi's message, like that of many leading religious figures who attained widespread exposure in the early 1990s, lived on among his followers. They converted others by playing his taped sermons, numbering 1,000 and officially illegal, and the chain continued.

Egyptians who had the money and resources spread his religious fervor. Movie stars, dancers, and television presenters surrendered their fame and fortunes to the cause. One opened an orphanage to make up for the sins of her former life; another gave up stardom to organize her own Koranic *dars* for the rich. A third actress donated an apartment worth 100,000 Egyptian pounds and established a medical clinic for the poor. The conversion among the famous was so widespread that secularist critics began accusing Kafi of belonging to an international network of extremists who paid rich women to veil. It was their only defense, and one that smacked of revenge, rather than reason. The women were already millionaires, so why would they be lured by bribes from the likes of Kafi?

While the spotlight remained fixed on Kafi's more illustrious followers, thousands of Egyptian were rebuilding their lives behind the scenes after their own exposure to "Dr. Omar," as he was affectionately called. Suzanne, a confident middle-aged woman who holds a doctorate in biology and is married to a wealthy lawyer, opened a Koranic school for children in Heliopolis. I met Suzanne when I first arrived in Cairo through her son, a student at the American University who looked like a holdover from the University of California at Berkeley in the 1960s. He wore his curly, frizzy hair in long, dangling cornrows, a style rarely seen in Egypt, and his mild, contemplative manner was a stark contrast to the cacophony engulfing a majority of his giggling peers. At the time, Suzanne was a regular at Kafi's *dars* in Dokki, despite wisecracks from her son and equally westernized husband. Whenever I asked Suzanne's son, Ahmed, about her activities, he would laugh, roll his eyes, and say, "Please don't call her and get her started on all this religious stuff."

I indeed phoned Suzanne in 1998 to inquire about the progress of her school. The enrollment had increased, she reported, as a result of a small advertising campaign. She had rented an adjoining room to the main class-room to offer courses in other subjects besides religion. The school had re-ceived an official seal of approval from the *sheikh*s at al-Azhar. The endorse-ment in turn produced a small state stipend for the teachers. But the bulk of teachers' salaries, rent of the building, and all other expenses was paid out of the pocket money Suzanne received from her job in a nearby hospital and from her husband's salary. Her husband did not encourage her religious activity, but he never stood in the way of her beliefs, even at his own expense. Once Suzanne began following Kafi, she started fasting and praying more frequently and reduced the number of meals she prepared for her family.

"I wanted to give something to my religion in return for being shown the way by Dr. Kafi," Suzanne told me one hot June afternoon. All of this is because of him," she said proudly, as she gave me a tour of the school.

Suzanne found religion in much the same way as many other Egyptians from her generation. As thousands migrated to the Persian Gulf states to earn wages as much as ten times higher than in Egypt, they were exposed to societies more religious and conservative than their own. In Saudi Arabia, for example, veiling is mandatory. Throughout the Gulf region in general, social norms among men and women are more restrictive than in Egypt, and most activities revolve around religion. When Egyptians became involved in these societies, they too became more religious.

Suzanne became drawn to Islam while her husband was working in Ku-wait in the 1980s. Her brother had just died, and she derived spiritual comfort from a Kuwaiti woman who encouraged her to learn the Koran. Suzanne had never read the Muslim Holy Book, and the experience inspired her to devote her life to Islam. She began wearing the veil, and when she returned to Egypt, she continued her religious activities until she found Sheikh Omar Abd al-Kafi. "I love my religion and my country," Suzanne told me in the same breath, revealing the strong associations between Islam and Egyptian nationalism she had clearly developed in her mind.

I left Suzanne that afternoon in a morbid mood. Sheikh Mohammed Mat-wali Sharawi, Egypt's most beloved religious figure, had just died. As we watched flashbacks of the *sheikh's* long life on the television set at the school, she burst into tears. "He was such a good man. Someone like him comes along only once in every century."

Sheikhs Sharawi and Abd al-Kafi have been largely responsible for shaping the new image of the ideal Islamist woman in Egypt. Their religious lessons, Friday sermons, television programs, and widely distributed literature serve as guides, particularly for urban middle-class women, who, over the last twenty years, have turned toward Islam to redefine their duties in the family and their status in society. Sheikh Sharawi began in his first televised ad-dresses in the 1970s to broaden the parameters of Islamic womanhood, in order to respond to the demands of the modern world. For the first time in Egypt, the slumping economy made it necessary for urban women to work; men could no longer serve as sole breadwinners. Sharawi was one of the first contemporary Islamic leaders to expand the definition of an "Islamic woman" from one who should strive to be culturally authentic to one also entitled to the civil liberties and rights guaranteed for men. Women, according to Sharawi, should be equal to men, but should never cross the line that divides and differentiates the sexes, particularly in family matters. Kafi's general message and objectives were similar: A woman could be both modern and Islamic at the same time.

Egypt's Islamists have focused much of their attention on women in the struggle to create an Islamic society. For them, the national debate is not one between tradition and modernity, but how to define appropriate limitations on modernity. Many of Egypt's Islamists believe women should have the right to education and employment. But they also believe the priority must lie with the family. Their primary concern is not the balance of power between men and women, but how to preserve the interaction between the sexes that guarantees procreation and the continued existence of the Muslim family unit. As in many Western societies, the central question among Egypt's Islamists is how to reconcile the inherent rights of women with the responsibilities in life only they can fulfill. Women also play a vital role as "bearers of culture," the key to the perpetuation of the faith. For the Islamists, the main threat from the West is cultural, rather than political and economic. Protecting the traditional duties and roles of women is key to Islam's very survival in a world increasingly influenced by Western values.[1]

The link between Islam and modernity is not new to the women's movement in Egypt, but it has evolved dramatically to fit the changing economic times. In the 1970s, when women entered the workforce in greater numbers, the division that once existed between secular career women on one side and homebound, religious traditionalists on the other began to evaporate. Suddenly, more and more women sitting behind desks in government offices were veiled. Likewise, professors, lawyers, and doctors were also engaging in religious activism in universities, the syndicates, and through less official channels. By expanding the limits of religious debate, and creating a place for feminism within the Islamic agenda, religious activists succeeded in attracting to the Islamic cause middle- and upper-class women, once virtually driven by economic and social forces out of the religious camp.

At the same time, the religious revival offered traditionalists an acceptable social life outside the isolation and seclusion of their homes. By the 1990s, just as young middle and upper-middle class professionals were attending religious lessons at night after work, so too were traditionalists, formerly housebound, congregating with their female friends for lessons in the mosques in the afternoons. Such impromptu gatherings have become commonplace at many mosques, including the central mosque at al-Azhar during lunchtime, where women sit in circles on the floor eating tomato and cucumber sandwiches as they await the sermons delivered by local *sheikhs*.

Zeinab al-Ghazali, who founded the Muslim Women's Association in 1937 and later joined forces with Hasan al-Banna and the Muslim Brotherhood, worked for decades to fuse the roles of women as devoted wife and mother and as devout believer. She led weekly seminars for women in mosques and organized sessions in her home for many professionals and university students. But she also broadened the model for women through her own example as the female counterpart to al-Banna. She received powerful politicians in her home; she publicly opposed the Brotherhood's cooperation with Nasser and the Free Officers after the 1952 revolution; and she and her network of women served as liaisons between the Brotherhood and the outside world in 1954, after many of the society's leaders were imprisoned. Ghazali was arrested in 1965 and initially sentenced to death for her political activities. The sentence was reduced to life in prison, but she was released in 1971 as part of President Sadat's goodwill gesture toward the Muslim Brotherhood.

Ghazali was ahead of her time in believing that there could be rights for women within Islamic societies, a view that is just now being articulated among Islamic feminists. She believed Islam offered women "everything—freedom, economic rights, political rights, social rights, public and private rights," though these rights were not manifest in Islamic societies.[2]

She also emphasized the vital role for women in the Islamic movement: "Women (are) . . . a fundamental part of the Islamic call. . . . They are the ones who build the kind of men that we need to fill the ranks of the Islamic call. So women must be well educated, cultured, knowing of the precepts of the Koran and Sunna, informed about world politics, why we (Muslims) are backward, why we don't have technology. . . . Islam does not forbid women to actively participate in public life. It does not prevent her from working, entering politics, and expressing her opinion, or from being anything, as long as that does not interfere with her first duty as a mother, the one who first trains her children in the Islamic call."[3]

Now frail and living with a few female relatives in her Heliopolis home, Zeinab al-Ghazali takes comfort in seeing the efforts of her half century crusade bear fruit. At eighty-two years old, she still receives visitors, provided the meetings occur shortly after her morning medication when she is most alert. When I visited Ghazali, she was wearing her trademark white headscarf and thick black eyeglasses. She relived her romantic days as an activist alongside Hasan al-Banna, even as she strained to remember dates, events, and anecdotes. "Now you have young girls leading families to Islam. The future of the Islamic movement is guaranteed because today's youth are leading the way," she told me. "I always encouraged women to wear the veil, because it is important for women to be religious. It is through them that men find Islam and this influences the family to be religious."

The discourse concerning feminism within Islam has evolved since Ghazali's time and undergone serious reexamination by activists across the political spectrum. Heba Raouf Ezzat, an Islamist lecturer at Cairo University now earning her doctorate at Oxford, has taken the debate to new heights, arguing that women's rights existed within Islamic texts and Islamic law during the time of the Prophet. Raouf Ezzat's arguments rest as much on her endorsement of Islam as a prescription for the modern woman as they do on her condemnation of Western feminist ideas. She adamantly rejects the Western concept of feminism, arguing that it has pigeonholed women into narrow roles, given them fewer choices, and created division between the sexes. Furthermore, according to Raouf Ezzat, implicit in Western-style women's liberation is a challenge to the Church as the regulator of social norms, given the contradictions between the feminist movement and the Church on issues such as abortion, divorce, and birth control.

By contrast, she turns to the Islamic texts when arguing that women's rights were guaranteed since Islam was founded in the seventh century. The language in the Koran refers to humanity as "insan," which in Arabic means person or human being, and can be either masculine or feminine. In her book, *The Woman and Political Work: An Islamic Perspective*, Raouf Ezzat frequently quotes verses of the Koran to support her argument. Among her citations is the following: "And their Lord hath accepted of them, and answered them: 'Never will I suffer to be lost the work of any of you, be he male or female, ye are members, one of another'" (3:195). Although Raouf Ezzat is well known in intellectual circles, and has written extensively about the subject, her line of reasoning has yet to filter down into the general society.

As in most Muslim societies today, the veil and its surrounding symbolism provide the most prominent vehicle for debating women's rights. If the role of women offers one of the main venues for the struggle between today's Islamists and secularists, then the *hijab*, the *khimar*, and the *niqab*—the progressively more conservative veils among Egyptian women—clearly represent the trophies of war. Reformists as early as the turn of the century, such as the prominent feminist Qasim Amin, were opposed to veiling, and Egyptian women in the 1920s were the first in the Arab world to call for abolishing it altogether. By the early 1950s, women's liberation had made its public debut, with women taking on more public roles and adopting Western-style fashions; over time, miniskirts became more common than headscarves. When asked if Western dress violated religious principles, women generally agreed that their fashions were not un-Islamic. In fact, they argued, women were not expected to veil during the early Islamic period, except the Prophet's wives who lived near a mosque and were exposed to men attending prayers. Between the 1930s and the 1970s, a majority of women embraced their new public role and rejected traditional stereotypes.

Wearing a head veil, the *hijab*, gained support in the early 1970s in response to growing Western influence and a reciprocal rejuvenation of Islamic identity. Islamic groups in the universities, which denounced Western values and mores and made the creation of an Islamic society their ultimate goal, encouraged female students to wear the veil. Such Islamic dress was one of the symbols of the new movement. It denoted uniformity and solidarity and clearly separated those students within the movement from those outside. Islamic groups fought hard at times against university administrators to permit students to wear the *niqab*—a practice the authorities opposed. When young women were banned from entering the campuses in full veil, the Islamists often staged protests in their defense. Given the leading role within society of campus Islamic groups, it was only natural that many among the general population would soon follow their lead.

Veiling has become pervasive. In the early 1990s, schoolgirls began wearing the *hijab* in far greater numbers than ever. The Minister of Education issued a decree in 1994 saying that girls should refrain from veiling in the primary schools. The decision unleashed national strife that had been brewing beneath the surface. Clashes erupted between parents who insisted their daughters attend classes with veils and teachers who felt obliged to comply with the government's decree. Officials dismissed some students in Cairo and other cities who refused to obey the new requirement. A number of parents filed lawsuits against the education minister, challenging his decision. The state in turn sacked teachers who encouraged the veil in primary schools, and sketches of schoolgirls wearing the *hijab* were removed from textbooks about religion.

The state's action set off a flurry of criticism from Islamists. The *fatwa* committee of al-Azhar publicly confronted the minister, arguing that covering everything except a girl's hands and the feet was necessary after puberty, according to the Islamic texts. Eventually, Education Minister Hussein Kamal Baha al-Din backed away from his decision, and rewrote the policy to say that schoolgirls could be veiled, provided they had parental permission in the form of a note from their fathers. However, even this requirement was never enforced, as the great majority of girls reported to school in *hijab* and it seemed impractical to demand written notes from thousands of parents. He won a belated victory, however, when the courts agreed to a second ban he had issued that prohibited the full-length *niqab* in schools and universities.

During my years in Egypt, I was deluged from all sides with explanations for women taking the veil. The three favorites among secularists, including one cabinet minister, were, first, that women were too poor to buy shampoo or go to a hairdresser. Covering their hair was a cheap, easy remedy. Second, women were frustrated with their roles as housewives and turned to Islam out of boredom. Once veiled, they instantly acquired a new status in life as women of religion. And third, the women's husbands forced them to veil as a means of control and domination in a sexually repressed society.

But the women who follow Abd al-Kafi and other *sheikhs* like him give the lie to these myths. They are certainly wealthy enough to buy shampoo or visit a coiffeur. Many were university-educated, and could have careers if they chose to do so, and their status in Egyptian society was already elevated. The evidence is clear in their memberships in country clubs, their designer fashions, and frequent trips abroad. In many cases, their husbands, who play active roles in their lives, objected to the headscarves and preferred their wives to show off their well-groomed hair and sculpted health club figures.

By appearing for lessons in their homes, or at the very least appearing on popular television programs, the *sheikhs* helped create informal networks among women who otherwise might have remained isolated and alone in their search for the latest religious imperative. The increased access to members of the *ulama*, who were no longer mythical figures cloistered inside the grand halls of al-Azhar, made a significant difference to the spread and pace of Islamization among Egyptian women. In the case of Abd al-Kafi, his notoriety developed quickly among the rich because he was one of them. He often advised his followers at an exclusive shooting club in Mohandiseen, while sipping tea in the landscaped gardens. He lives in a brick compound of apartments in Dokki, which only the affluent could possibly afford. He keeps a fashionable wardrobe and wears designer eyeglasses. In response to criticism that his appearance was ostentatious, he once sneered: "Do I have to wear a torn *gallabiyya*? What is wrong with a religious figure wearing decent clothes and looking neat?"

Kafi was a pragmatist. He refused to allow his religious ideas to freeze him in time. By the late 1990s, he had deliberately left behind the stinging sermons from his Dokki days. He realized some of his comments that sparked outrage then were no longer appropriate in the postmilitant days of the late 1990s. When I first met him in 1994, he refused to look me in the eye. The entire interview was conducted with Kafi's gaze fixed above my forehead on the door of his study. In no time, I was trapped in a nervous twitch, wondering if I should look into his wayward eyes, or at the ground, or settle on a more neutral spot. Adding to the tension was his body language, which made it clear that each question was one question too many.

Our second meeting in 1997 proved that Kafi had adapted to the changing times. He was calm, personable, and willing to talk freely about sensitive subjects. He had trimmed his gray beard, and he was dressed in a white shirt starched to perfection, and gray trousers. The urgent tone behind every word he once uttered had given way to a ruminative note. It was as if he had participated in a revolution, and, in hindsight, once the fervor and passion had subsided, was prepared for corrective action. He looked me squarely in the eye, and tried convincingly to moderate the ideas that led him into exile from the pulpit.

He began the conversation with complaints about Americans' negative perception of Muslims. He told me he had joined in a letter-writing campaign with *sheikh*s in the United States to protest a story in the *Los Angeles Times* concerning the persecution of Christians in Egypt. He handed me a copy of the story. I read it, and agreed that the correspondent, based in Cairo, had exaggerated not only the level of tension between Muslims and Christians in Egypt, but across the Middle East.

The subject provided me with the perfect entree to discuss one of the chief reasons Kafi had been placed under house arrest. His enemies had used his comments about Christians as their main ammunition to get him banned from preaching.

"Why did you say Christians should not be greeted with Islamic sayings, such as *'al-salam aleikum?'* " I asked.

"This is not my idea. The Prophet said this. It is a greeting for Muslims only, but it doesn't mean you shouldn't greet Christians. This is why you say 'Good morning.' The Prophet used to say to Christians, 'Peace be upon those who follow the right path.' "

His answer was interrupted with a knock on the door. Kafi's young son Omar opened the door slightly and squeezed his small dark head in the crack to summon his father to the adjacent apartment where the family lived. Kafi excused himself, explaining that his wife was not at home and he was taking care of his children. When he returned a few minutes later, he carried with him a tray of tea and biscuits. It was further evidence of Kafi's makeover. Rarely did I visit a man in Egypt who prepared tea himself. If there were no wives to serve the tea, there were teaboys, and if there were no teaboys, there was no tea.

Kafi began talking about his wife. They had met in 1984, when she was teaching in the arts faculty at Cairo University. The attraction was mutual: She wanted to marry a man of religion, and Kafi was impressed by her youth, beauty, and the fact that her father and grandfather were both Islamic scholars. Mrs. Kafi continued working after they married, despite protestations from her husband. Many Egyptian university professors and instructors had left to work in the Persian Gulf, where they earned higher wages, and Mrs. Kafi wanted to take full advantage of the shortage in the local teaching market. She quit only when she became pregnant with their first child.

I asked Kafi if I could speak to his wife alone. I wanted to know if her version of events matched his, if she regretted giving up her career, and how she viewed a woman's role in Islam. He arranged a meeting for me, and one day we drank tea together in Kafi's study. "Omar said he believed a woman shouldn't work, according to Islamic teaching," explained Mrs. Kafi, a soft-spoken woman. And he told me, 'I can't tell women not to work if my wife is working.' I stalled for three years before making a decision and took a leave from the university, but then I made my decision that I would not pursue a career."

I asked Mrs. Kafi if her father would have financed her university education if he had known she would never have a career. "Of course," she shot back, insulted that I had posed the question. "Islam says that women shouldn't be ignorant. I plan to enroll my daughters in the best schools, no matter whether they eventually have careers or not."

During my next meeting with Sheikh Kafi, I asked him specific questions about women's role in Islam.

"Do you believe woman should work or should stay at home?"

"If it is necessary economically for a woman to work, she should work. But if not, she shouldn't.... Women are like crystal. You shouldn't be too hard on them, and they should be respected more than men. This is the essence of women, not what the West's idea of a woman is. There is a *hadith* which says every house must have a woman. My wife's work at home, taking care of children and everything else, is hard work. It's a twenty-four-hour-a-day job."

"Why do people call you the women's *sheikh*? Was this your intention?"

"I don't know how this happened," Kafi replied. "I always preached to men and women, even before I preached in Dokki. Perhaps the difference between me and other *sheikh*s is that they tend to direct their teaching to men. But the Koran addresses both men and women, and the Prophet addressed men and women. I explain to women what their rights are in Islam."

"But what is the reason you attracted so many thousands of worshippers?" I asked.

"I remember one Ramadan when approximately 100,000 people came to hear me, and they closed Dokki. I realized then it was a special kind of love between me and the people. The next day the papers wrote that the Islamists control the streets.... There is no way I alone could have convinced all these people to love me. There is something in me that God has deliberately planted."

A preordained gift from the divine is the reason many *sheikh*s give for their unrelenting activity. Once God's will has been determined, it becomes reality that must be defended and protected at all cost. Egyptians firmly believe that God micromanages all affairs on earth, from the most prosaic to the most significant. When you ask a plumber if he can fix a leaky pipe, or the salesclerk if a new refrigerator can be delivered, the answer is predictably *Inshallah*, or God willing. To try to pin down a precise reply is to suggest man has the power to control such events, which is considered sacrilegious.

Dozens of women I interviewed who followed Kafi believed God sends signals to his followers that, once correctly identified, must be followed. Mona, the hostess of the *dars* in Zamalek, convinced her mother to wear the veil only after she had difficulty sleeping. She took her insomnia as a sign from God that her life was in disarray.

"I convinced my mother to go to Mecca," Mona said. "She didn't tell me at the time, but she had made a deal with God. She told God, 'If you accept me, lightning will strike.' We were eating at a restaurant and lightning struck, and it began to rain. It never rains in Mecca. My mother couldn't believe it. That's when she put on the veil."

For DelJane, the message came while she was in the middle of a modeling job on the beach. "I was standing in the modeling shoot with women who looked like prostitutes, and I became so depressed. I didn't know why. I am intelligent, I have a good figure, and I am the youngest teacher at City University. But I had to ask myself what was wrong, and I thought it must be my relationship with God.

"I knew I must become religious. What was I supposed to tell God when he asked me what took me so long to find Islam? That I had a fashion show?"

Religious women of all classes took comfort in the many famous actresses, belly dancers, and singers who have taken the *hijab* over the last ten years, giving up their glamorous lives and fat salaries in order to become better Muslims. In Egyptian culture, actresses, singers, and other women who perform in public—and thus for men—have always had a seedy reputation, not far removed from that of common prostitutes. So veiling among the stars is the ultimate vindication for pious women. The Egyptian cinema, the Hollywood of the Arabic-speaking world, links Egypt culturally and linguistically with the rest of the Middle East in ways that would never be possible otherwise. The movie industry is as much a part of the country's national identity as the pyramids. Although the stars circulate in a heady world few Egyptians could ever fathom, they carry a sense of familiarity that transcends the gulf between their universe and that of the impoverished but infatuated fan. They are referred to in the press and public by their first names—Yousra, Shadia, Lucy, Fifi, Yasmin. Their faces are splashed over enormous cartoon-like billboards in central Cairo, their voluptuous figures spilling out of low-cut dresses across the skyline and giving all of downtown an intoxicating aura of kitsch.

When such stars repented in public for lives filled with debauchery, materialism, and temptation, the Islamic movement scored a major moral victory. Not only had the symbols of Western-style decadence caved in, but in giving up their careers, the actresses and singers embraced the traditional roles they had once publicly rejected as full-time mothers and wives. "When there is a lot of sin and corruption around us, people return to religion to rid themselves of corruption," Sheikh Sharawi once explained in a discussion of actresses taking the veil. "When people suffer from contradictions, they rely on religion to solve their dilemma."

For some stars, taking the veil was a return to their cultural and religious identities, rather than a radical departure from their roots. "All those artists who quit art, quit willingly. Every artist is originally a Muslim Egyptian woman. In other words, they were not atheists and became believers, nor were they unbelievers and converted to Islam. But they were suffering from lack of understanding, or their minds and hearts failed to know what was right and what was wrong," Kafi said.[4]

Yasmin al-Khayam, once a popular Egyptian singer, for example, is the daughter of Sheikh al-Hosary, an Azhari who ran a mosque in Cairo's Agouza district along a street named in his honor. When Yasmin began following Sheikh Kafi, for whom she became an unofficial spokeswoman in the early 1990s, she established a center for reading and memorizing the Koran in her father's mosque. She also held religious lessons twice a week for women in the neighborhood that included counseling from various *sheikh*s.

Like many stars who were targets of the sensationalist press, which obsessively chronicled their turn toward Islam, Yasmin became a bit reclusive by the late 1990s. Her followers likewise were trapped in a web of paranoia. The constant badgering, scathing attacks, and ridicule from leftist journals and magazines left deep wounds. Middle-aged and confident in her decision to reclaim her religion, Yasmin shied away from discussing with outsiders her convictions or her close association with *sheikh*s such as Kafi. When I visited one of her religious lessons in 1997, she at first welcomed me, convinced I planned to convert to Islam. But when I began taping the speech delivered by the evening's guest speaker, Sheikh Yahya Ismail, the Azhar conservative who was a leader in the renegade Scholar's Front, the recorder prompted bursts of anger and accusations. The women attending the religious lesson assumed I was working for Egypt's state intelligence service or the CIA. I was driven from the mosque, and Yasmin, who had promised a private interview, refused to see me again, insisting I must be an Israeli spy.

Kafi told me a few months later he had been instructed by the authorities to halt all contact with movie stars or any type of public personality. For him, the threat was further evidence that he had become a pariah in the eyes of the state, fearful of both his influence and his elevated constituency. Kafi lived with the same heavy fear many Islamists carried around with them: One day, without warning, the authorities might issue the order to cart them off to jail. For some, the fear was an invitation to test just how far the authorities could be pushed. One young Islamist, under surveillance for many years, told the intelligence brigade who followed him around Cairo: "I sleep better at night, knowing you are always watching me." But Kafi dealt with his foreboding by being extremely cautious. He never again counseled the stars, not even on the confidential line he had hooked up to sidestep the state intelligence's bugging devices.

Kafi's mark, however, imprinted on the wide circle of women who once attended his sermons and religious lessons in Dokki, had a powerful ripple effect. Kamila al-Arabi, a former television announcer who had been fired for wearing the veil, opened an orphanage, an impressive modern structure equipped with cheerful toys, small bunk beds, a cafeteria, and playground. The day I met her, she was busy on the telephone ordering new equipment to run her school. A large staff of young women cared for the dozens of children, playing in their rooms and eating their lunch in decorated halls far more lavish than most Egyptian houses.

Arabi never attended Kafi's *dars*, but she mingled with his converts, and eventually began offering her own weekly religious lessons to those who traveled in the circle of the "women's *sheikh*." Without the benefit of formal Islamic education or instruction, Arabi was a freelance *imam*, who offered advice she declared "Islamic" but would likely fail the test of the *ulama*. In this way, she was no different from the street *sheikh*s of Imbaba who were quick studies and who spread their own religious interpretations, however idiosyncratic they might be.

At a *dars* she held one evening in Mohandiseen in the home of a Kafi follower, Arabi's warnings about death, temptation, and sin were melodramatic enough to achieve the shock value she clearly sought. The young women, packed in the living room of the house in a standing-room only crowd, were mesmerized by her words and often nodded in agreement as if they were attending a faith healing session with an evangelical preacher. They were searching for religious guidance, and they took it wherever they could find it. So much the better that it was delivered in the comfort of a modern apartment, among a socially acceptable group of their peers.

"Does anybody have a notice that guarantees when one will die? If so, go to the graduation parties, the dances. Have drinks with friends. Have fun of all sorts. However, I'm afraid you'll die while doing this, and these things are not in obedience to God," Arabi advised. "There are a lot of bad things taking place, because we are not maintaining our religion."

Distinguishing between good and evil was the key to being a good Muslim, Arabi told her fans. One young woman asked: "I like to listen to the songs of Raghib Alama [a popular Lebanese singer]. Is this forbidden?"

"I don't know what these songs are," Arabi replied. "But the question is, do these songs waste our time or not? They do waste our time, but if I tell you they are forbidden, and music is forbidden, and television is wrong, and the satellite dish is wrong, and videos are a curse, you will never attend religious lessons again."

When one woman asked about the importance of veiling, Arabi confidently pronounced on one of the most complex and vexing issues facing modern Muslims. "God ordered us to take the veil.... Take the veil, even if you are not convinced, because you might die before you are convinced.... I wonder why some women are convinced of the goodness of nudity. Why is it difficult to be convinced of God's orders, while it is easy to be convinced of the devil's temptations?"

Arabi, an attractive woman with small features and light skin, took the veil at the height of her career. First she wore the *hijab* for two years, and then adopted the *niqab*. When I met her at the orphanage she had established in the district of Maadi from donations and personal funding, Arabi told me she had been wearing the *niqab* for six years, and she explained her transformation from television star to self-proclaimed *imam*.

"I had a religious upbringing. We were punished if we didn't fast. Egyptians are brought up on religion, but we think it's tradition. When I got older, I used to pray until dawn, and then go to the television station and work. One day I was reading the Koran and I started to cry, and I said to myself, 'Something is missing in my relationship with God.' I decided that showing my hair was against the rule of God, and that was the start.

"I was inspired by God directly, not by a *sheikh*. My husband was against me wearing the veil. He wanted me to look elegant. But finally he gave in."

While millions of men and women across the Muslim world consider veiling a duty in Islam, religious scholars debate whether the custom is indeed a religious requirement. Various forms of veiling are found in many religions, but the practice has emerged as the most evocative aspect of contemporary Islamic revivalism. In Egypt, the debate has pitted al-Azhar's conservative *sheikhs* against their more modernist rivals. It has prompted state-appointed judges in Egypt's highest courts to issue rulings that contradict state policies. Veiling has also become a measure of a woman's honor, dignity, nationalism, and devotion to Islam.

The Koranic debate largely centers on the following verse, which remains open to broadly varied interpretations: "And say to the believing women that they should lower their gaze and guard their modesty; that they should not display their beauty or ornaments except what they must ordinarily appear thereof; that they should draw their veils over their bosoms and not display their beauty except to their husbands, their fathers, their husbands' fathers, their sons, their husbands' sons, their brothers or their brothers' sons, or their sisters' sons, or their women, or the slaves whom their right hands possess, or male servants free of physical needs, or small children who have no sense of the shame of sex (24: 31)."[5]

This verse, however, poses a central question: Should all Muslim women be held up to the same standard as the wives of Mohammed? After all, critics point out, elsewhere the *hadith*s make a distinction between ordinary women and those of the Prophet's immediate family.

Perhaps the loudest voice against mandatory veiling belongs to Mohammed Sayyed Ashmawi, a former Egyptian judge. He argues that the Prophet's pronouncements on veiling were limited to his own wives and should not apply to the general community of believers. The *hadith* most often cited to support the institution of veiling, Ashmawi asserts, was issued only to advise Muslims on proper conduct when visiting the Prophet's household and not as a directive to women in general. Although serious Islamist thinkers in Egypt have discredited Ashmawi, his position on the veil is supported by a majority of secularists.

But the debate over veiling is not limited to Egypt and has for many contemporary Islamists throughout the Muslim world moved beyond formalistic interpretation of the Koran and the *hadith*s to take on a specific message for modern life. Veiling should be obligatory, they say, to keep relations between the sexes proper and avert *fitna*, or chaos within society sparked by a woman's power to engender uncontrolled lust among men. For these Islamists, veiling is also a rejection of Western mores and a shield against the invasion of Western-bred corruption and immorality. A leading Iranian cleric, Morteza Motahhari, who was assassinated in 1979, explains this aspect of veiling in his book, *On the Islamic Hijab*: Will men work better in an environment where the streets, offices, factories, etc. are continuously filled with women who are wearing makeup and are not fully dressed, or in an environment where these scenes do not exist? ... The truth is that the disgraceful lack of *hijab* in Iran before the Revolution ... is a product of the corrupt western capitalist societies. It is one of the results of the worship of money and the pursuance of sexual fulfillment that is prevalent among western capitalists."[6]

With so much political, social, and emotional capital invested in the veiling of women, it is no wonder that the institution has been thrust to the foreground in those Middle Eastern societies most closely associated with the rise of Islamic activism. From Tehran to Istanbul to Cairo, the *hijab* serves as the most potent homegrown symbol of the power of the Islamists, far more accurate and telling than Western cliché images of the bearded *mujaheddin* praying next to his Kalashnikov. Engage almost any secularist Iranian, Turk, or Egyptian in even casual conversation and the subject will inevitably turn to the practice of veiling.

Iranian women looked to the 1979 Islamic revolution, as did many segments of the population, as an alternative to the Shah's corrupt and Westernized regime. Educated urban women took the veil as a symbol of their dissent, but many never expected veiling to become permanent. About one and a half years after the revolution, Ayatollah Khomeini declared that he would like to see women in "modest" dress, and soon thereafter veiling became mandatory. The Islamists argued that women had lost their honor and dignity under the Shah, who openly embraced a Western value system. Rich Iranian women, famous worldwide for their love of extravagant designer fashions and opulent jewelry, were suddenly the targets of the mullahs. In contrast to the self-indulgent and highly Westernized Iranian women of old, the showpieces of the Shah's regime, the ideal woman as popularized by the Iranian sociologist Ali Shariati should be noble, chaste, and antimaterialistic.[7] The new image of the model woman was part of cleansing Iranian culture and society of the dreaded disease of *gharbzadegi*, or occidentosis.

Twenty years after the Islamic revolution, many Iranian women in the middle and upper classes are shedding as much of the veil as they dare. They are pushing to the limits a window of social and political reforms since President Mohammad Khatami came to power in August 1997. Their well-to-do sisters in Egypt, meanwhile, are taking to the veil in increasing numbers. This stark contrast illustrates the great difference between Iran, a country whose Islamic system was largely imposed from the top down, and Egypt, a society that is creating an Islamic order from the bottom up, with genuine support from the general population.

In nearby Turkey, not long ago the center of the vast Islamic Ottoman Empire and once home to the highest authority in Sunni Islam, veiling has also emerged as one of the most contentious and divisive issues facing the country. In fact, efforts by Turkey's first elected Islamist prime minister, Necmettin Erbakan, to ease restrictions in 1996 on veiling in government offices and on university campuses—part of a package of symbolic but largely hollow "Islamist" reforms—kicked off a wave of hysteria in the mainstream press and helped doom his government. Secularist forces backed by the powerful army forced Erbakan from office in June 1997 and outlawed his Welfare party.

Turkey's debate over the veil dates from the earliest days of the republic, pulled together from the remnants of the Ottoman Empire. Kemal Ataturk, secularist founder of modern Turkey, outlawed the fez—the brimless felt cap that allowed the wearer to touch his head to the ground in prayer—and other forms of Islamic dress for men in his famous "hat speech," delivered in a small Black Sea coastal town in 1925. He used similar appearances to actively discourage the veil. Although never banned outright, headscarves and other forms of veiling were eventually barred from government offices, parliament, state universities, and all public institutions.

Ataturk, who had little time for religion himself, viewed the cloak, the veil, and the fez as vestiges of a failed and outmoded order. Modern Turks were Europeans and as such they should wear suits, ties, and proper hats with brims. Women should not hide their hair or their legs. In his presidential palace in the new capital of Ankara, Ataturk schooled a generation of nation-builders in European ways. Women in low-cut dresses danced, drank, and smoked in public. As later happened in Egypt under Nasser, a secularist "look" emerged from Turkey's political theater, particularly for women.

Yet the veil never vanished completely; it simply remained in seclusion, out of sight and out of mind of the Kemalists, in the towns and villages of the Anatolian steppe. The Turkish peasantry is nothing if not conservative and it would take more than the undoubted dynamism of Ataturk to eliminate the traditional veil, or *turban*. Widespread migration to the major urban centers over the recent decades has seen a profound diffusion of Anatolian culture into Ankara, Istanbul, and other big cities, a process aided by good roads and communications links. Along with their foods, their customs, and their large families, the Anatolian masses brought the veil to the heart of the cities.

"When I was growing up in Istanbul, I had no idea what was a *kebab* or *lachmacun*," a fifty-year-old woman international banker told me at a reception in Istanbul. "We never heard of such foods. And we never saw anyone in the *turban*. We were part of Europe," she added with a faint sigh. Others like her bemoan the loss of Istanbul's "Byzantine" flavor, that mix of Turkish, Greek, Armenian, Jewish, and Italian influences now submerged by a flood of cultural and religious nationalism. This process has been so complete that modern Turkey is today 99 percent Muslim.

Unlike Egypt, where society is caught up in a profound transformation, the rise of Islam in Turkey reflects a long overdue redress of the balance of power between a Europeanized elite and the traditional masses. Despite their defeat at the hands of the army and their secularist political allies, Turkey's Islamists remain a powerful presence. And veiling remains as problematic for Turks as ever. Islamist university students, banned by the secularist officials from wearing either veils or the small "Islamic" beard in the ID photographs required for taking examinations, show no signs of ending their periodic protests, which frequently include clashes with security forces. Islamist lawyers, doctors, and professors, meanwhile, continue to challenge the ban on headscarves in courtrooms, state hospitals, and classrooms, often invoking Turkey's public endorsement of universal human rights, including freedom of religion, in support of their demand.

In May 1999, a newly elected Islamist member of parliament caused an uproar when she tried to wear her headscarf inside the halls of Turkey's Grand National Assembly, a move seen by many in authority as a direct assault on official secularism. The deputy, Merve Kavakci, was chased from the hall by jeering leftwing deputies while the conservative majority sat in embarrassed silence. The cabinet later stripped her of her Turkish citizenship, after an inquiry found that she had obtained a U.S. passport while living in America. Kavakci has appealed the decision.

Despite the ebb and flow of Turkey's debate on the veil, it is essentially a static situation, framed more by enduring forces of class and tradition than by the dynamics of religious revivalism. The "conversion" of a leading Turkish celebrity aside, the broader movement toward Islam and the veil among well-off, educated women resembling Mona, DelJane, and Suzanne is virtually unthinkable in Turkey. The dividing lines between the secular and the religious are too deep, too rigid. Nor is the common Egyptian tableau of a veiled daughter walking with her "uncovered," Westernized mother likely to be encountered anytime soon in the streets of Istanbul or Ankara, where often only the older women of a family are veiled.

It is the fluidity of Egyptian society, as well as its long-standing relationship to religion, that helped create the current climate of the Islamic revival, conditions lacking in Turkey and, to a large extent, in the Islamic Republic of Iran. The disenfranchised of Imbaba, the dissident *sheikhs* of al-Azhar, the emerging Islamist professional classes, university students, and a broad spectrum of women have all emerged as distinct and vital players in this drama. In a society that places so much emphasis on the role of women as "bearers of culture"—as the guarantors of the health and survival of the community of believers—it is perhaps this latter constituency that harbors the greatest long-term danger to the secular regime now in power. Ayatollah Khomeini, who must rank as one of the greatest revolutionary tacticians of the twentieth century, understood the vital role of women in the Islamic movement: "If women change, the society changes." This is all the more so when the women in question are educated, rich, and powerful.

For his part, Kafi was convinced that it was his access to the upper echelons of society, rather than the specific content of his sermons and lessons, that drove the state to ban him from the pulpit and place him temporarily under house arrest. "No one told me the reason," he explained, four years after his ban. "But I think the main reason was that I had infiltrated a certain class of society—businessmen's wives, the wives of cabinet ministers, actresses. The state didn't like this."

7

COURT OF PUBLIC OPINION

asr Hamed Abu Zeid was always a reluctant professor of Islamic studies. As an undergraduate in Cairo University's Faculty of Arts in the early 1970s, he had every intention of steering clear of such a sensitive subject. There were enough examples for him to know that the road ahead would be filled with professional, and even personal, risk. Rationalist Islamic thinkers, such as the poet Taha Hussein and the scholar Sheikh Mohammed Ahmad Khalafallah, had been persecuted by the religious authorities at al-Azhar for their maverick interpretations of the Koran and the holy texts decades earlier. In Hussein's case, al-Azhar attacked his book *Pre-Islamic Poetry*, and he was removed from a position he held at Cairo University in 1931 by Egypt's then prime minister. Unless he were inclined to confine himself to a literal interpretation of the Koran, something the young Abu Zeid was not prepared to do, he risked academic suicide at the hands of traditionalist scholars and their powerful backers among the *ulama*. But by the time he began his career as an assistant in the department of Arabic, Faculty of Letters, a university committee had decided that the shortage of professors in Islamic studies had reached crisis proportions. Abu Zeid was instructed to devote his masters and doctoral research to the subject.

Almost exactly twenty years later, Abu Zeid's career came to an abrupt end precisely as he had feared. He was denied a promotion within his department, amid charges that his scholarly works were blasphemous under Islam. Exhibit A was his latest book, *Critique of Islamic Discourse*, published in 1992. But unlike most of the other scholars who had dared to challenge traditional interpretations of the holy book, Abu Zeid's ordeal did not remain within the confines of the Ivory Tower. Abd al-Sabour Shahin, a *sheikh* in a popular Cairo mosque and a professor who had voted against Abu Zeid in the promotion vote, helped take the case to court.

Backed by a team of Islamist lawyers, in 1993 Shahin charged Abu Zeid with heresy. The lawyers used an almost forgotten principle of Islamic law called *hisba*, allowing them to take legal action against a fellow Muslim to defend the faith; they argued that because Abu Zeid's writing had made him an apostate, he could no longer remain married to his Muslim wife, the scholar Ibtihal Yunis. The Egyptian Appellate Court agreed and invalidated their marriage. The verdict left the couple with no choice but to flee Egypt for the West. They now live in exile in the Netherlands.

The court ruled that, in his writings, Abu Zeid had denied that the Koran was the word of God as revealed to the Prophet Mohammed. He had cast doubt on the existence of heaven and hell, saying such ideas were based on legend. And he rejected the Muslim belief that the Sunna, the traditions of the Prophet, were handed down from God.

The Abu Zeid case exploded across the rarefied world of Arab secularist intellectuals, with aftershocks felt as far away as the literary *salon*s of London, Paris, and New York. It also unmasked an Egyptian legal system in turmoil after more than a century of tug-of-war between competing demands of Westernization dictated from above and religious authenticity driven from below. Foreign human rights and literary associations, including the influential PEN literary societies, were quick to label the affair a violation of freedom of expression. They compared Abu Zeid's plight to that of author Salman Rushdie. In 1989, Ayatollah Ruhollah Khomeini issued a *fatwa*, or religious edict, calling for Rushdie's death for blaspheming the Prophet in his novel *The Satanic Verses*. The *fatwa* said: "I announce to the courageous Muslim believers of the world that the author of the book, *The Satanic Verses*, which is against Islam and the Prophet and the Koran, be condemned to death." Khomeini's order extended to the book's publishers as well. "I ask all brave Muslim believers that wherever they find these people immediately execute them so that no one else will dare insult the sanctities of Muslims and whoever is killed in this path is a martyr." Islamic groups placed bounties on his head, and Rushdie was assigned a twenty-four-hour security detail by British authorities.

But the essence of the case brought against Abu Zeid was never about Western notions of civil liberties or freedom of expression. Instead, the Cairo courts chose to address some of the most contentious philosophical issues facing contemporary Muslims: What limits should modern-day Muslims recognize in interpreting the Islamic texts? Can this process of interpretation, or *ijtihad*, be adapted to historical change, or is it locked in time? If *ijtihad* is permitted, who should be authorized to conduct this process? Should individuals be allowed to declare someone an apostate on behalf of the *umma*, the Muslim community of believers? After all, those filing the case against the professor were not personally harmed by his writings, the traditional standard for bringing an action in civil courts. In a direct appeal to the overriding authority of the holy texts, the plaintiffs based their case on the Koranic injunction that every Muslim has a responsibility to promote good and combat evil for the benefit of the community of believers.

The Abu Zeid affair, a public relations disaster for Egypt's image in the West, revealed the structural weaknesses of a legal system patched together from the Ottoman and colonialist periods. Like other central institutions of Egyptian life, including the universities, al-Azhar, and the professional unions, the court system was slipping away from the secularist regime. And as with these institutions, much of the turmoil within the judiciary can be traced back to mistakes and miscalculations of Egypt's secularist masters.

Chief among these was a 1971 decision by President Sadat to give in to demands from the Islamists, as part of the payoff for their devout anticommunism, for a constitutional amendment declaring Islamic holy law, the *sharia*, to be "a principal source of legislation." In 1980, the same clause was strengthened further, making *sharia* "*the* principal source of legislation." While Islamist jurists contend, with considerable justification, that this amendment has never been properly implemented, its effect was to throw all of Egyptian jurisprudence into question. As a result, modern secularist notions, including the state's right to restrict Islamic dress in public schools or ban the practice of female circumcision, were opened up to legal challenge by a growing corps of Islamist lawyers and magistrates.

For the Islamists who accused Abu Zeid of apostasy, the debate came at an opportune time. The militant movement was at full strength, and moderate Islamists were making significant progress in promulgating the importance of being a good Muslim. At Cairo University, well-organized Islamic student groups were demanding that the state be ruled according to a strict reading of *sharia* law. Outspoken voices within the faculty also participated in the religious revival by means of activities within their clubs. Intellectual debate that had once centered on the Enlightenment and Western intellectual history shifted its focus to Islamic philosophy and the reinterpretation of the Islamic texts. Leading proponents of Islamic studies were bolstered by the *sheikh*s at al-Azhar, who made public their determination to safeguard the substance and direction of religious discussion.

It was in the midst of this highly charged environment that Abu Zeid faced his accusers. At first, his lawyers advised him to apologize for his writings and reaffirm that he was a believer. According to Islamic law, this would have blocked any attempt to declare him an apostate. But Abu Zeid refused on principle; he felt such a course would set a dangerous precedent for courts to inquire about a person's faith, which he believed to be a violation of civil liberties. He refused even after one of his lawyers quit in protest, warning that the case would be lost if Abu Zeid did not affirm his devotion to his faith and drop his defense of freedom of expression. "I told him to go to court and say he is a Muslim, and he refused, saying, 'If I do this they will say I wasn't a Muslim in the past,'" the lawyer, Amira Bahi al-Din, told me.

Under the influence of both Egyptian and foreign human rights advocates, Abu Zeid miscalculated the direction the legal debate would take and assumed the case would turn only on his right to free speech, regardless of whether his ideas could be considered heretical. He also misread the emerging trends among contemporary Egyptian courts, assuming the judiciary would be bound by Western legal tradition to distinguish between religious and civil law. Until his case, court decisions seemed untouched by the growing Islamization of society at large; like many intellectuals critical of the religious revival, Abu Zeid lived in a state of denial, taking comfort in the mistaken notion that the renewal of Islam was limited to a few marginal groups.

The Giza Court of First Instance, the lower court, had boosted Abu Zeid's early optimism. The court dismissed the petition against him by relying on rules applicable in civil courts, arguing that his accusers had no personal interest in the effect of his writings and therefore lacked standing in the matter. By the time the case was appealed by the plaintiffs, it had become a scandal. Abu Zeid assumed that the state would intervene in the Appellate Court decision to save face in front of the Western world and avoid a replay of the Rushdie affair. By that time, Islamic groups stretching from Pakistan to Iran, Afghanistan, Algeria, and the Gaza Strip were calling for Rushdie's death and the execution of other writers who had insulted the Prophet or questioned the authenticity of the Islamic texts. The U.S. and British governments had turned Rushdie into a cause célèbre, using Khomeini's *fatwa* to justify a foreign policy that condemned Islamic activism around the world. Iran believed this policy ignored the basic laws in Islam regarding the holy texts and the Prophet. Many moderate theologians to this day believe expression in Islam is not absolute. Therefore, Rushdie should be judged according to Islamic law, not Western standards of free expression and human rights. Many in the Islamic world saw the Rushdie affair as a convenient weapon deployed by the West to brand Iran a pariah state and denounce political Islam as barbarian.

When considering Abu Zeid's case, the Egyptian courts were indirectly influenced by the Rushdie affair. The courts were experiencing the same religious transformation as the universities, the syndicates, the *ulama*, and society in general. The courts and the *sheikh*s were engaging in a bit of role reversal: while the doctors of religion at al-Azhar were exceeding their authority by passing judgment on which aspects of life should fall under the scrutiny of the *sharia* code, the judges likewise were overstepping their own traditional mandate and entering the realm of religion. Faced with questions relating to religion, they took it upon themselves to decide proper Islamic behavior. Al-Azhar and the courts reinforced the opinions held by conservatives in both institutions that society must be protected from intellectuals who questioned the basic tenets of Islam.

In keeping with the trend that was gathering pace in Egyptian society, the Appellate court decided that the Abu Zeid case should be considered in accordance with *sharia* rules. The court took advantage of an ambiguity in Egyptian jurisprudence. In 1955, Egypt abolished its *sharia* courts, but blurred the distinction between religious and secular law. After 1955, the state insisted that civil courts continue to apply the same rules as the *sharia* courts in matters of personal status, domestic and religious endowments. When the constitution was amended in 1980, making the *sharia* the primary source of legislation, it was due to political rather than religious considerations. In pushing through the amendment as a concession to the Islamists, Sadat failed to consider the long-term effects. The Appellate Court decided that the rules of Hanafite jurisprudence, one of four leading schools of law under Sunni Islam, should be applied in the Abu Zeid case. Those rules recognize every Muslim's obligation to resort to *hisba*. Thus, the main issue at stake was not the fate or freedom of Abu Zeid and his wife, but the public interest of the Muslim community.

The court's decision to refer to the *sharia* resurrected a debate that had continued intermittently since the 1980s. For years, officials in the parliament and the government had stalled Islamist requests to change those Egyptian laws seen as inconsistent with the *sharia*. Once again, the debate focused on the degree of *sharia* application and the definition of Koranic law itself. Secularists argued that the *sharia* was simply a set of ethical codes. Judge Mohammed Sayyed al-Ashmawi, a leader of the secularist position at the far left of the debate, argued that the Koran provides no provision for a system of government or a system for appointing rulers and no electoral system. All these institutions are left for people to decide. In 1985, he asked: "Do we want to go back to the days of sedition, deviation and oppression, which were perpetrated in the name of religion? True religion has nothing to do with that! Let everyone know that this *dawa* is a political movement, using religion as a mask and the *sharia* as a veil in order to achieve its political goals."[1]

Many of the country's most respected jurists, however, called for full implementation of Islamic law. This was seen as more compatible with Egypt's Islamic culture and heritage than Western codes, largely imported from France. Egypt was fundamentally an Islamic society, they argued, and as such it required an appropriate legal code derived from the Islamic texts and the accompanying Islamic institutions of jurisprudence.

"We want to apply *sharia* for so many different reasons," said Ahmed Kamal Abu-Magd, a former cabinet minister under Sadat and today one of Egypt's most respected lawyers. "One, it complements our own culture, our own belief, because in Islam you cannot at all separate *sharia*, which are injunctions ordained in the Koran and the Sunna, from their historic Islamic teachings; it is a personification . . . of the orthodox principles of the faith in real life. How can we become politically independent while we continue to be dependent on the culture of others, transplanting it into the world of Islam where it may produce very different products?"[2]

Tariq al-Bishri, head of the High Administrative Court and the man who extended the powers of al-Azhar to the cultural realm, has written extensively on the application of the *sharia*. During the years of national debate, Bishri became the counterpoint to Ashmawi. He believes Egypt has not gone far enough in its application of the *sharia*, but he also emphasizes that Islamic law can be applied in degrees. "When we ask for the application of the *sharia* we are not asking to relive a past historical era. We are simply asking to draft from the *sharia*, as a divine condition and original laws, and to learn from all the historical experiences that occurred after the 'message.' One is aware that the application of the *sharia* is never perfect because it is man-made according to time and place, according to history. Therefore, our movement will always strive toward the ideal realization of the revealed *sharia* law."[3]

The views of al-Bishri and Abu-Magd were shared by far more conservative Islamists. Abd al-Sabour Shahin was preaching the same message from his pulpit in Cairo's Amr Ibn al-As mosque. *Sheikh*s in al-Azhar's Islamic Research Academy used the Abu Zeid case to renew calls for full implementation of the *sharia*. Yussef al-Badri, a freelance radical cleric who was the noisiest voice in declaring Abu Zeid an apostate, also joined the chorus. Badri was a former member of the national parliament, but when he left office he decided to take his political activity outside the system. In the late 1980s, when many Egyptian Islamists were beginning to transport their ideas to the United States, he had preached in a mosque in New Jersey. But since then, the U.S. government had placed him on a blacklist and denied him a visa, leaving Badri to concentrate all his efforts in his native land. Before the Appellate Court verdict was handed down, Badri called on Abu Zeid to change his mind. "Islamists are not criminals or terrorists. We have no guns, bombs, sticks or chains, no power but our faith. . . . If Zeid were to renounce his writings we would happily embrace him as our brother."[4]

Judge Faruq Abd al-Aleem Mursi wrote the sixteen-page verdict against Abu Zeid. Like so many other Egyptian professionals and technocrats, Abd al-Aleem Mursi had spent years in economic exile in the arch-conservative society of Saudi Arabia, where he had come into direct contact with the kingdom's austere *wahabbi* brand of Islam. The decision concluded that Abu Zeid's writings constituted apostasy beyond any doubt.

The court cited the following passage in his *Criticism of Religious Discourse* as evidence that the professor had contradicted the teachings of the Koran: "The text, [the Koran] from the moment it descended over the Prophet has been transformed from being a divine text to a human understanding because it changed from revelation to utterance. The Prophet's understanding of the text represents the first stages of transformation to an interaction of the text with a human mind." In other words, the revelations of God had entered the realm of human discourse—and thus implicitly lost their divine nature— once they entered the consciousness of the Prophet Mohammed and were then delivered up to mankind.

According to court documents, these passages led the judges to conclude that Abu Zeid was guilty as charged. "This proves that the defendant denies the divinity of the Koran and emphasizes that it is a human text." The court's logical conclusion was that Abu Zeid was an apostate, adding, "An apostate is someone who rejects one of God's orders or those of His Prophet. This puts him outside the realm of Islam whether the rejection is based on doubt or unwillingness to submit. For God has ruled that those who do not submit to the Prophet are not faithful."

The final section of the verdict scolded the professor for spreading his ideas to his students. "Abu Zeid has turned his back on Islam and moreover he exploited his job as a professor teaching university students and started to teach these lies against the book of God and compelled his students to study these books."

Abu Zeid clearly intended to criticize modern Islamic thought, but he never meant to deny his Muslim faith. Instead, he argued that modern Islamists refused to acknowledge that even the Koran was relevant to a certain historical time period and was progressive for the time in which it was written. Therefore, the same progressive approach of the Koran should be applied in the modern world. In his latest book, Abu Zeid declared an intellectual war against the "self-serving, preconceived ideological reading" of the Koran by contemporary Islamists who were "guided literally by the heritage of the past, in order to give them the historical depth, and consequently the legitimacy they lacked."[5]

The afternoon I met Abd al-Sabour Shahin, long after the Abu Zeid case had ended, he was just as adamant in his position as he had been in the heat of the legal battle. He received me in his office at Cairo University in the Dar-al-Ulum faculty, historically a breeding ground for Islamist students. His office was bare, and his laser voice filled the emptiness in the room. By that time, Shahin had risen to pariah status among the guardians of free expression. He was associated with those branded as "extremists," lumped together with the Yussef al-Badris and the Omar Abd al-Kafis. As a graduate of al-Azhar University and a child influenced by the teachings of Hasan al-Banna, Shahin had the classic background of a contemporary Islamic activist. He had managed to hold on to his position as a professor; it was never in jeopardy, he said, "because the university was one hundred percent behind me in the Abu Zeid case." But in the Amr Ibn al-As mosque, where the state had direct control, Shahin was banned from preaching after the Abu Zeid trial.

As he sat behind his desk stroking his short beard, a wry smile fixed on his face, I asked him if he would bring a *hisba* case against another writer like Abu Zeid.

"Did you deny Abu Zeid the right to freedom of expression?" I asked.

"It wasn't me who banned him," he replied in a measured tone. "All the courts were with me. In the West, they don't allow someone to insult Jesus. In America, you are not allowed to insult the Jews. Freedom in religion is not absolute. If someone shows that they are against Islam, I will fight. Anyway, banning Abu Zeid's books made him famous. No one had ever heard of the man before we took him to court. Now, look at him. He is famous, living a nice life in the West."

"Do you believe Farag Foda should have been killed?" I asked him. "And what do you say to your critics who believe that, through your condemnation of writers like Abu Zeid, you encourage extremists to strike against them?"

Shahin did not rise to the bait. "All these cases should be handled by the courts. The Farag Foda case should have been settled in court."

Shahin certainly was considered a man on the periphery of the Islamic movement. But his views on this subject were no different from those held by the most well-reasoned, progressive ayatollahs in Iran who made similar arguments regarding Salman Rushdie. "Blaspheming the Prophet is unlawful in Islam," Hojatolislam Mohsen Kadivar, a religious scholar in Tehran explained to me when discussing the *fatwa* against Rushdie. "It is no different than other religions. In Christianity, you are not allowed to insult Jesus Christ. . . . This issue has nothing to do with freedom of expression."

In an interview in 1997 from his exile in the Netherlands, Abu Zeid said his case showed a lack of solidarity among Muslims. "Where is the unity in Islam now? I mean would someone like to say where it is? It is an illusion. We have to learn, not only Muslims, but the whole world, to respect differences. I think diversity is not something evil, it is a wealth, richness, and it should be emphasized. We can't lose our unity because we are different. . . . God created us different in order to understand each other, not to fight each other."[6]

One of Abu Zeid's lawyers, Khalil Abd al-Kareem, raised perhaps the most profound question in the aftermath of the verdict, one that lies at the heart of the judicial and religious debate. Kareem declared that the judge had, in effect, issued a *fatwa* against Abu Zeid, not a legal opinion. "The judge of the court of appeals has entered into very dangerous territory, that of accusing a professor of Koranic studies in the faculty of arts of apostasy, without being himself qualified for it. Does the judge who has issued the *fatwa* in the robes of a verdict know the book of God and know its invalid verses from valid ones and know the Sunna? . . . He may be knowledgeable about local positive laws, but he has no right to issue a *fatwa*."[7]

With the successful prosecution of Abu Zeid behind them, the Islamists declared their readiness to use the *hisba* statute against other prominent writers who they believed had blasphemed Islam. Yussef al-Badri, the renegade *sheikh*, presented a list of forty potential targets, among them the Nobel laureate Naguib Mahfouz. At first, cases involving writers such as Abu Zeid were brought only by Islamists on the periphery of the movement. The Muslim Brotherhood did not consider Yussef al-Badri a member, and the *sheikh*s at al-Azhar tried to distance themselves from his personal crusades. But over time, the opinions of figures on the margins came to coincide with those within the mainstream Islamic movement.

For the secularists, the verdict was enough of a shock. They feared the Islamists would be inspired to begin a witch hunt to cleanse society of intellectuals who did not share their views. The pursuit of such writers and thinkers was termed "intellectual terrorism" by the secular press. If not for the *hisba* statute, Abu Zeid's faith would never have been put on trial. Thus, the secularists worked to prevent *hisba* from ever being used in such cases again. They based their campaign on the argument that *hisba* is not stated in the Koran, but was established as a *hadith* under the Abbasid dynasty when its forces were fighting Persian rebels.

The People's Assembly, or parliament, answered the secularists' call by passing a law in January 1996 prohibiting individuals from using *hisba* in civil courts to break up the marriages of writers and intellectuals accused of heresy. Only the state's general prosecutor now has the right to file such cases, according to the new law. Individuals wishing to file petitions based on *hisba* must first present the complaint to the general prosecutor. If the case is accepted, it is pursued by the prosecutor's office and the private plaintiffs take no part in the legal proceedings. The attorney general has the final say in whether a case will be filed in court and has thirty days to reverse decisions by state prosecutors. The new law was drafted to ensure state control over *hisba* cases, and to make it impossible to take petitions directly before judges whose sympathies may lie with the Islamic cause.

In tactical terms, secularists backed by the central authorities and the loyalist parliament appear to have successfully de-fanged the *hisba* statute, but they have made no strategic inroads against growing Islamic influence within either the legal profession or the judiciary. This development reflects the increasing demands of the broader society for an Islamic system that addresses their personal and religious values on the one hand and the particular vulnerability of the legal system to the Islamist message on the other. "It is not without reason that today's Islamic radicalism can attack contemporary (legal) systems and denounce an almost total forgetfulness of the Islamic *sharia*. For the advocates of radical Islam, the abandonment of the *sharia* is synonymous with depersonalization and loss of culture," wrote legal scholar Bernard Botiveau.[8]

Secular legal systems based in large measure on European law have existed throughout much of the Muslim world since the nineteenth century. In Egypt during the British occupation, new codes were first introduced by the Mixed Courts in 1876, created after much international negotiation to hear cases involving foreign interests. The Egyptian state was eager to reduce or eliminate the power of foreign consuls to preside over legal matters involving their own citizens. In exchange, it was forced to accept European codes and jurists. Seven years later, this trend spread to the new National Courts, which had jurisdiction over civilian and criminal cases involving Egyptians.[9] With the creation of the National courts, the *sharia* courts were restricted to matters of personal status, such as marriage, divorce, and inheritance, and remained that way until they were eventually combined with the National Court system in 1956.

These early changes attracted scant protest at the time, exciting little if any resistance to what many contemporary Egyptian Islamists now regard as the debasement of the sacred *sharia* and its relegation to second-class status behind an alien, imported legal system. Some scholars say that a secular legal system was so readily accepted because the *sharia* was never in fact the prevailing rule of law in the Muslim world. For them, the relatively smooth introduction of European law and the partial abandonment of the *sharia* suggest that preexisting codes were based more on tribal law, custom, and the edicts of rulers than on holy Islamic texts. But other experts have suggested that it was the later degradation of the traditional legal institutions and the scholarly and theological methods that made up Islamic jurisprudence as a whole that sparked the modern-day backlash. The introduction of elements of European law only emerged as a central political and social question when the institutions and practices accompanying implementation of the *sharia* came under threat—a much more recent phenomenon and one that continues to this day.[10]

Whatever the role of the *sharia* courts in Egyptian history, there is little doubt that demands among modern Islamists for the return of *sharia* law stem from a feeling that Islam was shunted aside at the hands of foreign rulers in the name of a now-bankrupt "modernity." From their vantage point, the return of Koranic law is a return to cultural authenticity and a rejection of Western intrusion. In modern Egypt, the demand to reinstate the *sharia* became more urgent during the 1950s, when the Muslim Brotherhood was enjoying considerable political power. Abd al-Qadir Awda, an ideologue in the Brotherhood and a civil judge, claimed that Muslims were obliged to be ruled under the *sharia* and to combat laws that contradicted it.[11] Awda was executed in Nasser's massive crackdown on the Brotherhood, but he inspired those who followed him. By the 1970s, the Islamic movement sought to reconcile the contradictions between Western, positive law and the *sharia*, even if this meant rewriting parts of the legal code. As long as states such as Egypt continue to avoid changing laws to accord more fully with the *sharia*, Islamists will continue to find legal loopholes, such as the *hisba* statute, to bring cases before personal status courts or into a realm in which the *sharia* can be applied.

Since the early 1990s, two other emotive issues before Egypt's courts, the veiling of schoolgirls and the practice of female circumcision, reflected this struggle to redirect important social, religious, and cultural matters back into the realm of the traditional *sharia*. After the scandal sparked during the 1994 UN Population Conference by the CNN broadcast that showed a ten-year-old girl being circumcised, Egypt's Minister of Health issued a decree banning circumcisions from being performed in public hospitals, but not private ones. In July 1996, a subsequent health minister declared that no licensed medical professional could perform the operation unless it were required for health reasons.

Once again, buoyed by public outrage over the ban, a coalition of Islamists, including conservative *sheikh*s from al-Azhar, Islamist lawyers, and the freelance crusader, Sheikh Yussef al-Badri, took the state to court. The lawsuit, filed by Badri, claimed that the ban was a violation of the *sharia*, which he said calls for Muslim girls to be circumcised. Public debate between the Islamists and human rights activists reached a fever pitch after the Grand Sheikh of al-Azhar, Gad al-Haq, issued a *fatwa* calling on the government to execute anyone who opposed the practice. The Egyptian Organization of Human Rights in turn filed a lawsuit against Gad al-Haq, who is appointed by state authorities.

The opinion of the *fatwa* committee at al-Azhar contained a phrase many found outrageous. Writing for the committee, Sheikh Atiyah Saqr cited a famous narrator of the *hadith*s named al-Bukhari, who lived about 1,000 years ago. In discussing one *hadith*, al-Bukhari said circumcision was as "natural" as shaving a woman's pubic hair, shaving hair under the armpits, clipping a mustache, or trimming one's fingernails—all commonly associated with Islamic mores.

The general consensus among scholars is that the practice of female excision is pre-Islamic and originated in Africa, witnessed by the fact that it is unknown in many other Islamic societies. Circumcision is most common today in Sudan, where it is referred to as "pharaonic circumcision" and in countries located in the Horn of Africa. The tradition in Egypt is well documented before the Arab invasions. A Greek papyrus of 163 B.C. notes the excision of a young girl "according to the custom of Egyptians" as a premarital rite.[12] The Greek geographer Strabo visited Egypt in 25–24 B.C. and reported that "one of the customs most zealously observed by the Egyptians" was that they "circumcise" their boys and "excise" their girls.[13]

Once the CNN program had exposed to the world the fact that circumcision of girls remained widely practiced in Egypt, the state was compelled to act. Until then, the authorities had taken no steps to actively eliminate the rite, despite pleas from human rights groups and nongovernmental organizations. But with the world spotlight on Cairo, officials were lodged in a political dilemma. To take no action would lead the world to assume that Egypt was a backward country that condones medieval practices proven to be medically harmful. But to ban the practice risked giving the Islamists a weapon to turn society further against the state, whose official position was being championed by women's rights groups, the secularist press, and human right's organizations. Before the CNN program, women's groups had worked quietly behind the scenes to change public opinion and decrease the rate of female circumcision. But once they were forced to publicly defend their position, any hope of convincing women not to circumcise their daughters was lost under the crush of religious absolutism.

Shortly after he became the Grand Sheikh of al-Azhar, Mohammed Sayyed Tantawi, following in the footsteps of many grand *sheikh*s before him, tried to give religious sanction to the state's position in order to shield the government from the wrath of the Islamists. He declared: "The Prophet's sayings concerning female circumcision are either weak or doubtful. . . . I myself didn't circumcise my daughter, circumcision is a habit. Whoever wants to undertake it, that is fine. He who doesn't want to should not be forced to do so."[14]

Instead of changing public opinion, Tantawi lost credibility as the country's designated *imam*. His position was directly at odds with conservative *sheikh*s in al-Azhar's Islamic Research Academy who issued a statement shortly after the UN Population Conference saying that female circumcision is legal in Islam and cannot be considered a crime. Tantawi's remarks also contradicted earlier comments he had made as the Mufti of Egypt when he said he favored a mild form of circumcision. Few believed he had suddenly changed course. But it did not matter; Egyptians were able to find confirmation for their belief elsewhere, among the dozens of other prominent *sheikh*s who told them what they wanted to hear. Egypt's Islamists and the faithful, who circumcise an estimated 97 percent of all Egyptian girls, cited the *hadith*s when making their case that the practice is a religious requirement. One *hadith* often cited is when Umm Atiya al-Ansariyya reports that the Prophet enjoined a female circumciser in Medina: "Do not destroy it completely for that is more favorable for the woman and preferable for the husband."[15] This *hadith*, however, is considered "weak" because of a dubious chain of transmitters extending from the Prophet to the present day, and many scholars doubt its authenticity. The Prophet's instructions to the female circumciser holds a slightly different interpretation in a *hadith* with a separate Shi'ite chain of authority, addressed to a woman named Umm Habib: "If you perform the operation, do no crush or uproot it, but rather take only a small portion for that is easier for the woman (literally it makes her face more radiant) and more favorable for the husband."[16]

This latter interpretation is the one held among a majority of Islamists in Egypt. By clipping only the foreskin of the clitoris, the Islamists believe the religious duty is fulfilled and the girl endures less physical duress from the operation, making it more humane. For centuries, Egyptian villagers have taken the foreskin and wrapped it in a loaf of bread before casting it into the Nile River—a custom believed to ensure the girl's fertility.

Many Islamist leaders I met over the years favored this limited form of circumcision, not out of a belief that it was necessary for fertility but to control a woman's sexual desires. Once the clitoris is clipped, an intense orgasm is nearly impossible. Islamists believe that if a woman's sexual desires are controlled, the rate of extramarital affairs will be limited and the sanctity of the Muslim family preserved. Married men who may be inclined to seduce women will find fewer willing partners. Clipping only the foreskin of the clitoris also allows women to have normal intercourse with their husbands, the Islamists say. The full form of female genital mutilation scars girls so severely that intercourse and childbearing are often so painful that women avoid them. The Islamists believe this is not in the interest of the Muslim community.

One booklet written by a *sheikh* at al-Azhar and distributed outside Cairo mosques discusses the benefits of circumcision. An uncircumcised woman is "unnatural," the author, Sheikh Mohammed al-Sayyed al-Shinnawi writes. He then goes on to list the drawbacks of an uncircumcised woman: unstable sexual appetite that may lead to sin; repeated tension and mental disturbance for the woman; repeated contact with clothing (especially for those who wear tight clothing) that may lead to a heightened sexual appetite. This in turn stirs up body cells, which may lead to infections or even cancer.[17] The author also argues that Egyptian females, more so than those in other countries, need to be circumcised. "Doctors in Egypt say the outer sexual organs of Egyptian women tend to be larger than those of women in other societies. Hence, the need for circumcision of most women in Egypt."[18]

In June 1997, the Administrative Court answered Yussef al-Badri's challenge to the Health Minister's decree banning circumcision. The court canceled the decree based on a legal technicality: Any ban should have been proposed by the health minister in the form of draft legislation and then approved by the parliament, the court said. The minister had no authority to declare the practice illegal. The health ministry then appealed the decision to the High Administrative Court. The court disagreed with the Islamists, saying that circumcision is not required in the Koran and is not a stipulation in the *sharia*. Therefore, it is not the personal right of Muslims to circumcise their daughters. By ruling that the matter did not fall under the *sharia*, the court applied positive law to the case and concluded that the practice harms the human body and is not medically necessary. The court declared that the matter was within the authority for the health minister to decide, and the ban he had issued should stand.

Among the lawyers representing the state in the case was Seleem al-Awa, one of the country's brightest lawyers and a leading figure among the Islamists. Al-Awa is respected for being able to put aside his religious beliefs when deciding legal matters. In the months of debate, al-Awa wrote extensively on the subject in the press and spoke out on television programs. In 1996, al-Awa explained his position in the Islamist newspaper, *al-Shaab*. "My opinion is clear. There is no evidence on the permissibility of female circumcision or it being a duty according to the *sharia*. . . . This is purely a medical issue that has nothing to do with religion. . . . Medical experts agree it is a harmful practice, especially on the psychological side. Based on the prophet's saying, 'No harm, no damage,' this practice should be stopped."[19]

Unlike the Abu Zeid case, the *sharia* argument was much more difficult to apply to circumcision; the practice was certainly well established throughout society, but it had no precedent in the Koran and only a tenuous claim on legitimacy from the collected *hadith*s. Nonetheless, many Egyptians involved in the case were surprised by the final outcome, overlooking perhaps the political and social dimensions at work that made victory at the appellate level more problematic. Chief among these was the varying composition of the different courts. One of Egypt's most respected jurists told me that judges in the lower courts were more inclined generally to side with the Islamists. The judges in these courts did not rise or fall based on their politics, and they generally reflected the opinions of society at large rather than those of the ruling secularist elite. It was logical, therefore, that they would side with popular opinion in the circumcision case. Once the matter reached the High Administrative Court, where judges are far more politicized, the state's position and reputation played a role in the decision, the jurist explained. Even Yussef al-Badri appeared less than surprised when the final decision was handed down in December 1997: "This isn't my case, it's a case for all Muslims. I will continue to battle and protect Islam through legal means."

The ruling drew far more attention in Western capitals than in Cairo. Egyptian doctors, the Islamists who had filed the lawsuit, and society at large knew the state had no plans to enforce the ban. Egyptians had been circumcising their daughters for centuries. The operations were performed in state hospitals and clinics and everyone was comfortable with the practice until the Western feminists, NGOs, and human rights activists intervened. The minister had issued his decree in part to calm Western hysteria. Once the outside world was content that action had been taken, life would continue as before. As with many other aspects of daily Egyptian life, a practice popularly seen as part of a good Muslim lifestyle—and backed up by so many impeccable Islamic jurists and scholars—could not be eradicated simply by government fiat.

Moreover, the health ministry decree provided doctors, who most certainly would continue performing the operations, with a convenient loophole. One clause in the order said that circumcision was permitted in cases of "medical necessity." For many doctors, particularly those who consider themselves Islamists, all girls must be circumcised to remain healthy. Without the operation, the clitoris grows and dangles outside the body, and can cause infections. When asked why women in most of the world who are not circumcised remain healthy without the operation, these same doctors often had no reply.

Mounir Mohammed Fawzi is a gynecologist and an activist who led the fight to permit circumcision. Several telephone calls were required to convince Dr. Fawzi to see me. He believed I was working for the U.S. Central Intelligence Agency and I failed to convince him otherwise. His accusations came at the end of my research, by which time I had found myself caught up in a breathtaking range of conspiracy theories. I had been variously accused of spying for the U.S. government, working for Egyptian—or even Israeli—intelligence, and conspiring with underground groups trying to discredit Islamic organizations. I had little patience left for another inquisition, and I told Dr. Fawzi as much. "I am surprised that someone as educated as you would fall victim to such a ridiculous conspiracy theory," I snapped over the telephone, during my final attempt to secure an appointment to see him. "If you don't want to be interviewed, fine. But I am not going to lend credibility to your silly ideas by defending myself. I'm tired," I told him, and abruptly ended the conversation. He phoned the next day and set a date for our meeting.

On a blistering afternoon in June 1998, I hailed a cab from downtown to Dr. Fawzi's clinic in a wealthy part of Heliopolis. For days, the *Khamaseen*, the seasonal dust storms blowing sand in from the desert, had swept through the city. Cairenes close the louvered wooden shutters to their apartments, as part of the seasonal ritual, and stay secluded indoors to escape the hot winds and swirling sand. But I knew if I delayed a few days until the weather improved, he would likely change his mind.

When I walked into his modern clinic off a small commercial street, he greeted me with a smile. He was amicable enough and offered the obligatory cup of tea. I felt slightly foolish over losing my temper the day before. As I expected, he was a bit embarrassed at first to discuss circumcision with a woman. But I had dressed in a long-sleeved shirt and baggy trousers, despite the heat, knowing it would put us both at ease. I decided to ignore his reluctance and forge ahead, as if I were a man conducting the interview.

"Why do you believe a woman should be circumcised?"

"Women have strong sex drives. The only way to ensure order in society is to contain their sexual desires. Also, it has been proven scientifically that women are healthier if they are circumcised, and they have healthier babies. The clitoris can cause infection."

"But don't you think it is unjust to deprive women of having intense orgasms by clipping the clitoris?" I asked, shuffling in my seat after uttering words I knew were a bit extreme for his taste.

"No. This is why there is so much immorality in the West," he replied, in a matter-of-fact tone. "At a young age, girls begin having sex. When they are older they tempt men because they can't control their desires."

Dr. Fawzi told me most of his patients who circumcised their daughters were middle- to upper-class Egyptians. The mere fact that 97 percent of all Egyptian females were circumcised proves its religious significance, he told me. During the years I had spent in Egypt, I was often surprised when I asked educated, well-off Egyptian women if their mothers had circumcised them. They often said yes. Once, I tried to persuade an Egyptian acquaintance who was arranging the operation for his six-year-old daughter to resist social pressure and consider the pain she would have to endure. But he dismissed my concern, and announced to me a few months later that the operation had taken place inside his home and his daughter was fine.

Despite the court ruling, the state and society had made their own implicit agreement. Doctors would continue performing circumcisions, parents would continue believing it is necessary, the *sheikh*s would go on proclaiming the practice an Islamic duty, and human rights groups would claim victory. The state was content at having done its part before the Western world in technically banning circumcision, and CNN took credit for exposing the practice and preventing suffering. But officials had no intention of enforcing the prohibition. How could they when society was never planning to comply with the court decision? The broad span of religious interpretation on display in

Imbaba and in communities across the country dictated proper religious behavior, no matter how distorted that interpretation might be. Given this reality, why would the state take on a political battle it was certain to lose to
the Islamists? "Even if the state believed strongly enough in enforcing the
ban, what are they going to do, send policemen around to clinics like mine
and try to put me out of business?" asked Dr. Fawzi.

If the state and its Islamist critics were prepared to brawl in open court
over the most private details of female sexuality and its proper place in society,
they were certainly fated to confront each other over the highly public institution of veiling. In the early 1990s, when Egyptians were beginning to publicly express their growing religious sentiment, more and more young girls
were arriving at schools wearing various forms of veils from the *hijab* to the
niqab. A tug-of-war developed between teachers and their students. In some
primary and secondary schools, teachers demanded that young girls remove
their *hijab*. In other schools, they made the *hijab* mandatory, but in most
schools teachers were discouraging girls from wearing the *niqab*. By 1994, the
newspapers were filled with stories each day on the struggle under way.
"Shameful Incident in a School in Alexandria!" read one headline in the
newspaper *al-Ahrar* in November 1994. The report concerned a headmistress
in Alexandria who ordered twenty-four schoolgirls to remove their veils. The
students' parents protested, saying the headmistress should remove her own
veil first, before imposing the rule on her students. "Is it permitted in Islam
to Impose the *Hijab* by Force?" read another headline in the same newspaper
in January 1993, reflecting the national debate. The article reported that officials in Shubra al-Khemia, a district in Cairo, were forcing female students
to wear the veil.

The state education minister at first tried to bring order to the schools by
stating publicly that the veil was not compulsory and was not part of the
school uniform. School officials were told they could not prevent girls who
were not veiled from attending classes. In May 1994, minister Baha al-Din
issued a formal decree banning the *niqab*. The less-extreme *hijab* was also
banned in primary schools, but permitted in secondary schools with a written letter of permission from the girl's father. Baha al-Din said the decree
was aimed at preventing some "extremist" teachers from forcing students as
young as six years old to wear the veil. He then transferred 2,000 teachers
who were identified as encouraging veiling to administrative jobs outside the
classrooms. The decree sparked a flurry of criticism. The *fatwa* committee
of al-Azhar called on Baha al-Din to rescind his opinion. The committee
referred to the Koran and Sunna in arguing that Muslim girls must be covered, except for the face and hands, after puberty. "To impose a penalty on
a Muslim girl who observes God's order in this matter, by depriving her of
education and preventing her from going to school . . . is to punish obedience

to God's orders and to encourage disobedience to God Almighty," the *fatwa* committee ruled.

The Islamists urged parents to turn to the courts to reverse the decision, and many did just that. Dozens of suits were filed by outraged parents across the country, making the civil courts the final arbiters of the question: Do the Islamic texts require adolescent girls to be veiled, and if so, should the state impose laws to comply with these texts? Some parents filed suits directly against the education ministry; others challenged individual school administrations, once their daughters were denied entrance to class because they were wearing the *niqab*. When Islamist lawyers representing the parents made their cases in the courts, they argued that the *sharia* must provide the basis for any legal decision. One lawyer who represented parents in the courts was Abd al-Haleem Mandour, long-time representative of Sheikh Omar Abd al-Rahman and many other members of the *Gama'a al-Islamiyya*. For Mandour and lawyers like him, the battle was not legal but religious. "The government argued it was the ministry of education's right to decide school uniforms the same way the ministry of interior decides the uniforms of police officers and soldiers. In response, I pointed out the difference between God's right to decide on a certain uniform and the state's decision. "The court supported God's decision over the state," Mandour explained.

In August 1994, the Cairo Administrative Court ordered the suspension of Baha al-Din's decree banning the *hijab* in primary elementary schools without written parental permission. The court said the *hijab* was part of the school uniform and was a "general freedom" protected by the Egyptian constitution. It said the minister exceeded his powers in issuing the decree and the matter should have first been considered by the parliament. Fahmy Huweidy, an Islamist writer, commented at the time: "With the new ruling, students are allowed to wear the *hijab* without conditions or obstacles.... Public opinion and the *fatwa* committee of al-Azhar made the minister change his mind."[20]

Most of the cases filed against the state concerned the *niqab*, which hides all but the eyes. Some fifty such cases were filed in Cairo courts alone. About 100 other cases were filed by women battling to wear the *niqab* in universities. The court in the end was far less sympathetic to the Islamic argument about the *niqab*, saying there was no evidence in the Islamic texts making it mandatory.

Baha al-Din soon softened his stance. Under a torrent of attacks, he assured Egyptians that no student would be denied entrance to school for wearing the *hijab*, even if she did not have parental permission. In an interview with Baha al-Din, I asked him why the state fought so hard against society's wishes to wear the *hijab* and the *niqab*. He explained that the no-veiling position was a way to eradicate Islamic expression at an early age. The same thinking, he told me, prompted the education ministry to remove pictures of veiled girls from textbooks. "If girls in the primary schools are not veiled and they continue this way for five years, they will never veil. But if you veil from early childhood, then it will be a way of life, and there will be no return."

He also explained that the state believed veiling was used as a symbol by Islamic groups to convince other Egyptians and the outside world of their growing influence and power. "They [Islamic groups] want to tell public opinion and the outside world that they have a majority of support and to claim that all those girls wearing the veil are part of their organization. This is not true. Many girls and women are wearing the veil for economic reasons. They can't afford to go to the coiffeur. In the villages, wearing a cloth around your head is a tradition. It has no religious origin at all."

The courts continued to rule in individual cases filed against particular school and university administrators. In October 1995, a group of Islamist students won a case against Helwan University. The Administrative Judiciary Court in Cairo invalidated a decision by Mohammed al-Gawhari, the university president, forbidding women in *niqab* from entering the university. "Muslim scholars have not banned the wearing of the *niqab* although they have agreed that showing a woman's face was not forbidden. This is why wearing the *niqab* remains a matter of personal freedom and should not be banned or forbidden," the court said.

The Education Ministry appealed the August 1994 decision, and after a two-year battle the Supreme Constitutional Court issued a verdict which stands today. In May 1996, the court declared Baha al-Din's 1994 decree "fully legitimate." The court said: "Personal freedom (of individuals) does not deny the legislator the prerogative to order a unified dress code for certain groups of people in certain places." In an interview, the counselor to the Supreme Constitutional Court said the decision applied to both the *hijab* and the *niqab*. "We do not believe that there is a text that strictly requests Muslim women to take the *hijab*. It is all a matter of different interpretations of the text."[21]

The final decision put a halt to any possibility that parents could continue to sue the state. It gave the education ministry power over the school uniform and hence the power to ban the *niqab*, which the court declared was not an Islamic duty. Nonetheless, the wishes of society prevailed over those of the state. The education ministry officially required parental permission for secondary schoolgirls to wear the *hijab*, but it allowed that requirement to lapse. To venture out into the streets of Cairo, Mansura, Suez, or nearly any large Egyptian town when school recessed in the afternoon was to witness a parade of young girls wearing *hijab*. It was senseless to force millions of fathers to write notes, when it was so obvious that the veil was part of the preferred uniform.

The innate pragmatism that yielded an unwritten truce over the issue of veiling, for many a question of lifestyle, was nowhere in evidence when it came to matters of dogma. In making an acclaimed film based on the biblical figure Joseph, who is also revered by Muslims, Egyptian director Yussef Chahine violated Islam's ban on the depiction of any of the prophets. His film *The Emigrant* collected eight Egyptian film industry awards and played to packed movie houses. It also fell afoul of the Islamists, who initiated a series of court fights to ban the film.

Backed by the opposition daily *al-Shaab*, Islamist lawyers filed suit against Chahine, Egypt's most famous film director, to enforce a demand from the *sheikh*s of al-Azhar that the film be withdrawn for its depiction of the prophet Joseph, known in the Koran as Yussef. Chahine's characterization of the central figure named Ram, taken from the story of Yussef, breached the general code of respect Muslims reserve for religious figures. A Cairo court agreed in December 1994, beginning a cycle of appeals.

In later court rulings upholding the ban, jurists noted that "Ram" was pictured in sensual scenes, kissing and seducing young girls. His family, they said, did not believe in God. Chahine's defense primarily focused on a hair-splitting argument that neither the courts nor thousands of moviegoers believed. The character of Yussef, he argued, was not a characterization of the prophet, but an allegorical figure he had created once inspired by the Koranic story. Chahine used this defense in an effort to avoid being accused of violating a 1983 decree issued by al-Azhar that barred the depictions of the prophets in television, film, or theater productions. Chahine tried to convince his critics that the film was autobiographical: Ram, like Chahine, emigrates to another country and then returns to Egypt.

By the time the case had completed its trek through four Egyptian courts in late 1996, the primacy of religious sensibilities over artistic freedom had been well established. The most decisive court opinion declared that the *sharia* is crystal clear on prohibiting the depiction of the holy prophets or stories relating to them. Egyptian law was unclear on the matter, and the court ordered the country's legislators to "rapidly intervene" and pass a law that would comply with the *sharia*'s intent. This will show, the court said, "that Islam remains above all else."

This was certainly not what secular intellectuals wanted to hear. Chahine, much like the novelist Naguib Mahfouz, was a national symbol of Egypt's acceptance into the Western world. A veteran director who was in his late sixties at the time, Chahine had won numerous awards at foreign film festivals, including Cannes. During the two years of his court battles, his case attracted significant support among secularists whose fear of the Islamic revival hindered any true understanding of its philosophy and ideas. Like his fellow secular crusaders, Chahine's misreading of what was happening to him was reflected in his response to the court decisions: "We should talk first before using arms against each other. We can all see what is happening in Algeria because of a lack of democracy. Innocent people are being killed, including intellectuals and journalists."

Chahine was using the most alarming argument of the secularists, often whipped out when Egyptian reality failed to meet their expectations: If the Islamists continue to be permitted to voice their opinions in institutions such as the courts and al-Azhar, Egypt's secular intellectuals would all soon be dead. Like Salman Rushdie, Chahine failed to acknowledge the Islamic world's general consensus about freedom of expression, which is that such liberties are not absolute. Freedom of expression cannot be applied to a discussion of the most sacred figures and precepts in Islam. Across the Muslim world, the film was criticized for personifying the prophet. In Indonesia, the Ulama Council called on the government to ban the film from moviehouses. The film was also banned in Saudi Arabia. Even the Grand Sheikh of al-Azhar, Tantawi, surmounted his own cautious inclinations to support the case against Chahine. In the course of the court battle, al-Azhar forced Chahine to cut some scenes in the film, even though in the end the censorship did not help his legal defense.

The pitched battle over *The Emigrant*, which often played like a soap opera in the local press, was driven in part by the central role of Egyptian cinema in the cultural, social, and political life of the entire region. Cairo is home to the biggest film industry in the Arab world, its output a staple in cinemas from the Gulf to the Maghreb. Many Arabs master the guttural dialect and earthy humor of the Egyptians solely through exposure to exported films, a sure sign of the power and influence of the cinema. Thus, the industry has found itself at the center of Egypt's cultural wars. Yussef al-Badri, the gadfly *sheikh* from al-Azhar, helped file suit in 1994 against Cairo cinemas for displaying posters of scantily clad women. The *sheikh* and his allies also took on other films, including one that allegedly depicted Islamist lawyers in an unfavorable light.

Secularists also turned to the cinema in the early 1990s, seeking to exploit the undoubted power of the moving image against the Islamists and, in particular, against the armed militants who were then creating havoc throughout Egypt. Film star Adel Imam's *The Terrorist*, released in 1994, took aim at the alleged hypocrisy of the Islamist activists, lampooning them more as interested in sex and material comfort than the struggle for the true faith. The central character, a militant in hiding, entertains sexual fantasies about Western images of women, from Barbie dolls to the pop star Madonna. Hit by a car and then nursed back to health by members of a wealthy secularist family who rescue him from a Cairo street, the terrorist develops a taste for "the good life," depicted here in scenes of the young daughters doing aerobics in tight leotards, a football match featuring the Egyptian national team, and the general ease of the affluent suburbs.

Battered by adverse rulings on social issues such as the Abu Zeid case, the screening of taboo films, and the veiling and circumcision of girls, the secularist state has taken a series of measures to avoid a similar fate in the most sensitive criminal cases, those involving alleged Islamic militants. Since 1992, the Egyptian government has increasingly used its emergency law powers to steer cases against suspected militants away from civilian courts, which it feared might not be able to provide the kind of swift and decisive justice it deemed necessary, and into military tribunals. President Mubarak issued the first such order, Decree 370, in October of that year to send two landmark "terrorism" cases to the Supreme Military Court in the coastal city of Alexandria.

The president defended his actions as justified by the threat the militants posed to Egypt's vital tourist trade, the ability for militants to intimidate civilian judges, and the demands of society at large to end violence in the name of religion. Besides, such orders were well within the scope of the state of emergency, renewed periodically by parliament. But there was another, equally compelling reason: The state was losing confidence that the criminal justice system could resist the tug of the broader Islamic movement. Military courts, as part of the executive branch and subject to strict army discipline, were far less likely to go their own way than civilian tribunals. This was particularly important in many of the militant trials, where evidence against some of the accused was less than compelling and the state's need for deterrence clearly overrode demands for fairness and due process of law.

According to the U.S.-based human rights group Middle East Watch, the three-member military panel heard charges against a total of twenty-eight civilian defendants in the two Alexandria trials. Defense lawyers and rights advocates challenged Decree 370 as unconstitutional and demanded that the trials be heard before civilian judges. The rules of military law were too strict, they argued, with inadequate safeguards for defendants' rights and no avenues of appeal, as required under Egypt's international treaty obligations. The Supreme Administrative Court, however, ruled definitively in May 1993 that the president had been within his legal rights when transferring the cases to military courts. Meanwhile, the Alexandria verdicts had come in. Eight defendants were sentenced to death, all but one *in absentia*. Thirty-one others were given prison sentences, four of them life terms, and nine were acquitted.

Four months later, the Egyptian authorities decided to refer all cases involving attacks on tourists and tourist sites to the military courts. A whole new cycle of arrests, trials, and executions soon began. Again, defense lawyers and rights groups protested. There was too little attention to due process, too much room for torture and abuse, too few guarantees for the accused, they argued. To this day, military courts remain a central weapon in the state's struggle with the militants. They stand as a constant reminder that the ruling secularist elite can no longer count on the very institutions their forefathers created to support a Western-style and "modern" state.

8

TO IRAN AND BACK AGAIN

The lonely drive from Tehran to the Shi'ite holy city of Qom, an hour and a half of monotonous scrublands punctuated by bursts of religious enthusiasm, offered the perfect time to reflect on my long journey through Egypt's own Islamic landscape. There was little else to do but stare into the expanse as it opened up to the right and left of the superhighway linking the political capital to the intellectual center of the Islamic Republic. Our underpowered Paykan sedan periodically passed even more underpowered buses, jammed with pilgrims. The sandy hills ranged along the roadway were dotted with crude mosaics spelling out the names of Shi'ite holy figures: "Ya, Ali" or "Ya, Fatima" and signed by army units, police detachments, and student groups.

Only one landmark provided any real distraction: a massive mausoleum complex, with gilded domes as garish as those darting into the Moscow skyline from the edge of Red Square. This is where Ayatollah Ruhollah Khomeini lies buried, where weeping pilgrims journey by bus at least once a year from their provincial towns. Khomeini's body lies in a massive tomb. When worshippers make the visit, they touch the tomb, hoping his spirit will surface and transport them to a more peaceful state of mind.

But peace has been hard to come by in the Islamic Republic. Twenty years after the revolution, Iran remains the greatest single example of both the success and the failure of political Islam. The militant clerics and their supporters who brought down the monarchy constructed a religious state, but it is still an open question whether they created a religious society. I set out to experience this paradox for myself, and Qom seemed the perfect place to start.

The city itself is hardly remarkable. It's reputation as an ancient holy site and, later, the center for resistance to the Shah is commonly overstated. Yet it undoubtedly represents part of the bedrock, both organizationally and spiritually, of modern-day Iran; no pilgrim in search of the essence of the Islamic Republic can afford to pass it by. There have been mullahs in Qom for centuries, and when I first caught sight of them as I approached the city center, the contrast between their long multilayered tunics with an aura of the Islamic Middle Ages, and the electronic shops, the souvenir kiosks selling plates with pictures of Khomeini, and other trappings of the modern world was jolting. Somehow it was different from seeing a nun gliding over the cobblestones of Rome or a Hasidic rabbi hurrying through New York's Times Square.

The turbaned mullahs glide with uniformed posture, their backs upright and their cloaks flowing neatly to keep pace with their movements. Some wear open-backed flat leather shoes, restricting their stride. Others prefer bright yellow slippers resembling those commonly seen in Morocco and believed to enhance fertility. Many of the women practice a balancing act, clutching their black *chadors* underneath their chins or over their mouths while carrying their handbags or sacks of groceries. Just as I stared out the window of my taxi, the people of Qom stared back. I nervously adjusted my own full-length black robe, my Egyptian-made *chador-e arabi*, and glanced at myself in the car mirror to make sure all my hair was covered.

Everything about Qom's exterior tells the story of its inner self. It is a company town, where the industry is religion. Just as laborers once filed to their jobs on assembly lines or steel mills in cities like Detroit and Baltimore, young seminarians flock to the classrooms of Qom to pursue a grueling curriculum that prepares them for future positions of power and influence. Pious Iranians arrive in busloads to tour the city's holy shrines and leave some money behind for good works and upkeep of the sacred places. The most famous shrine, the tomb of the sister of the Eighth Imam, has been a destination for pilgrims for centuries. But the city's importance lies more with its present than with the role it played for Shi'ite Muslims in the past. It is the ideological center of the faith, a designation won when Khomeini returned to Iran from exile in February 1979 and made Qom his headquarters.

Like the pilgrims, I too journeyed to this seat of political Islam. Qom was my last stop in search of Islam's rejuvenation. There was no better vantage point to understand the religious revival in Egypt than the place where Islam established its greatest hold in the twentieth century and put to rest 2,500 years of monarchical rule. Iran was the example, the catalyst bringing Shi'ites and Sunnis to the religious well, even if the substance of their belief continued to divide them.

Qom is the breeding ground for the political vision that helped drive and perpetuate the Iranian revolution. The contrast with al-Azhar and other institutions of Egypt's religious life could not be more striking. Where Qom thrives on bringing structure and an official interpretation to Islam, Egypt struggles with many competing interpretations from a variety of sources. Within the Egyptian state, there were those authorities trying to establish legitimacy based on their own reading of Islam, and others through the representation of the popular will. At al-Azhar, there were *sheikh*s trying to promote the official state interpretation and others who, feeding on the support of the masses, were charting a new course. Private mosques spread a living Islam that met the needs of the Egyptian population at large without the often stultifying influence of the official *ulama*. These distinctions have pushed Iranian and Egyptian societies in very different directions.

Religious interpretation in Qom is guarded as the exclusive preserve of certified scholars and their pupils. This interpretation is so absolute that a grand ayatollah and one-time successor to Khomeini is now under house arrest in Qom for deviating from the establishment's reading of Shi'ite political philosophy. This offers a striking example of what some thinkers have identified as the distinction between the ideological society of Iran and a religious society such as Egypt.

One of the major functions of the Shi'ite clerical establishment is to preserve its role as the ultimate judge in matters of religious doctrine and practice. There are no Yussef Badris or Abd al-Sabour Shahins fighting against state policy. It simply is not allowed. By the time I moved to Iran in June 1998, public debate over religion, civil society, and foreign policy was freer than it had been since the Revolution. Yet there were only a handful of clerics licensed to deliver the weekly *khutba* in central Tehran. Others who spoke out regularly in the press ventured carefully through the minefield of religious interpretation. If they strayed too far, they were surely silenced.

Iran's best-known and most controversial Islamist intellectual critic, Abdolkarim Soroush, has spelled out the political and social implications of these divergent paths, an observation seemingly borne out by recent history. Before my journey to Qom, I went to see Soroush to learn more about his ideas. At the time, he risked arrest for speaking openly. He had already lost his teaching post at Tehran University; he was beaten on numerous occasions by hooligans who believe he is subversive; and his passport had been confiscated temporarily to prevent him from leaving the country. As a thinker who focuses on the philsophy of religion, Soroush explained that the clerical establishment has failed to "Islamize" Iranian society. Instead, through a strict interpretation of religion, the mullahs have created a national identity that reduces Islam to little more than an ideology. This national mindset was important in creating the Islamic Republic but since then the establishment has failed to move forward. A state like Iran, where one official interpretation of religion predominates, must put ideological purity ahead of such concepts as human rights. Conversely, religious societies, with their broadly accepted notions of social justice, imply a greater possibility for democratic forms of government, and they interpret the Koran and the Sunna in harmony with society's needs and changing understanding of religion.[1]

The Iranian clerical establishment controls the seminaries, which serve as breeding grounds for future clerics who will rise to state positions. This interdependence, according to Soroush, encourages the seminary to reaffirm the state's religious theories and forces aspiring clerics to become apologists for the state. There is little hope for maverick ayatollahs to emerge who might challenge the ruling dogma, as in the case of the increasingly assertive *sheikh*s at al-Ahzar who constantly issue *fatwa*s contrary to state policy.

I returned to Qom several times in 1997 and 1998 to test out Soroush's theories. I met ayatollahs from all sides of the political spectrum, and during each visit I posed variations of the same questions: Did the revolution bring religion, not just ideology, to Iran? Would the system in Iran, imposed by the clerical establishment, ever manage to integrate religion into society to the degree that it is carried out voluntarily in Egypt? And, conversely, would the revival in Egypt, imposed by society, ever become powerful enough to establish a theocratic state? For twenty years, the ayatollahs had told the world they wanted to export their revolution, and for twenty years the world had waited. When the Islamic Group, or GIA, became more and more powerful in Algeria, the ayatollahs rejected their form of Islam. When the Taliban took hold of Afghanistan, Iran openly opposed their interpretation of the faith, even to the point of verging on open warfare along their shared border. So what type of Islamic renewal did the ayatollahs actually have in mind?

The first ayatollah I ever met kept an office in the Imam Khomeini Research Institute, a massive complex on a quiet street in Qom. When I entered, a cluster of men greeted me warmly, and everyone seemed to know I had come for an interview. I was escorted into a reception room. A large table with at least a dozen chairs around it was covered with fruits and pastries. The position of the chairs and the large spread of local delicacies suggested there had been many guests before me, with more to come.

I had come to see Ayatollah Mohammad Taqi Mesbah-Yazdi, a conservative who was gaining a reputation as a leading philosopher of the right-wing. It was December 1997, seven months after Mohammed Khatami had been elected president. Everyone was capitalizing on the image of a "new Iran," ushered in with Khatami's landslide victory. President Khatami seemed to draw supporters from a broad cross section of society. Even fallen aristocrats who had suffered severely when their properties were confiscated and their fortunes taken from them at the revolution had favorable things to say about the new president. Young people sitting in cafes in mixed company, a violation of the moral code, were always eager to express their gratitude at the new openness in society, possible only through Khatami's reforms. But when I asked Iranians if they lived in a religious society, the answer was rarely about Islam and more often about their distaste for the system.

Even some conservatives were jumping on the reformist bandwagon, provided they could keep from offending their staunch supporters. Conventional political labels were becoming more and more confusing in Iran, as the clerical factions split and regrouped in new combinations. Some hardliners suddenly were opposed to the old conservative establishment and were supporting Khatami's drive for a civil society. Ayatollah Mesbah-Yazdi was one such mullah at the intersection of right and left. He had a reputation of being a rightist. But in recent interviews with foreign journalists he had voiced support for change, as long as it did not undermine the basic principles of the revolution.

Mesbah-Yazdi wore layers of overcoats. He had a salt-and-pepper beard, but his smooth skin made it difficult to guess his age. When I asked him if Iran was still planning to export the Islamic revolution, it became clear he had spent time with foreign journalists. He managed a diplomatic response while indirectly blaming the lack of revolutionary progress on Western influences. "We wanted to export the thought behind the revolution, not to meddle in the affairs of other countries. What succeeds in one society may not succeed in another society. It is important to note that after the Islamic revolution western countries tried to prevent us from exporting the revolution. In Algeria, they saw Islam was powerful and they wanted to get rid of it. They had an election. The Islamic party won and they banned them from power."

Certainly, Iran's revolution had provided inspiration for the two primary trends within Egypt's Islamic movement, the militant groups and the moderate Islamists who had transformed society. Just as the Iranian revolution was under way in the late 1970s, Egypt's *Gama'a al-Islamiyya* split on university campuses and the militant movement was born to implement the slogan "change by force." When President Sadat allowed Iran's dethroned Shah to be admitted into Egypt for medical treatment in 1979, students across the country staged protests. Further evidence in the eyes of the Islamists that Sadat had betrayed his religion, this was a major landmark along the road to his assassination.

Militancy flourished in the early 1980s through the proliferation of unlicensed mosques and unofficial preachers in certain districts of Cairo and in Upper Egypt. In 1981, of 46,000 mosques, only 6,000 were under the control of the Ministry of Religious Endowments.[2] The militants were popular in communities such as Imbaba, where residents felt abandoned by the state. Their primary aim was the establishment of an Islamic government along the Iranian model. But from the beginning, the militants in Egypt had only a remote chance of achieving their goals. There was no charismatic leader, such as Ayatollah Khomeini, at the head of their opposition movement. Their best-known spiritual guide was Sheikh Omar Abd al-Rahman, who, like the militants themselves, existed on the margins of society. Many of the early militants came from the lower middle classes and were either students or low-income workers.

The Iranian revolutionary passion that inspired Egyptian groups like the *Gama'a* began fizzling back home in the 1990s. The student movement that traces its roots to the heady days of the U.S. embassy takeover, what Khomeini termed the second revolution, now says it has no quarrel with Americans. In fact, members of the *Daftar-e Tahkim-e Vahdat*, the Office to Consolidate Unity, have discarded their bare-knuckle intimidation tactics and now preach a gospel of political pluralism and free speech. This same movement, which claims 50,000 members on campuses across Iran, on November 2, 1998, held a remarkable commemoration of the embassy seizure, abandoning traditional chants of "Death to America" in favor of pleas for mutual respect and renewed cultural and political ties with the Great Satan. As I mingled with the crowd of women students, my black robe nearly identical to theirs, there was a palpable sense of excitement at meeting a real-life American. They tried to utter a few words in English and said in Persian that it was good that an American was living in Iran. *Daftar* activists have emerged as a leading force behind President Khatami, whose electoral campaign in May 1997 swept to victory on a platform of "political development" and respect for the rule of law. Former and present leaders of the movement are mainstays at pro-reform rallies, their speeches the target of hardline reprisals and their every word catalogued in pro-Khatami newspapers.

It is far too early to predict the prospects for Khatami's bid to create a "civil society" within Iran's existing Islamic system. Critics point to the authoritarian nature of many Iranian institutions, the supremacy of clerical rule over all elected office-holders and, most daunting of all, a perceived innate conflict between Islam and democracy. But to witness the Khatami reforms firsthand is to be struck by their fundamental assault on what once appeared immutable pillars of the *ideological* state. One by one, the institutions of ideological control are under attack: limits on press freedom are pushed back by the day; the Special Court for Clergy, with no due process for clerical defendants, has been challenged as unconstitutional; and scholars are debating whether the supreme clerical leader, whose powers dwarf those of the president, should be chosen directly by the people rather than by an obscure body of senior Shi'ite theologians.

The changes taking place in Iran threaten to undermine the regime's monopoly over religious interpretation, swinging the balance of power back to the fundamental moral, political, and religious convictions of society at large. Nowhere is this more evident than in the current debate raging in the daily press, the Friday prayer sermons, and the corridors of political and theological power over the definition and appropriate limits to personal and political freedom. Conservative clerics such as Ayatollah Mesbah-Yazdi argue that anything approaching Western notions of freedom is by definition in conflict with religion, which imposes divine duties, limits, and responsibilities on man. For their part, Khatami and his supporters assert that freedom is an integral part of faith and that Western liberal democracy, stripped of its un-Islamic excesses, has much to offer Iran. Likewise, Khatami has called on the Revolutionary Guards and other coercive elements to relax their grip on the nation's youth; moral suasion, not the threat of lashes or imprisonment, will lead the young to a proper Islamic lifestyle.

The retreat of the forces of ideology at home has been accompanied by an easing of Iran's revolutionary zeal in foreign policy. Relations with the archconservative Sunni kingdom of Saudi Arabia are improving steadily, while full diplomatic relations with Britain, long hostage to the Rushdie affair, have been restored. Mesbah-Yazdi's tacit admission that the days of pan-Muslim revolution were over before they ever really began demonstrates the degree to which Iran's effort to normalize ties to the outside world has the backing of the entire establishment, including the conservatives. In fact, it is clear that had the traditionalist candidate defeated Khatami in the 1997 presidential elections, U.S.–Iranian relations would be much further along; instead, the right appears determined to deprive the moderate president, for as long as possible, of the political windfall from what would clearly be a popular move with most ordinary Iranians.

Two decades earlier, the Iranian revolution seemed an answer to the prayers of so many faithful throughout the Muslim world, repelled equally by the godless communism of the East and the commercial idols of the decadent West. However, the years of forced consolidation of clerical power, the devastating war with Iraq, and the debilitating isolation imposed by a hostile outside world have taken much of the shine off the Islamic Republic. More important, they have revealed the great underlying weakness of an Islamic revival imposed from the top down—its lack of permanence and inevitable tendency to cave in once the revolutionary moment has well and truly passed.

The forces of *Gama'a al-Islamiyya* and *Jihad*, once seen as a serious threat to the Mubarak regime in Egypt, have run aground on this same revolutionary logic. The failure of militancy to gain political or religious support in Egyptian society and destabilize the government was brought into focus with the 1997 Luxor massacre, when fifty-eight tourists and four Egyptians were killed. As the initial horror of the militants' brutal actions, including hacking to death some of their victims and mutilating the bodies, faded over time, it became clear that the spectacular assault was more of a last gasp than a victory in the war with the state. When the last of the broken bodies were identified and sent home, nothing remained but the empty, nihilist center of the militants' ideology. It was clear to all they had nothing left to offer.

Society was so revolted at the level of violence, unprecedented in the history of militancy in Egypt, that *Gama'a* leaders quickly dissociated themselves from the attack. A *Gama'a* statement declared the perpetrators to be a "rogue element" within the group, and the organization vowed to stop targeting tourists, a strategy that had been in play since at least the 1980s. "Exiled *Gama'a* leaders were surprised by what happened at Luxor and were shocked by the large number of victims and the mutilation of some of the dead, which violates the principles of legitimacy, humanity, and politics of the *Gama'a* in Egypt," read one communiqué. Montassir al-Zayyat announced publicly he was resigning temporarily from his work as their lawyer and unofficial spokesman.

Two of the militants were students at the University of Assyut in Upper Egypt, another unusual aspect of the attack. The sociological profile of militants in the 1990s stood in sharp contrast to that of their predecessors in the 1970s. Many in the 1990s were not university educated; they came from more impoverished backgrounds and were less ideological. By the late 1990s, university administrators boasted that they had eradicated militancy from their campuses. But the Luxor attack renewed concern that the universities were once again becoming breeding grounds for extremism. The president of Assyut University tried to assure Egypt and the world that the two students were aberrations. "Really, we haven't (had) at all any trouble in the university and we haven't any Islamic groups since five or six years ago and university life is proceeding well," he told the BBC.

Despite such assurances, commentators were horrified by the violence of the attack and they filled the newspapers with speculation that the militant movement may have made fresh inroads among Egyptian youth. Many blamed the government for failing to address the economic and social needs of the country's young generation. After Luxor, the state was compelled to make changes to a system centered on police repression. The interior minister resigned, officials released prisoners convicted of militancy, and detainees held for years in jail without charge were also set free. Officials vowed to reconsider their general policy, which they indirectly admitted had caused hostility and resentment among the young who might not have become disaffected if they had believed there was an avenue of political participation. Officials were also criticized for ignoring pleas from the *Jihad* and *Gama'a al-Islamiyya* a few months earlier in the summer of 1997, when the two groups called for direct negotiations with the government in exchange for a cease-fire. Sheikh Omar Abd al-Rahman endorsed the proposal from his prison cell in New York. But the state rejected the request for negotiations, saying the plea was proof that the militants had been defeated and there was no need for talks.

A few months after the Luxor attack, I had a meeting with Montassir al-Zayyat. By that time, the fallout of Luxor had been picked apart and analyzed to death in Egyptian newspapers and on television. There were conflicting reports over whether the *Gama'a* had split as an organization in the aftermath of the attack. Zayyat explained that there was no split within the group, but that the movement was separated between those living in exile and those in Egyptian jails.

I asked him why the militants had failed over twenty years in their stated goal to overthrow the government and create an Islamic state. Zayyat explained that some of the most capable and insightful Islamists of the 1970s, such as Esam al-Eryan, had joined the Muslim Brotherhood and created a brain drain at the start of the militant movement. During the years that followed, the strategists failed to stick to a consistent plan. "A lot of time passed with no clarity of vision. Too much energy was put into having clashes with the government, simply for the sake of having clashes. And the armed struggle forced them to lose popular support within society."

The afternoon of the Luxor massacre I was on the campus of American University in Cairo, just as I had been during the previous attack, which occurred in September 1997, at the Egyptian Museum in Tahrir Square only a few blocks away. I walked out of the university main gate and hailed a cab. All around me, Egyptians were cursing the violence. They stood in crowds in the middle of downtown, waving their hands in the air and looking past one another as they shouted in anger and frustration. When I got into the cab, the passengers sitting next to me all talked about how the militants had tarnished the reputation of Egypt, a country that prides itself on its hospitality to foreigners.

Egyptian society's response to the militants has taken many different turns over the last two decades. If at first the militants won sympathizers among ordinary individuals, each spectacular massacre or attack chipped away at this temporary support. Even the militants' attempted assassination of President Mubarak in June 1995 in Addis Ababa inflicted much harm on their cause. It was perhaps one of Mubarak's most difficult summers. He had just approved a new law on libel, which his opponents considered another obstacle to creating a civil society, and his government had been criticized more than usual for corruption. But Egyptians interpreted the attack on Mubarak's life as an affront to their strong nationalist feelings, and an embarrassment in front of the world community. Mubarak's most vehement critics, including the Muslim Brotherhood, condemned the assault and society at large displayed an unusual burst of support for the president. Thousands of well-wishers gathered outside the presidential palace in Cairo. Programming on television indulged in an orgy of adulation for Mubarak in replays of the gunfire attack on his motorcade, his frightened expression after his escape, and his triumphant return to Cairo. But Mubarak never seized on the rare moments of his surging popularity to make the constructive changes his critics had demanded for much of his presidency. Soon, it was business as usual.

This inability on the part of Mubarak and his secularist allies to channel any newfound popularity, however fleeting, reflects the overriding logic of the moment. Egypt's militants may have lost the war, but the state has certainly not emerged victorious. The last gasps of the armed struggle, which the Luxor massacre may well come to represent, must be seen as the failure of militancy, not the success of the secularist regime. In fact, the shortcomings and systemic weaknesses are more apparent today than ever. They are obvious in the growing erosion of civil liberties in Egypt, a process that began in earnest in 1992, just as the militant movement was at the peak of its power. The militants may have failed to overthrow the state, but they indirectly pushed the government toward totalitarianism. In this way, the militants have achieved a victory in discrediting the state in the eyes of its own people.

Examples of totalitarian tactics used in the name of combating the "militant threat" abound. The most glaring example was the state's decision in 1992 to refer cases in which civilians are charged with "terrorist acts" to the military courts. From 1992 through 1996, seventy-four civilians were sentenced to death by military judges. Since the early 1990s, an estimated 10,000 to 20,000 political prisoners have been held in jails.[3] Of this number, an estimated 1,000 of the detainees were arrested in 1992 in the raid on Imbaba, according to human rights lawyers. The interior ministry also has the right to arrest and hold anyone without charge for thirty days, under the emergency law renewed periodically since 1981.

For much of the 1990s, the typical routine practiced by security forces in arresting young men who they claimed were militants was well documented by human rights organizations. In February 1994, during the course of reporting these incidents, I visited one neighborhood where security forces had cordoned off blocks of apartments and then shot to death a group of young men. The state's explanation in newspapers was in direct contradiction to the accounts witnesses gave me when I went to the scene of the crime the next day. The state claimed a shoot-out had occurred, but residents living in the poor neighborhood called Zeinhom told a tale of horror in which security forces rounded up four young men and then shot them to death. The bodies of the victims were then dumped on the street, where a machine gun and bombs were placed beside them as fabricated evidence that a gun battle had occurred. The Egyptian Organization of Human Rights confirmed the eyewitness accounts I had collected in a report issued shortly after the killings.

"The inhabitants of Barkat Qarun Street heard the screams of young men and witnessed a large number of individuals wearing civilian clothes holding four persons, one of whom faced the wall while the other three were moved into a truck resembling a furniture removal vehicle. Shooting was then heard coming from inside the truck. . . . Egyptian human rights representatives observed traces of blood near the bodies, but an amount which was too small to confirm the belief that the three were shot in the same location where they lay," the report concluded. "This cycle of violence and counter violence endangers human rights, which cannot be practiced in a society where the state does not respect the law or function within it."[4]

By 1997, the state had turned its unlawful tactics on lawyers representing defendants charged with political crimes. Lawyers were arrested arbitrarily in the course of duty. Sixty-six lawyers were detained either for practicing their jobs or for their political activity, according to the Arab Center for the Independence of the Judiciary and the Legal Profession. Another fifty-seven lawyers who were detained went missing, according to the same report, issued in April 1998 by the Arab Center. Assaults on lawyers "became more common," including beatings at police stations, as did threats lodged against the jurists and their families for defending political activists.

The state crushed efforts by those opposition elements seeking to create a civil society that would permit a multiparty political system and freedom of the press. The law on political parties was revised in 1992 to block any group from conducting political activity before they have been permitted to form a political party. A government commission must approve new parties, a lengthy process that often takes years. Party aspirants can appeal the commission's ruling to an administrative court, but these courts generally side with the state.

Former members of the Muslim Brotherhood, the young generation of leaders who were active in the syndicates, tried to form the "Wasat" party. Among the founders was Abu al-Ela Mady, the dynamic leader of the engineering syndicate whose earlier attempts at mainstream politics were stymied by the forced closure of his professional union. Another founder was one of the country's most respected leaders in the Christian Coptic community. They aimed to run candidates in national and local elections in parliament and municipalities. But the state accused Mady of using the party as a front for the Muslim Brotherhood. Officials also argued that religious parties were not permitted. After years of appeals and legal wrangling, the authorities issued a final ruling in 1998 that killed off any chance for the "Wasat" generation to participate in the political process.

Even if opposition parties, such as Wasat, were permitted, their participation in free and fair elections could hardly be guaranteed. During the parliamentary poll held in 1995, not one of 150 Muslim Brotherhood candidates who ran as independents or under the Islamist-oriented Labor Party won a seat. Widespread fraud and vote-rigging were conducted openly to ensure an overwhelming victory for Mubarak's National Democratic Party.

Even before the election was held, the state eliminated from the running the most credible Islamist candidates, such as Esam al-Eryan, by arresting them on bogus charges and putting them in jail. During election campaigning and in the period between the first and second rounds of voting, the authorities arrested 1,392 Islamist campaign workers, supporters, and poll-watchers, according to the Egyptian Organization of Human Rights. The state wanted to avoid a repeat of the 1987 poll, when the "Islamic Alliance" of the Muslim Brotherhood and the Liberal and Socialist Labor parties won sixty seats in the 360-member People's Assembly.

In response to calls for more press freedom, the state passed amendments to the penal code in May 1995, imposing stiff penalties on "publication crimes," such as printing "false rumors" or "defamations." The law was designed to stop criticism of Mubarak, high-level members of his administration, and Mubarak's sons, who were often accused of corruption in the opposition press. Just one year after the law was passed, ninety-nine journalists and editors had been charged, and in some cases sentenced by lower courts.[5] One editor was Magdi Hussein of *al-Shaab* newspaper and one of Egypt's most influential Islamist writers. Opposition to the law was fierce, even among prominent editors from *al-Ahram* newspaper, the state's mouthpiece. In June 1996, the law was abolished in the first significant retreat by the authorities from their repressive policies. But Magdi Hussein did not escape unscathed; he served several months in jail.

It may seem ludicrous to argue that militant Islam has failed, or that the Egyptian government overreacted to the threat, given its potential for social mayhem. If anything, the worldwide network of radical Islam stretching from Pakistan, Sudan, Afghanistan all the way to New Jersey under the supervision of Osama bin Laden, the rich Saudi renegade, certainly suggests the opposite. The bombing of U.S. embassies in Africa in 1998 and bin Laden's vows to strike against American interests show his strength and the determination of his adherents, one of whom is Ayman al-Zawahiri, the exiled leader of the Egypt's *Jihad* organization. The Taliban's conquest of the vast majority of Afghan territory, and it's strict interpretation of *sharia* law, which has resulted in a policy of stoning adulterers and hanging political dissenters, illustrates radical Islam imposed from above. In Algeria, the relentless bloodletting of tens of thousands of innocent civilians at the hands of the Islamic Group is all done in the name of Islam.

But violence, not ideology or belief, is the common thread linking these movements and groups. Just as these movements condemn Jews and Americans, they exhibit the same venom toward their Shi'ite neighbors. In a statement that alarmed the world in early 1998, bin Laden and al-Zawahiri called for the creation of a World Islamic Front for a *jihad* against Christians and Jews. The Iranians issued a similar call after the revolution twenty years ago to bridge the divide between Sunni and Shi'ite Muslims. But bin Laden's aim to create a worldwide *umma* with his army of nomadic militants scattered across the globe is farther from reality today than it was at the time of Ayatollah Khomeini. Militant movements no doubt will continue to flourish, but their success in unleashing havoc on the world should not obscure their failure to create a global, or even regional, religious community.

The grassroots religious revival in Egypt provides the most solid evidence to date that a failed militant movement in no way spells the death of Islamic revivalism. In fact, the moderate Islamists leading the grassroots revival in Egypt have benefited indirectly from the militants' brutality. The moderates were the counterpoint to the militants, a viable alternative between the radicalism that was giving Islam a bad name and the authoritarian state. In this way, Egypt's voluntary, broad-based religious revival is likely to strengthen in the new century and offer an example to Muslim societies torn between repressive governments and militant extremism.

The only outstanding question is to what degree the religious revival will take over Egyptian society. Will the power of the conservatives at al-Azhar reduce state-appointed Grand Sheikhs, such as Tantawi, to little more than figureheads with no real religious authority? Will judges and lawyers continue to implement decisions and laws more in line with the *sharia*? Will government ministries issuing decrees relating to social policy be forced to defer to the courts and to al-Azhar?

One of the first Islamic scholars I met when I moved to Cairo told me that Egypt was undergoing an Islamic revolution that was peaceful and quietist. "We don't need to overthrow the state, because we are achieving our aims without violent insurrection," he said. One of the keys to the success of Egypt's revival has been the gradual creation of an Islamic order that has no rigid recipe, no monopoly on religious "truth." The same upper-class Egyptian who drinks wine or alcohol socially considers himself a believer. The same young woman who pours herself into tight stretch pants also wears the headscarf or the veil. Such things often lead Egyptian secularists to conclude that the country's religious revival is superficial or at most temporary. But in reality Egyptians have created flexibility within their religion in keeping with their relaxed philosophy about life in general.

During the holy month of Ramadan, a time for sacrifice, reflection, and fasting, the elaborate festivities held in Egypt are renowned throughout the Middle East, so much so that Lebanon has begun to copy some of Egypt's Ramadan traditions. Egyptians gain so much weight during this month of fasting that the health ministry issues advisories warning people of the hazards of overeating. Egyptians indeed observe the Koranic injunction to fast during daylight hours, but from sunset until dawn the country engages in a massive orgy of food and fun. Does this make them less Islamic than their Muslim neighbors? In their eyes, the answer is an emphatic no.

For contemporary Egyptians, it is the integration of their faith and their society that counts, not rigid interpretations or attempts at a codification of an Islamic state ideology. Humble neighborhoods like Imbaba have largely gone their own way, led by unofficial *sheikh*s and street preachers, toward a popular notion of Islam. This grassroots revival has proven so powerful it has coopted members of the official *ulama* at al-Azhar, long a pillar of Egypt's ruling elite and the center of gravity for the world of Sunni Islam. The senior *sheikh*s, in turn, have provided the grassroots movement with theological, social, and political legitimacy.

Likewise, the growing professional middle class has turned its back on many of the trappings of Western-style "development," preferring to make room for Islamic notions of justice, family, and social cohesion. University campuses keep alive the Islamic dream, despite the state's best efforts to stamp it out, by brute force if necessary. Educated, wealthy women are increasingly turning to Islam, depriving the secularists of what might seem like a natural constituency for their modernizing aspirations. Even the judicial system, originally created as a counterweight to the religious courts to help integrate Egypt into the Western world, can no longer be counted on to fulfill its appointed duty.

Such institutions as the universities, the professional syndicates and the courts all owe their very existence to Egypt's attempts to carve out a Western-style identity, one characterized by the separation of the state from religion. The new campuses, with room for all, were designed to churn out the generations of skilled citizens the state needed to compete in the modern world. The professional middle class would provide social and political stability and act as the engine of development. The courts would underpin a contemporary society. As we have seen, all three failed in their assigned roles. The distinction between state and religion, Western history's imposition on the East, has become increasingly untenable. The Cairo lawyers' syndicate, once a hotbed of Western leftist ideology, summed it up at a public celebration of the Islamist victory in union elections: "Yes, we want it Islamic." The less politically minded, perhaps, take refuge in the core creed of Islam, which makes no room for the secular deity of the state: *"There is no God but God, and Mohammed is his Prophet."*

NOTES

CHAPTER 1: THE NEW FACE OF ISLAM

1. Bernard Lewis, *The Middle East: 2000 Years of History from the Rise of Christianity to the Present Day* (London: Weidenfeld & Nicolson, 1995), p. 149.
2. P. J. Vatikiotis, *Islam and the State* (London: Routledge, 1991), p. 90.
3. Ibid.
4. Ibid., p. 95.
5. Sayyid Qutb, *Milestones* (Cedar Rapids: The Mother Mosque Foundation, n.d.), p. 9.
6. Cited in Jalal Al-e Ahmad, *Occidentosis: A Plague from the West*, trans. Robert Campbell (Berkeley: Mizan Press, 1984), p. 13.
7. Gustave Flaubert, *Flaubert in Egypt: A Sensibility on Tour*, trans. Francis Steegmuller (Chicago: Academy Chicago, 1987), p. 79.

CHAPTER 2: STREETS OF GREEN

1. *Al-Wasat,* December 21, 1992.
2. Ibid.
3. Ibid.

CHAPTER 3: THE FOUNT OF ISLAM

1. Malika Zeghal, *Gardiens de L'Islam: Les oulemas d'Al Azhar dans l'Egypte contemporaine* (Paris: Press de Sciences, 1996), p. 17.
2. Ibid., p. 49.

3. Gilles Kepel, *Muslim Extremism in Egypt: The Prophet and the Pharaoh*, trans. Jon Rothchild (Berkeley: University of California Press, 1986), p. 175.

4. P. J. Vatikiotis, *The History of Modern Egypt: From Muhammad Ali to Mubarak* (Baltimore: Johns Hopkins University Press, 1991), p. 18.

5. Ahmad S. Bin Salamon, *"Reform of Al-Azhar in the 20th Century"* (Ph.D. diss., New York University, 1980), pp. 13–14.

6. Ibid., p. 23.

7. Ibid., p. 15.

8. Ibid., p. 21.

9. Ibid.

10. Cited in Vatikiotis, *History*, p. 39.

11. Ibid., p. 43.

12. Cited in Philipp Thomas and Moshe Perlmann, eds., *A Guide to Abd al-Rahman al-Jabarti's History of Egypt* (Stuttgart: Franz Steiner Verlag, 1994), 3:26.

13. Salamon, p. 58.

14. Ibid.

15. Richard P. Mitchell, *The Society of the Muslim Brothers* (New York: Oxford University Press, 1993), p. 230.

16. Ibid., p. 212.

17. Ibid., pp. 213–14.

18. Zeghal, p. 47.

19. Daniel Crecelius, "Al-Azhar in the Revolution," *The Middle East Journal* 21, no. 1 (1966): 39.

20. Kate Zebiri, *Mahmud Shaltut and Islamic Modernism* (New York: Oxford University Press, 1993), pp. 26–27.

21. Zenghal, p. 102.

22. Patrick D. Gaffney, *The Prophet's Pulpit: Islamic Preaching in Contemporary Egypt* (Berkeley: University of California Press, 1994), p. 34.

23. Ibid., p. 35.

24. Crecelius, p. 41.

25. Ibid., p. 42.

26. Magda Ali Saleh Rabi'i, *Al-Dawr al-Siyassi lil-Azhar* (Cairo: Cairo University Political Research Studies Center, 1992), p. 30.

27. Ibid.

28. Robert Bianchi, *Unruly Corporatism: Associative Life in 20th Century Egypt* (London: Oxford University Press, 1989), p. 182.

29. R. Hrair Dekmegian, *Islam in Revolution: Fundamentalism in the Arab World* (Syracuse: Syracuse University Press, 1985), p. 84.

30. Gaffney, p. 114.

31. Vatikiotis, *History*, p. 422.

32. Kepel, pg. 98.

33. Ibid., p. 80.

34. Ibid.

35. Ibid., p. 99.

36. Ibid., p. 100.

37. Fatima Mernessi, *Beyond the Veil: Male-Female Dynamics in Modern Muslim Society* (Bloomington: Indiana University Press, 1987), p. 15.

38. Ibid., p. 42.

39. *al-Hayat*, April 6, 1996.

40. *al-Musawar*, March 29, 1996.

41. Ibid.

42. *al-Hayat*, May 15, 1996.

43. Kepel, p. 172.

44. Ibid., p. 175.

45. Cited in Steven Barraclough, "Al-Azhar: Between the Government and the Islamists," *Middle East Journal* 52, no. 2 (1998): 242.

46. Cited in Egyptian Organization for Human Rights, Report no. 125, n.d.

47. From a censored interview in 1996 with the *Middle East Times*, made available to the author.

48. Steve Negus, "Azhar Rebels Against Mosque Law," *Middle East Times*, June 9–15, 1996.

CHAPTER 4: THE PROFESSIONALS

1. R. Hrair Dekmajian, *Islam in Revolution: Fundamentalism in the Arab World* (Syracuse: Syracuse University Press, 1985), p. 82.

2. Mitchell, p. 152.

3. Ibid., p. 29.

4. Ibid., p. 279.

5. Ibid., p. 180.

6. Moheb Zaki, *Civil Society and Democratization in Egypt, 1981–1994* (Cairo: Konrad Adenauer Stiftung, 1995), pp. 186–87.

7. Ibid., p. 187.

8. Report by the Central Apparatus for Statistics and Mobilization, 1994.

9. Clement Henry Moore, *Images of Development: Egyptian Engineers in Search of Industry* (Cairo: The American University in Cairo Press, 1994), p. 13.

10. Ibid., p. 17.

11. Ibid., p. 215.

12. Sami Zubaida, *Islam, the People and the State: Essays on Political Ideas and Movements in the Middle East* (London: Routledge, 1989), p. 48.

13. Osman Ahmed Osman, *Safahat min Tajribati* (Cairo: Al-maktab al-Misri al-*hadith*, 1981), p. 359.

14. Ibid.

15. Ibid., p. 364.

16. Ibid., p. 363.

17. Moore, p. 219.

18. Ibid., p. 221.

19. Amani Qindil, "Al-Jaraim al-iqtisadiyya al-mustahdatha fi al-niqabat al-mihniyya: Diras halla li niqabat al-muhandisin," in *Naadwat al-jaraim al-iqtisadiyya al mustahdatha* (Cairo: al-markaz al qawmi lil-buhuth al ijtimaiyya wa al-jinaiyya, 1994), p. 321.

20. *al-Ahrar,* February 26, 1995.

21. Amani Qindil, *Al-dawr al-siyasi li jamaat al masalih fi Misr: Dirasa Halla li niqabat al-atibba 1984–1995* (Cairo: Centre for Political and Strategic Studies, 1996), p. 61.

22. *al-Ahrar*, February 10, 1992.

23. For a comprehensive overview of Egyptian human rights abuses, see Middle East Watch, *Behind Closed Doors: Torture and Detention in Egypt* (New York: Human Rights Watch, 1992).

24. *al-Shaab*, February 26, 1993.

25. *al-Shaab*, May 5, 1995.

26. Centre for the Independence of Judges and Lawyers, *Egypt: The Sequestration of the Bar: Report of a Mission, 10–16 March, 1998* (Geneva, 1998), p. 36.

CHAPTER 5: SCHOOL OF REVOLUTION

1. *al-Dawa*, no. 31, 1978.

2. *al-Dawa*, August 10, 1977.

3. Ahmed Abdalla, *The Student Movement and National Politics in Egypt* (London: Al-Saqi Books, 1985), p. 43.

4. Ibid., p. 46.

5. Hagai Erlikh, *Students and University in 20th Century Egyptian Politics* (London: Frank Cass, 1989), p. 177.

6. Abdalla, p. 152.

7. Ibid., p. 153.

8. Ibid., p. 183.

9. Ghada Hashem Talhami, *Mobilization of Muslim Women in Egypt* (Gainesville: University Press of Florida, 1996), p. 53.

10. al-Dawa, no. 23, 1977.

11. al-Dawa, no. 54, 1977.

12. al-Dawa, no. 17, 1977.

13. Hisham Mubarak, Al-Irhabiyyoun Qadimoun: Dirasa Muqarana bayn mawqif al-Ikhwan al-Muslimoun wa Gammat al-Jihad min Qadiyyat al-Unf (1928–1994) (Cairo: Markaz al-Maorousa lil-Nashr wa al-Khidmaat al-Suohufiyeh, 1995), p. 133.

14. al-Dawa, no. 10, August 1977.

15. al-Dawa, no. 18.

16. Mubarak, p. 138.

17. Hamied Ansari, Egypt: The Stalled Society (Albany: State University of New York Press, 1986), p. 185.

18. Abdalla, p. 228.

19. The exchange between Sadat and the students was recorded and later made available to the author.

20. Cited in Rifat Sayyed Ahmed, al-Nabi al-Musallah (London: Riyad al-Rayyes Books, 1991), p. 129.

21. Ibid., p. 191.

22. al-Dawa, no. 50.

23. al-Dawa, November 1980.

24. Nemat Guenena, "The 'Jihad': An 'Islamic Alternative' in Egypt," Cairo Papers in Social Science, vol. 9, monograph 2 (Cairo: The American University in Cairo Press, 1986), p. 62.

25. Ibid., pp. 67–69.

26. Ibid., pp. 68–69.

27. al-Wafd, November 5, 1988.

28. al-Shaab, December 6, 1988.

29. Liwa al-Islam, no. 42, November 1987.

30. Data files on Islamic Activism, unpublished study by the Ibn Khaldun Center, Cairo, p. 55.

CHAPTER 6: TAKING THE VEIL

1. Yvonne Yazbeck Haddad and John L. Esposito, eds., Islam, Gender and Social Change (New York: Oxford University Press, 1998), p. xvi.

2. Leila Ahmed, Women and Gender in Islam: Historical Roots of a Modern Debate (Cairo: American University in Cairo Press, 1993), p. 198.

3. Ibid., p. 199.

4. Al-kawakeb, April 13, 1993.

5. The Meaning of the Holy Qur'an, trans. Abdullah Yusuf Ali (Beltsville, Md.: Amana, 1989), pp. 873–74. With annotations.

6. Cited in Valentine M. Moghadam, *Modernizing Women: Gender and Social Change in the Middle East* (Boulder: Lynne Rienner, 1993), p. 89.

7. Ibid.

CHAPTER 7: COURT OF PUBLIC OPINION

1. *Akhbar al-yom*, June 29, 1985.

2. *Ahram Weekly*, February 9–15, 1995.

3. Tariq al-Bishri, *Al-Wadi al-Qanouni al-Muaser bayn al-Shariah al-Islamiyya wa al-Qanun al-Wadei* (Cairo: Dar al-Shorouq, 1996), pp. 74–75.

4. "Zeid Faced the Power of Our Faith," *Middle East Times*, June 23–30, 1995.

5. George Sfeir, "Basic Freedoms in a Fractured Legal Culture: Egypt and the Case of Nasr Hamid Abu Zayd," *Middle East Journal* 52, no. 3 (1998): 411.

6. *Middle East Times*, January 12–18, 1997.

7. *People's Rights* (Cairo: Legal Research and Resource Center for Human Rights, 1995).

8. Bernard Botiveau, "Contemporary Reinterpretations of Islamic Law: The Case of Egypt," in *Islam and Public Law*, ed. Chibli Mallat (London: Graham & Trottman, 1993), p. 262.

9. Nathan J. Brown, "*Shariah* and State in the Modern Muslim Middle East," *International Journal of Middle East Studies* 29 (1997): 360.

10. Ibid., pp. 364–65.

11. Ibid., p. 371.

12. Jonathan P. Berkey, "Circumcision Circumscribed: Female Excision and Cultural Accommodation in the Medieval Near East," *International Journal of Middle East Studies* 28 (1996): 21.

13. Ibid., p. 23.

14. *al-Hayat*, November 11, 1997.

15. Berkey, p. 25.

16. Ibid., p. 26.

17. Mohammed al-Sayyed al-Shinnawi, *Khitan al-Bannaat bayn al-Sharia wa al-Tib* (Cairo: Dar al-Qalam lil-Turath, n.d.), p. 57.

18. Ibid., p. 71.

19. *al-Shaab*, November 1, 1996.

20. *al-Hayat*, September 12, 1994.

21. *al-Ahram Weekly*, May 23, 1996.

CHAPTER 8: TO IRAN AND BACK AGAIN

1. For an overview in English of Soroush's work, see Valla Vakili, "Debating Religion and Politics in Iran: The Political Thought of Abdolkarim

Soroush," Council on Foreign Relations Occasional Paper Series, no. 2, 1996.

2. Ansari, p. 129.

3. Eberhard Kienle, "More Than a Response to Islamism: The Political Deliberalization of Egypt in the 1990s," *Middle East Journal* 52, no. 2 (1998): 222.

4. Report of the Egyptian Organization for Human Rights, February 20, 1994.

5. Kienle, p. 223.

SELECTED BIBLIOGRAPHY

Abdalla, Ahmed. *The Student Movement and National Politics in Egypt.* London: Al Saqi Books, 1985.

Abrahamian, Ervand. *Khomeinism: Essays on the Islamic Republic.* London: I. B. Tauris, 1993.

Ahmad, Jalal Al-e. *Occidentosis: A Plague from the West.* Translated by Robert Campbell. Berkeley: Mizan Press, 1984.

Ahmad, Rifat Sayyid. *Al-Nabi al-musallah.* London: Riad el-Rayyes, 1991.

Ahmed, Leila. *Women and Gender in Islam: Historical Roots of a Modern Debate.* Cairo: American University in Cairo Press, 1993.

Ali, Said Ismail. *Dawa al-Azhar fi al-Siyasa al Misriyya.* Cairo: Dar al-Hilal, 1986.

Ansari, Hamied. *Egypt: The Stalled Society.* Albany: State University of New York Press, 1986.

Antoun, Richard T., and Mary Elaine Hegland, eds. *Religious Resurgence: Contemporary Cases in Islam, Christianity and Judaism.* Syracuse: Syracuse University Press, 1987.

Arjomand, Said Amir. *The Turban for the Crown: The Islamic Revolution in Iran.* New York: Oxford University Press, 1988.

Arkoun, Mohammed. *Rethinking Islam: Common Questions, Uncommon Answers.* Translated and edited by Robert D. Lee. Boulder: Westview Press, 1994.

Al-Azmeh, Aziz. *Islams and Modernities.* London: Verso, 1993.

Baer, Gabriel. *Egyptian Guilds in Modern Times.* Jerusalem: The Israel Oriental Society, 1964.

Barraclough, Steven. "Al-Azhar: Between the Government and the Islamists." *Middle East Journal* 52, no. 2 (1998): 236–49.

Berkey, Jonathan P. "Circumcision Circumscribed: Female Excision and Cultural Accommodation in the Medieval Near East." *International Journal of Middle East Studies* 28 (1996): 19–38.

Bianchi, Robert. *Unruly Corporatism: Associational Life in Twentieth-Century Egypt.* New York: Oxford University Press, 1989.

Bin Salamon, Ahmad S. *Reform of al-Azhar in the 20th Century.* Ph.D. diss., University of New York, 1980.

al-Bishri, Tariq. *Al-Wadi al-Qanouni al-Muaser bayn al-Sharia al-Islamiyya wa al-Qanun al-Wadei.* Cairo: Dar al-Shoruq, 1996.

Brown, Nathan J. "Sharia and State in the Modern Muslim Middle East." *International Journal of Middle East Studies* 29 (1997): 359–76.

Bulliet, Richard W. *Islam: The View from the Edge.* New York: Columbia University Press, 1994.

Crecelius, Daniel. "Al-Azhar in the Revolution," *Middle East Journal* 21, no. 1 (1966): 31–49.

Dekmajian, R. Hrair. *Islam in Revolution: Fundamentalism in the Arab World.* Syracuse: Syracuse University Press, 1985.

Eccel, Chris A. "Alim and Mujahid in Egypt: Orthodoxy versus Subculture, or Division of Labor?" *The Muslim World* 78, no. 3–4 (1988): 189–208.

———. *Egypt, Islam and Social Change: Al-Azhar in Conflict and Accommodation.* Berlin: Klaus Schwarz Verlag, 1984.

Eickelman, Dale E., and James Piscatori. *Muslim Politics.* Princeton: Princeton University Press, 1996.

el-Sayyid, Mustafa Kamil. "Le syndicat des ingenieurs et le courant islamique." *Monde arabe Maghreb Machrek* 146 (October-December 1994): 27–39.

Encyclopedia of Islam. Leiden: E. J. Brill, 1986.

Erlikh, Hagai. *Students and University in 20th Century Egyptian Politics.* London: Frank Cass, 1989.

Esposito, John L. *The Islamic Threat: Myth or Reality?* New York: Oxford University Press, 1992.

Esposito, John L., and John Donohue. *Islam in Transition: Muslim Perspectives.* New York: Oxford University Press, 1982.

Esposito, John L., ed. *Voices of Resurgent Islam.* New York: Oxford University Press, 1983.

Ezzat Raouf, Heba. *Al-Mara wa al-Amal al-Siyasi: Ru'ya Islamiyya.* Herndon, Va.: The International Institute of Islamic Thought, n.d.

Fanon, Frantz. *The Wretched of the Earth.* Translated by Constance Farrington. New York: Grove Press, 1963.

Fernea, Elizabeth Warnock. *Guests of the Sheikh: An Ethnography of an Iraqi Village.* New York: Doubleday, 1969.

———. *In Search of Islamic Feminism: One Woman's Global Journey.* New York: Doubleday, 1998.

Flaubert, Gustave. *Flaubert in Egypt*. Translated by Francis Stegmuller. Chicago: Academy Chicago, 1987.

Gaffney, Patrick D. *The Prophet's Pulpit: Islamic Preaching in Contemporary Egypt*. Berkeley: University of California Press, 1994.

Goldschmidt, Arthur, Jr. *Modern Egypt: the Formation of a Nation-State*. Cairo: The American University in Cairo Press, 1990.

Guenena, Nemat. "The 'Jihad': An 'Islamic Alternative' in Egypt." In *Cairo Papers in Social Science*, vol. 9, monograph 2. Cairo: The American University in Cairo Press, 1986.

Haddad, Yvonne Yazbeck. "The Qur'anic Justification for an Islamic Revolution: The View of Sayyid Qutb." *Middle East Journal* 37, no. 1 (1983): 14–29.

Halliday, Fred. *Islam & the Myth of Confrontation*. London: I. B. Tauris, 1996.

Hanafi, Hasan. "The Relevance of the Islamic Alternative in Egypt," *Arab Studies Quarterly* 1–2 (1982): 54–104.

Hodgson, Marshall G. S. *The Venture of Islam: Conscience and History in a World Civilization*. 3 vols. Chicago: University of Chicago Press, 1974.

Hourani, Albert. *Arabic Thought in the Liberal Age, 1798–1939*. Cambridge: Cambridge University Press, 1962.

———. *A History of Arab Peoples*. Cambridge: Belknap Press of Harvard University Press, 1991.

Huntington, Samuel P. *The Clash of Civilizations and the Remaking of World Order*. New York: Simon & Schuster, 1996.

Ibn Khaldun. *The Muqaddimah: An Introduction to History*. Translated by Franz Rosenthal. Princeton: Princeton University Press, 1967.

Juergensmeyer, Mark. *The New Cold War? Religious Nationalism Confronts the Secular State*. Berkeley: University of California Press, 1993.

Keddie, Nikki R. *Roots of Revolution: An Interpretive History of Modern Iran*. New Haven: Yale University Press, 1981.

Kedourie, Elie. "The Genesis of the Egyptian Constitution of 1923." In *Political and Social Change in Modern Egypt*, edited by P. M. Holt, pp. 347–61. London: Oxford University Press, 1968.

Kepel, Gilles. *Muslim Extremism in Egypt: The Prophet and the Pharaoh*. Translated by Jon Rothschild. Berkeley: University of California Press, 1986.

———. *The Revenge of God: The Resurgence of Islam, Christianity and Judaism in the Modern World*. Translated by Alan Braley. University Park: Pennsylvania State University Press, 1994.

Kienle, Eberhard. "More than a Response to Islamism: The Political Deliberalization of Egypt in the 1990s." *Middle East Journal* 52, no. 2 (1998): 219–35.

Kinross, Patrick. *The Ottoman Centuries: The Rise and Fall of the Turkish Empire*. New York: Morrow Quill, 1979.

Lewis, Bernard. *The Middle East: 2000 Years of History from the Rise of Christianity to the Present Day*. London: Weidenfeld & Nicolson, 1995.

———. *The Political Language of Islam*. Chicago: University of Chicago Press, 1988.

Maalouf, Amin. *The Crusades through Arab Eyes*. Translated by Jon Rothschild. New York: Schoeken Books, 1984.

Malat, Chibli, ed. *Islam and Public Law: Classical and Contemporary Studies*. London: Graham & Trotman, 1993.

Mernissi, Fatima. *Beyond the Veil: Male-Female Dynamics in Modern Muslim Society*. Bloomington: Indiana University Press, 1987.

Mitchell, Richard P. *The Society of the Muslim Brothers*. New York: Oxford University Press, 1993.

Moore, C. H. *Images of Development: Egyptian Engineers in Search of Industry*. Cairo: The American University in Cairo Press, 1994.

———. "Professional Syndicates in Contemporary Egypt." *American Journal of Arabic Studies* 3 (1975): 60–82.

Mortimer, Edward. *Faith & Power: The Politics of Islam*. New York: Vintage Books, 1982.

Mottahedeh, Roy. *The Mantle of the Prophet: Religion and Politics in Iran*. New York: Simon & Schuster, 1983.

Mubarak, Hisham. *Al-Irhabiyyoun Qadimoun: Dirasa Muqarana bayn mawqif al-Ikhwan al-Muslimoun wa Gammat al-Jihad min Qadiyyat al-Unf (1928–1994)*. Cairo: Markaz al-Maorousa lil-Nashr wa al-Khidmaat al-Suohufiyeh. 1995.

Osman, Osman Ahmed. *Safahat min tajribati*. Cairo: Al-maktab al-Misri al-hadith, 1981.

Osman, Wael. *Assrar al-Haraka al Tulabiyyah*. Cairo: Madkur Press, 1976.

Qindil, Amani. *Al-dawr al-siyasi li jamaat al masalih fi Misr: dirasa Halla li niqabat al-atibba 1984–1995*. Cairo: Centre for Political and Strategic Studies, 1996.

———. "Al-Jaraim al-iqtisadiyya al-mustahdatha fi al-niqabat al-mihniyya: dirasa halla li niqabat al-muhandisin" in *Naadwat al-jaraim al-iqtisadiyya al mustahdatha*. Cairo: al-Markaz al qawmi lil-buhuth al ijtimaiyya wa al-jinaiyya, 1994.

———. *Amaliyyat al-tahawwul al-dimuqrati fi Misr (1981–1993)*. Cairo: Markaz Ibn Khaldun, 1995.

———. "Al-nizam al-siyasi al Misri: al-taghayyur wa al-istimrar." In *Amal al-mutamar al-sanawi al-awwal lil-buhuth al-siyasiyya*. Cairo: Maktabat al-Nahadah al-Misriyya, 1988.

Qutb, Sayyid. *Milestones*. Cedar Rapids: The Mother Mosque Foundation, n.d.

Rabi'i, Magda Ali Saleh. *Al-Dawr al-Siyasi lil-Azhar*. Cairo: Cairo University Political Research Studies Center, 1992.

Reid, Donald M. "Educational and Career Choices of Egyptian Students, 1982–1922." *International Journal of Middle East Studies* 8 (1977): 349–78.

———. "The Rise of Professions and Professional Organization in Modern Egypt." *Comparative Studies in Society and History* 16, no. 1 (1974): 24–57.

Roy, Olivier. *The Failure of Political Islam.* Translated by Carol Volk. London: I. B. Tauris, 1994.

Schirazi, Asghar. *The Constitution of Iran: Politics and the State in the Islamic Republic.* Translated by John O'Kane. London: I. B. Tauris, 1998.

Sfeir, George. "Basic Freedoms in a Fractured Legal Culture: Egypt and the Case of Nasr Hamid Abu Zayd." *Middle East Journal* 52, no. 3 (1998): 402–14.

al-Shinnawi, Abd al-Azeez Mohammed. *Sowar min Dawr al-Azhar.* Cairo: al Jami' al-Azhar, 1971.

al-Shinnawi, Mohammed al-Sayyed. *Khitan al-Bannaat bayn al-Sharia wa al-Tib.* Cairo: Dar al-Qalam lil-Turath, n.d.

Singerman, Diane. *Avenues of Participation: Family, Politics and Networks in Urban Quarters of Cairo.* Princeton: Princeton University Press, 1995.

Sivan, Emmanuel. "The Islamic Republic of Egypt." *Orbis,* Spring 1987, pp. 43–53.

Springborg, Robert. *Mubarak's Egypt: Fragmentation of the Political Order.* Boulder: Westview Press, 1989.

———. "Patterns of Association in the Egyptian Political Elite." *Political Elites in the Middle East.* Edited by George Lenczowski. Washington: American Enterprise Institute for Public Policy Research, 1975.

———. "Professional Syndicates in Egyptian Politics, 1952–1970." *International Journal of Middle East Studies* 9 (1978): 275–95.

Talhami, Ghada Hashem. *Mobilization of Muslim Women in Egypt.* Gainesville: University Press of Florida, 1996.

Thomas, Philipp, and Moshe Perlman, eds. *A Guide to Abd al-Rahman al-Jabarti's History of Egypt.* Stuttgart: Franz Steiner Verlag, 1994.

Vakili, Valla. "Debating Religion and Politics in Iran: The Political Thought of Abdolkarim Soroush." Council on Foreign Relations Occasional Paper Series, no. 2, 1996.

Vatikiotis, P. J. *The History of Modern Egypt: From Muhammad Ali to Mubarak.* Baltimore: Johns Hopkins University Press, 1991.

———. *The Middle East: From the End of Empire to the End of the Cold War.* London: Routledge, 1997.

Viorst, Milton. *Sandcastles: The Arabs in Search of the Modern World.* New York: Alfred A. Knopf, 1994.

Voll, John O. "Islamic Dimensions in Arab Politics since World War II." *American Arab Affairs,* Spring 1983, 108–119.

Weber, Max. *The Protestant Ethic and the Spirit of Capitalism*. New York: Charles Scribner's Sons, 1958.

―――. *The Sociology of Religion*. Translated by Ephraim Fischoff. Boston: Beacon, 1963.

Zaalouk, Malak. *Power, Class and Foreign Capital in Egypt: The Rise of the New Bourgeoisie*. London: Zed Books, 1989.

Zeghal, Malika. *Gardiens de L'Islam: Les oulemas d'Al Azhar dans l'Egypte contemporaine*. Paris: Press de Sciences PO, 1996.

Zaki, Moheb. *Civil Society and Democratization in Egypt, 1981–1994*. Cairo: Konrad Adenauer Stiftung, 1995.

Zebiri, Kate. *Mahmud Shaltut and Islamic Modernism*. London: Oxford University Press, 1993.

Ziadeh, Farhat J. *Lawyers, the Rule of Law and Liberalism in Modern Egypt*. Stanford: Stanford University Press, 1968.

Zubaida, Sami. *Islam, the People and the State: Essays on Political Ideas and Movements in the Middle East*. London: Routledge, 1989.

INDEX